ROYAL HISTORICAL SOCIETY
STUDIES IN HISTORY
SERIES
No. 11.

ORDER AND EQUIPOISE
The Peerage and the House of Lords 1783-1806

Already published in this series

Copies obtainable on order from
Swift Printers., 1-7 Albion Place, Britton Street, London EC1M 5RE

ORDER AND EQUIPOISE

The Peerage and the House of Lords, 1783-1806

Michael W. McCahill

LONDON
ROYAL HISTORICAL SOCIETY
1978

The Society records its gratitude to the following, whose generosity made possible the initiation of this series: The British Academy; The Pilgrim Trust; The Twenty-Seven Foundation; The United States Embassy's Bicentennial funds; The Wolfson Trust; several private donors.

Printed in England
by Swift Printers Ltd
London, E.C.1.

TO MY MOTHER AND FATHER

CONTENTS

GRAPHS AND TABLES

ACKNOWLEDGEMENTS

I should like to thank the following for permission to quote from manuscripts in their possession: the Librarian, Birmingham Reference Library; the Trustees of the Matthew Boulton Trust; the Brotherton Collection which holds the Sydney/Townshend Papers; the earl of Clarendon and the Bodleian Library, custodian of the Clarendon Papers; the duke of Devonshire; the Earl Fitzwilliam, the Trustees of the Wentworth Woodhouse Estates and the City Librarian of Sheffield; the earl of Harewood; the earl of Harrowby and the Harrowby Manuscript Trust; the Trustees of the late duke of Portland and the University of Nottingham, custodian of the Portland Papers; the Viscount Sackville; the Earl Spencer; the earl of Verulam and the Hertfordshire County Record Office; the Wiltshire Record Office.

I am also grateful to the following persons and institutions for permitting me to use their collections and for providing me through their staffs with much helpful assistance: the Trustees of the British Library; the Buckinghamshire Record Office; the Essex Record Office; the Harvard College Libraries; the House of Lords Record Office; the Kent Archives Office; the marquess of Linlithgow and the Hopetoun Papers Trust; the National Library of Scotland; the Northamptonshire Record Office; the Public Record Office; the marquess of Salisbury; the Scottish Record Office; the Record Offices of East and West Suffolk.

Since I began working on my doctoral dissertation, from which this book has grown, I have received encouragement and criticism from Elliot Perkins at Harvard and Harold Hanham of the Massachusetts Institute of Technology. Professor Eric Robinson of the University of Massachusetts suggested new and interesting areas for research and later read the manuscript. I am also grateful to Professor Nancy Lyman Roelker of Boston University, Richard D. Brown of the University of Connecticut and Mr John Sainty for reading parts or all of the manuscript and for making helpful suggestions. Finally, I would like to thank Mr Maurice Bond, Clerk of the Records of the House of Lords, who at the outset helped me to shape and define my inquiries.

Ms Barbara Kaiser performed the laborious chore of checking some of my counts. For their typing and patience I thank Mrs Carol Ellis and Mrs Becky King. My wife, Barbara Ann, aided me in ways too numerous to describe: without her help, advice and support, I would not have completed this work. My final debt is to my parents: to them I dedicate this book.

ABBREVIATIONS

Add. MS	Additional Manuscripts (British Library)
AHR	*American Historical Review*
BIHR	*Bulletin of the Institute of Historical Research*
EcHR	*Economic History Review*
Eg.	Egerton Manuscripts (British Library)
EHR	*English Historical Review*
Hansard	Hansard's *Parliamentary Debates*
HL	House of Lords Records Office
HMC	Historical Manuscripts Commission
LJ	*Journals of the House of Lords*
Parl. Reg.	Debrett's *Parliamentary Register*
PH	*Parliamentary History*
PRO	Public Record Office
SHR	*Scottish Historical Review*
SRO	Scottish Record Office

1

THE HOUSE OF LORDS IN THE CONSTITUTION

The glory of the eighteenth-century constitution theoretically lay in the fact that the concept of mixed monarchy had been translated into reality. Thus were combined in three equal parts the monarchial, aristocratic and democratic elements of the nation. The peculiar nature of each component assured its independence and inspired the community with confidence in its ability to prevent other branches from gaining a monopoly of power.

Within this constitutional trinity the house of lords enjoyed an especially exalted position. 'It was', said Charles Fox, 'the balance that equalized and meliorated the powers of the other two branches, and gave stability and firmness to the whole'.[1] Endowed with special jurisdictions and ornamented by the splendid abilities, wealth and rank of its members, the house of lords was to be the constitution's equipoise, at once guarding against tyrannical ministers and curbing the excessive exuberance of the house of commons.[2]

In reality the house of lords seemed less pivotal to the functioning of the eighteenth-century political system. Governments enjoying royal sanction were unlikely to lose their majority in the upper house. Experienced politicians recognized that while the king supported his ministers, their lordships were unlikely to be active or obstreperous. Indeed, Fox, who had so lavishly described the lords' mission, unhappily concluded in the early years of the nineteenth century that that body was moribund. For him and his allies the supremacy of the house of commons was beyond question.[3]

Modern assessments of the lords' influence generally reflect the

---

1 *PH*, xxix, 409, 11 May 1791.

2 Among the authorities who discuss the constitutional mission of the house of lords are: T. Erskine May, *The Constitutional History of England since the Accession of George III, 1760-1860* (New York, 1876); Sir W. Holdsworth, *The History of English Law* (London, 1938), x; A.S. Turberville, *The House of Lords in the XVIIIth Century* (Oxford, 1927), and *The House of Lords in the Age of Reform, 1784-1837*, ed. R.J. White (London, 1958); C. Weston, *English Constitutional Theory and the House of Lords* (New York, 1965).

3 Lord Melville told a friend in 1804 that: 'It is clear that the House of Lords cannot turn out an administration so long as the King supports it. The Business must be done in the other house of Parliament.' Dacres Adam Papers, PRO 30/58/5, Melville to A. Hope, 5 Apr. 1804; Fox Papers, Add. MS 47564, fos. 197-8, Fox to Lauderdale [1804].

2

sentiments of eighteenth-century observers. Sir William Holdsworth is among the few scholars to have argued that the house of lords did mediate between crown and commons and did criticize the work of ministers and the lower house. Arthur Turberville, the most serious modern student of the lords, was far more restrained in his conclusions. For Turberville the significance of the upper house was revealed in the peers' control of parliamentary constituencies and their domination of the cabinet and important government departments. He dismissed the proceedings of the house as being relatively unimportant and believed that after 1760 George III transformed the former stronghold of whig oligarchs into a chamber which was increasingly submissive to himself.[1]

Historians working after Namier cannot assert, as Turberville did, that George III subverted the lords' independence. Still, the standard histories of this period along with many of the pertinent biographies and monographs share Turberville's underlying conviction that the house of lords was, during the reign of George III, subservient to the crown. Eighteenth-century political history is written under the assumption that power resided in the crown and the commons. The house of lords may occasionally have proved useful to ministers as a place to dispose of measures they did not care to oppose in the commons. Otherwise, it exercised little if any independent authority. Nor could it, for its members were, in the words of John Brooke, 'creatures of the Crown'?[2]

To justify their consigning the house of lords to relative obscurity, historians have fallen back upon a hypothesis which is purely whiggish. Throughout the late eighteenth century, it is argued, the lords was dominated by a 'party of the crown'. Because that group was so large, because its members — the newly honoured, the bishops, the courtiers and the representative peers of Scotland — were so beholden to successive governments, the house could not stand up to the crown as the commons did on some occasions.[3] Some scholars endeavour to

1 Holdsworth, *English Law*, x, 613-7, 626-9; Turberville, *Lords in the XVIIIth Century*, 482, 491-4. Cf. B. Kemp, *King and Commons, 1660-1832* (London, 1959), 68-9.

2 A. Briggs, *The Age of Improvement, 1783-1867* (New York, 1959), 96-7; R.K. Webb, *Modern England from the Eighteenth Century to the Present* (New York, 1969), 44-5; J. Cannon, *The Fox-North Coalition: Crisis of the Constitution 1782-4* (Cambridge, 1969), 125; R. Pares, *King George III and the Politicians* (Oxford, 1953), 39-43; J. Brooke, *King George III* (New York, 1972), 161.

3 D. Large, 'The Decline of the "Party of the Crown" and the Rise of Parties in the House of Lords, 1783-1837', *EHR*, lxviii (1963), 669-95; J. Ehrman, *The Younger Pitt: The Years of Acclaim* (New York, 1969), 44; D. Marshall, *Eighteenth Century England* (London, 1962), 52; Pares, *George III and the*

dilute or explain the illogical determinism of this view by citing their lordships' conservative inclination to adhere to the crown.[1] Only a very few perceive that men who were undoubtedly the king's friends could still in important instances act on their own initiative for well-defined political reasons.[2]

This last possibility, that the members of the peerage were relatively free agents who possessed distinct political interests and principles, is the point from which our study of the house of lords commences. A house whose members are freed from their supposed dependence upon the crown is itself naturally transformed. The crown's appendage takes on an independent existence, one whose nature it is the object of this book to identify. What was the role of the house of lords in the eighteenth century? To what degree were its members collectively able to shape the development of policy, to influence the course of political life and to maintain the balance of power at Westminster? Answers to these questions provide the means with which we can establish the lords' position within the English system of government. With them we can also more fully comprehend the strengths and weakness of a political order in which the house of lords was an important participant.

This investigation of the house of lords focuses on the years 1783-1806 for several reasons. The period opens with a constitutional crisis in which the house of lords played an important, if misinterpreted part. This upheaval went far to shape the character of the next twenty-three years, all the more because the leading combatants of 1783-4, William Pitt and Charles Fox, dominated English political life down to 1806. Thus, even while a host of forces were working to transform English life, the political nation continued to be preoccupied by the question of what constituted a proper balance between the crown and parliament. Of course this debate commenced before 1783. It continued after 1806, though the waning influence of the crown and the deaths in 1806 of Pitt and Fox deprived it of much of its former passion.[3] Between 1783

Politicians, 41-2; Turberville, *Lords in the XVIIIth Century*, 493; Webb, *Modern England*, 44-5. The popularity of the 'party of the crown' theory has not declined markedly even in recent years: Dr. Cannon, for example, found Large's article on this group to be an 'admirable analysis'. Cannon, *The Fox-North Coalition*, 125, n.2.

1 Ehrman, *Pitt*, 44-5; Marshall, *Eighteenth Century England*, 52; Pares, *George III and the Politicians*, 42; Turberville, *Lords in the XVIIIth Century*, 494.

2 P. Landford, *The First Rockingham Administration, 1765-6* (Oxford, 1973), 156-7; 163-70.

3 During the crisis brought about by the king's refusal to accept the Talents' bill permitting Roman Catholics to serve in the military, certain ministers proposed that the government carry the measure through the commons. Such action would not only pledge the lower house on the subject; it would force the king's hand. If

4

and 1806, however, it achieved a special intensity as rival factions strove to preserve or readjust the existing relationship between king and parliament. The nature, fervour and importance of this debate make these years particularly suitable as the setting for an examination of the political and constitutional role of the house of lords![1]

Other factors reinforced the central importance of these years for a student of parliament and its upper house. Between 1783 and 1806 the lords' membership grew substantially. While the new peers altered neither its social composition nor its political character, they brought with them resources of power which augmented the nobility's weight within the political system.[2] Such resources were especially useful in an era when the volume of legislation began to grow rapidly and when peers were asked to approve an increasing number of controversial measures. The revolutionary changes which occurred in these years subjected parliament and their lordships to repeated, difficult tests. An examination of the lords' conduct in the midst of such upheavals illumines the shortcomings but also the continuing vitality of eighteenth-century political institutions as they entered the industrial age.

The house of lords' constitutional mission was a conservative one — to preserve the classic balance of elements established at the revolution. Happily, the peers' political and social instincts amply qualified them for this task. All admired the political system which granted them so much authority, and if the whigs complained of the crown's growing influence, it was because they wished to re-establish the constitution's purity and, incidently, to restore themselves to power. With their vast estates, their social pre-eminence and their extensive political privileges the members of the peerage had an obvious interest in maintaining the

the bill were afterwards thrown out at his behest in the lords, ministers could go to the country complaining of his illegal intervention. However, Lord Grenville, the prime minister, refused to adopt such a course: it would only hurt the country by turning the king against his former ministers. Grenville's restraint contrasts sharply with Fox's acts in similar situations. *The Journal of Elizabeth Lady Holland (1791-1811)*, ed. Earl of Ilchester (London, 1908), ii, 215.

1 In order to establish the place of the house of lords in the eighteenth-century political system we shall focus our study on its political and legislative activities. The house will not be studied in its capacity as a court of law. By the late eighteenth century the judges controlled and directed the legal proceedings, unimpeded save in a very few instances by lay members. Highly specialized in its nature, ignored by most members and dominated by a very few, this aspect of the lords' business sheds little light on the rest.

2 The social antecedents of these new peers are discussed in Turberville, *The House of Lords in the Age of Reform*, 42-54; G.C. Richards, 'The Creations of Peers Recommended by the Younger Pitt', *AHR*, xxiv (1928), 47-54; F.M.L. Thompson, *English Landed Society in the Nineteenth Century* (London, 1963), 8-14.

5

stability of the existing order. Thus, as the forces unleashed by the French Revolution threatened temporarily to engulf England in revolution, the labels of whig and tory became meaningless, and men who two years yearlier had damned Pitt as a tyrant joined the majority to support the war and his efforts to quash sedition.

The crisis occasioned by the French Revolution dramatically illustrates the extent to which members of the peerage believed that the preservation of stability depended upon their steady adherence to the king's government. In quieter times some noblemen indulged themselves in systematic opposition, but the majority consistently eschewed this path. These last peers rejected the whig contention that the crown's expanding power had destroyed the constitution's balance: believing that the late eighteenth-century political system still embodied the essential features of the revolutionary settlement, they concluded that they could best preserve that condition by providing ministers with sufficient support to carry on the nation's business. Political upheaval disrupted the smooth functioning of the national administration; peers also believed that these convulsions encouraged politicians, intent upon their struggle for power, to propound innovative constitutional theories as a means of achieving their objective. But the possibility of disorder and constitutional disruption remained unlikely, they assumed, so long as the king's chosen ministers were able to fulfill their responsibilities.

Chapter 2 demonstrates that the majority of peers applied a commonly shared view of their constitutional duties consistently and with some effect. Their loyal adherence to the king's government contributed to the stability of the political world of Westminster and strengthened his administration's hold in the countryside. Moreover, in at least two instances the lords' activities had more far-reaching consequences. In 1801, but especially in 1783-4, George III found himself in conflict with politicians who commanded majorities in the lower house. Scholarly attention has focused in each instance on the struggles between the king, his ministers and the commons; the house of lords has either been ignored or dismissed as the crown's pawn. Yet, while the peers were not the most active combatants in these crises, their activities complemented and reinforced those of the king with whom they worked in partnership, not submission. Their attachment not only made it more difficult for politicians to force George III to accept changes which he disliked; in 1784 the peers also helped to restore that harmony between the closet, the cabinet and the commons which was the essential prerequisite for steady, effective administration.

The same conservatism which guided the peers' conduct in these constitutional crises shaped the legislative personality of their house. Normally the house of lords was a quiet, uncritical legislative body: its members followed the lead of the king's ministers and ratified whatever measures those men presented. When the lords deviated from their normal pattern of behaviour and assumed a more active stance, the consequences varied. Abolition and a host of less significant political and social reforms languished in the face of their opposition. Debates were sometimes foolish or cursory, and members succeeded in carrying amendments which weakened good measures or placed their own interests above those of the nation.

Yet, while the peers' conservatism may have prevented the house from becoming a focal point of the legislature, it did not inhibit them from exercising a positive influence on the legislative process. The house of lords was a useful second chamber: peers regularly corrected or clarified the text of measures sent up from the house of commons. More importantly, they were sometimes able to call local needs to the attention of ministers who would otherwise have remained oblivious of them when drafting important legislation. Nor was the house of lords leadenly obstructive of change during these years: privately initiated reforms on topics ranging from the laws of libel to clerical residence passed there as did Pitt's various bills for improving administrative efficiency, expanding commerce, governing the empire and readjusting Anglo-Irish relations.

Moreover, the house participated in the evaluation of the performance of successive ministers. Exploitation of available sources of information enabled the peers to amass an impressive body of material on a range of public bills and policies. This information was used both to justify and condemn controversial measures in debates. Because the house possessed a number of able statesmen, because the ranks of that group were continuously replenished during our period, the lords was able to serve as a forum for the intelligent discussion of important public issues. For the noble lords were prepared on certain occasions to question the capacity of the king's ministers. Differences over important issues frequently drove individuals to oppose politicians and governments which they had formerly supported, and very weak or inept administrations did engender enough opposition to jeopardize their control of the house of lords.

Only in one area, private and local business, did the house of lords emerge from the shadow of the more aggressive commons to take a leading legislative role. Private and local bills, which comprised about two-thirds of the legislation passed in each session during our period, reflect in part the social, economic and political changes which were taking place throughout Britain. Already thorough and efficient in its scrutiny of this business, the house moved in the 1790s to adopt a series of orders which at once tightened private bill procedures and facilitated the process by which legitimate promoters might obtain those bills. More importantly, the transformation of the chairmanship of the committees into a post whose occupant critically supervised the passage of such legislation insured that these measures would be subjected to a uniform and reasonably disinterested scrutiny and amended, where necessary, by a knowledgeable authority.

The lords' conservative character and loyal adherence to the king's government in part reflect the nature and quality of its leadership. Their exalted positions, formidable talents and personalities and close connection with George III enormously enhanced the powers of the law lords. By cleverly exploiting their prestige, these men were able to influence the house in two directions: their interventions added a much-needed element of precision to the lords' deliberations, but they also reinforced the chamber's conservative temper. The judges were the most powerful conservative force in the upper house and repeatedly gave direction and focus to their less articulate and less brilliant colleagues.

If the lawyers reinforced the lords' conservative temper, the king's ministers were in most instances able to overwhelm the whig opposition. Generally the government front bench was superior in terms of practical knowledge and debating skill to that of the opposition in these years. The small band of competent, well-informed peers that stood at the head of the government forces were recruited from the house of commons, and they derived their stature from their offices, their talents and, above all, from their intimate participation in the formulation of policy. The effectiveness of this group was further enhanced by their increasingly efficient direction. After 1790 the post of leader of the house was transformed into one whose occupant served as the chief spokesman for government's policies as well as the organizer of its forces. The leader's unchallenged direction of the ministerial majority and his ability to confront his opponents with authority and good sense gave coherence to the government front bench and additional strength to the government's position in the house of lords.

In comparison to their leading ministerial counterparts the titled grandees who led the whigs during these years seemed amateurish. Though they possessed a sense of decency and generosity which was often missing on the government side and adopted sound positions on a few issues, whig politicians tended to manage their forces poorly. They also lacked a detailed knowledge of leading national questions. Consequently, their attacks on ministerial policies often revealed their ignorance, their opportunism and sometimes even their incapacity to govern. Not until Grenville and Spencer joined their ranks did the whigs in the house of lords offer a consistently credible alternative to the administration.

Of greater importance than the leadership in moulding the character of the house was a rather amorphous collection of noblemen who stood by any government in which the king expressed his confidence. Some of these peers were members of groups normally included within the ranks of the 'party of the crown', but not all. Many owed the crown no particular obligation, and some Scots, bishops or new peers attached themselves to political factions or remained independent. As will be seen in chapter 7, the crown's adherents were not its bondsmen but instead the king's friends. Some looked for favours as rewards for past support, and many more felt a sense of obligation to their royal patron. But patronage was only one of the forces which bound members of this group together. Included within its ranks were men for whom service at court was a longstanding family tradition as well as those who were the personal friends of their sovereign. Above all, however, the king's friends were united by common political prejudices: hostile to the notion of reform, they also had a deep, even exalted respect for monarchial authority, and they deprecated opposition for its disruptive and disloyal proclivities. Individuals coveted or enjoyed the lush fruits of royal bene-ficence; others were bound to the king by friendship or family tradition; but without exception the king's friends shared a conservative political ideology.

Peers outside this group may have been somewhat more adventure-some politically, but they, like the king's friends, devoted only a small portion of their attention to parliamentary affairs. Much of the parliament's business was so limited in its scope that only the most diligent could find it absorbing. Moreover, a number of peers, because of their modest abilities, were incapable of making any constructive contribution to the conduct of business. Many too found that their extensive responsibilities as estate owners and local leaders prevented them from devoting themselves to the business of the house.

Few noblemen, in fact, acknowledged any obligation to follow the progress even of the most important legislation. An analysis of attendance records indicates that only major party confrontations, ceremonies or a few of the most controversial privately initiated reforms were likely to command the attention of a substantial portion of them. Even in these instances the largest number of peers were silent, sometimes inattentive participants who came to life only at divisions. Bills which touched upon personal or territorial interests might stir them to some activity, but in those instances most preferred to bring their influence to bear on cabinet ministers or members of the lower house, not directly in the house of lords.

The eighteenth-century peerage possessed stores of political power which neither the government nor the commons could ignore. Vast properties formed the basis for a territorial hegemony whose clearest manifestation was the nobility's large and growing parliamentary interest. This parliamentary interest and their other political resources enabled the noble lords to shape public or private bills through other channels than their own house. Many preferred to attain their legislative objectives through the agency of sympathetic ministers rather than by taking direct action on the floor of the house of lords: one letter or a short conversation with a minister often achieved the same purpose as a lengthy journey and endless hours in the house, and both concealed from the public view the unseemly spectacle of a peer criticizing his acknowledged leaders. Similarly, a friendly MP not only oversaw the passage of legislation in which his patron had an interest; because of the restriction barring lords from amending money bills, he was frequently better placed than his patron to make any necessary alterations.

The nobility applied its political resources to the service of the king as well as to the more personal requirements of its members. In quiet times the peers' members in the commons swelled an administration's majorities: most noble borough patrons were ministerial stalwarts, and their nominees or dependents, who normally followed the lead of their benefactors, were more inclined to support Pitt's government during the 1780s, for example, than the house as a whole. However, in the intermittent skirmishes between the crown and the commons, of which the 1783-4 crisis was the most important, the nobility's political might assumed even more crucial significance. In the early months of 1784 noble lords eschewed direct action as a body, and instead concentrated their energies on mobilizing public opinion in support of Pitt and on winning over individual MPs to his government. By using their personal influence in this manner, the peers helped to increase Pitt's following in the country and the commons without seriously dislocating the relations between the two houses. No other episode illustrates so vividly the extent of the nobility's political power and the manner in which it was used; the peers preferred to influence events indirectly and resorted to their own house in the last resort.

In order to place the house of lords in its proper perspective it is necessary to look beyond its proceedings and examine the manner in which the nobility applied its extensive political resources. While such an examination does not alter our conclusions about the lords' constitutional position, it demonstrates the peculiar importance of a house whose members were able in several critical instances to influence the outcome of events in the house of commons by rallying public opinion and by exerting pressure on their recalcitrant or inactive clients. A similar scrutiny of the peers' legislative conduct produces more surprising results. It shows first that the nobility was more actively critical and important in shaping policy than an analysis of its parliamentary conduct would indicate. It also substantiates a conclusion which can only be suggested on the basis of the peers' parliamentary activities — namely that these men were often active, effective patrons of individuals or groups which lacked direct parliamentary representation.

The range of the peers' patronage extended over a variety of groups and causes to include even the leading pioneers of the industrial revolution. Such breadth of activity reflects both a genuine desire to promote the prosperity of their neighbourhoods and an enlightened self-interest which in turn reflects the peers' careful assessment of their own economic and political needs. Often patrons were partners in or at least beneficiaries of projects whose implementation required legislative action; certainly those peers who cultivated electoral interests had to advance any legislation put forward by their constituencies or leading political supporters. It is remarkable, in fact, that some lords assumed that their effective performance as patrons would help to preserve a 'standard of true aristocracy' and thereby buttress the political and social order of their forefathers.

This last aspect of the peers' legislative character is both interesting and important. Conservative men seemingly distinguished by their legislative inertia suddenly appear as effective sponsors of measures which helped to bring about England's most fundamental and revolutionary economic transformations. As its chief beneficiaries the nobility naturally wished to preserve the *status quo* while at the same time harbouring within its ranks progressive entrepreneurs and realistic politicians who saw that their continued authority depended to an extent on their ability to move with the sentiments of their followers and dependents. At once detesting and encouraging change, the nobility was, in fact, slightly schizophrenic.

Yet, their active patronage of diverse communities and interests may in the short term have contributed to the stability that most peers desired. By enabling powerful but under-represented groups to obtain a portion of their legislative requirements in a period when parliamentary reform was impossible and the need for change extreme, the peers demonstrated the continuing vitality of the eighteenth-century political system. Unreformed as it was, parliament still could attend at least partially to demands of important segments of the national community.

As the nation's chief instrument of stability, the eighteenth-century peerage was unwilling to adopt a course of action which might disrupt the orderly functioning of government. Fortunately, peers could shape events indirectly because of their substantial political resources. Informal channels of influence were efficient. They were all the more appealing to men who were reluctant openly to take steps which might weaken the hold of the king's ministers. Without this ability to shape events through the cabinet or the commons it is unlikely that their lordships would have maintained their normally restrained, conservative posture in the house of lords.

Yet despite its members' restraint or seeming indifference the house of lords performed a series of important functions. In an age when the nature of the relationship between the crown and parliament provoked fierce debate, the house of lords stood forward as a formidable instrument of continuity and stability. Peers fulfilled their responsibilities as the constitution's equipoise consistently and, in 1783-4 and 1801, with considerable effect. They constituted during these years the main body of support for successive governments.

Even while the house remained a bulwark against disruption or substantial innovation, it participated critically and creatively in the business of government. As a group the peerage possessed a breadth of experience and knowledge which enabled its members to discuss and shape policy intelligently. Though their inclination was to support governments, their lordships demonstrated dramatically in 1804 that they were not prepared to suffer incompetent leadership. As legislators these same men helped at once to accommodate national legislation and public policy to the needs of a variety of interests and communities and to encourage measures which slowly transformed English society and economic practices. Finally, in an era when private and local bills constituted two-thirds of parliament's legislative business, the lords' capacity to define and implement an efficient, thorough procedure ensured that the house would dominate the scrutiny of such measures.

Policy, the course of politics, the very nature of the constitution — all in this period bear the imprint of their lordships' collective influence. That that influence was conservative is undeniable. However, it rarely lapsed into senseless obstructionism, and on occasions it proved to be creative, even daring. The undeniable importance of the lords' functions and achievements testify to its existence as an active, independent, sometimes vital participant in eighteenth-century affairs.

2

UPHOLDERS OF THE EQUIPOISE

The house of lords was composed almost exclusively of great land-lords. As a class these men were sated: they had neither major unrealized political ambitions nor serious grievances with the existing social and political orders. Understandably their overriding object was to conserve what already existed. 'As a person of property & a peaceable subject', wrote the second Lord Boringdon, 'I feel chiefly anxious that things sh^d be kept quiet', and his whig colleague, the third earl of Egremont, desired only to preserve 'a quiet state of the country'.[1]

The nobility accepted as an article of faith the idea of the constitution's general perfection. Partisan rhetoric which poured forth from the house of lords should not obscure the underlying unity of interest and principle which bound the peerage together. The third duke of Richmond, who was feared as one of the most radical reformers of the early 1780s, nevertheless proclaimed during the debates on the India Bill that it was the duty of the upper house to keep each branch of the legislature within 'prescriptions to which it was originally restricted'. Similarly, Lord Stormont, who had been one of the leaders of the whig opposition in the lords after 1784, protested in 1792 that the peers had a special obligation to thwart the designs of those who would 'level with the ground that venerable fabric that has so long been the pride and glory of this country, the admiration and envy of every other.'[2] Radicals and whigs as well as Pittites and courtiers complacently assumed that the underlying principles of their political system were of lasting validity.

Though the Foxite whigs shared the majority's essentially static view of the constitution, they were sincerely alarmed by the state of its current health. In particular, they lamented and attacked all evidences of the executive's growing influence. The party's primary object was to trim off the crown's more recent encrustations of power. During the 1780s most whigs believed that it was sufficient to eliminate needless sinecures, but in the 1790s the tone of their proposals became more radical. At the end of the nineties for example, Lord Holland proposed not only the abolition of all sinecures and many court offices, but also

1   Granville Papers, PRO 30/29/9, fos. 154-7, Boringdon to G. Leveson Gower, 7 Oct. 1801; H.A. Wyndham, *A Family History 1688-1837: The Wyndhams of Somerset, Sussex, and Wiltshire* (London, 1950), 309.

2   *PH*, xxiv, 506-9, 4 Feb. 1748; *ibid.*, xxix, 1571, 13 Dec. 1792.

a reduction in the size of the army and, most notably, an expansion of the suffrage. Whig prescriptions for reform were, however, purely remedial; neither Fox nor Holland wished to establish the full sovereignty of the people.[1]

Despite their essential moderation, the whigs never succeeded in convincing the majority of the upper house that the constitution's equipoise had been overthrown. On the contrary, most peers believed that the foolish notions and wild antics of the whigs and those radical groups with whom they associated themselves were the most serious threat to stability. Summarizing the views of his colleagues in February, 1784, Lord Fauconberg condemned Fox and his allies for violently assaulting the 'just prerogatives of the crown'. A decade later the moderate Lord Boringdon hinted darkly that

> there existed out of doors a large body of discontent capable of being directed & extended as might seem expedient to certain leaders by means of affiliated societies of secret organization, & unascertained extent, & whose connexion with the opposition was neither clearly avowed or disavowed by either party.[2]

Because the majority of peers believed in the constitution's continuing vitality, most were hostile to substantial political reform. Many were like the second Viscount Wentworth or the fourth earl of Sandwich' self-proclaimed enemies of all innovation. Portland, Fitzwilliam and other aristocratic whigs toleraged those measures which eradicated useless sinecures. But they, along with the greatest numbers of Pitt's supporters, abhorred their leaders' unfortunate plans for expanding the suffrage or redistributing parliamentary seats.[3]

This distrust of reform spread and hardened during the 1790s. Lord Grenville, in many respects a progressive man, viewed the consequences of innovation in apocalyptic terms: if the peers once 'opened the floodgate of innovation', he warned, 'the torrent of anarchy would spread so forcibly and so wide, that it would not be in the power of their lordships, by opposing their feeble hands as a barrier to destruction, to prevent the constitution from being overwhelmed in general ruin'. Violent

1 Holland House Papers, Add. MS 51571, fos. 13-4, Holland to Thanet [no date]. According to the duke of Leeds Fox believed that 'husbandmen & labourers thought so little of public matters that he should as soon think of consulting the sheep on the propriety of Peace as the people who had care of them or in general the lower orders of Peasantry.' Leeds Papers, Add. MS 27918, fo 313.

2 PH, xxiv, 502-4, 4 Feb. 1784; Morley Papers, Add. MS 48244, fos. 265-7, 'Memoirs of the Earl of Morley'.

3 The Noels and the Milbankes: Their Letters for Twenty-Five Years, 1767-1792, ed. M. Elwin (London, 1967), 262; PH, xxvi, 185-6, 5 July 1786; Wentworth Woodhouse MSS, F63 (c)-44, Portland to Fitzwilliam, 20 Aug. 1784.

as his words now seem, they accurately reflect the panic which seized his colleagues: his elder brother, the first marquis of Buckingham, feared that the slightest concession to the popular reforming spirit would provoke an outburst of radical proposals, and the Earl Fitzwilliam admitted his detestation of 'speculative innovations'.[1]

Their static concept of the constitution and their craving for stability eminently qualified the peers to be the upholders of the equipoise. The house of lords was the conservative branch of the legislature: as guardians of the system's traditional balance the lords were obliged to see that no innovation, no political upheaval disrupted constitutional practices from their established pattern. Of course the fulfillment of this trust required activity, even sacrifices, but the activity, the sacrifices were endurable because they were essentially so congenial to their lordships' political tastes. Conservatism gave birth to a coherent sense of the nobility's constitutional mission; it also stimulated the peers to watchfulness and exertion.

Between 1783 and 1806 the house of lords made its most direct and positive contribution to the preservation of stability by uniformly adhering to the king's government. Its members provided a substantial portion of that support in parliament and the countryside which enabled governments to function smoothly. So long as the king's ministers were able to carry on the nation's business, the peers assumed that their political system was operating effectively and that change was unnecessary. Few political reforms were, in fact, presented to parliament in these years, and the only major political innovation whose passage the peers obstructed even indirectly was Catholic emancipation. Support for established authority rather than belligerent opposition to political change was the means by which these men proposed to preserve the constitution's equipoise.

At no point during the late eighteenth century did the proceedings of the house of lords absorb the attention of the majority of peers. Graph I does not include the large number of noblemen who failed to attend the house at all.[2] Yet, even with the inactive portion of the peerage excluded from these tabulations, the median level of the

---

1 *PH*, xxxiii, 758-62, 30 May, 1797; *HMC, 13th R.*, iii, *Fortescue MSS*, ii, 338-9; Fitzwilliam Papers, Box 52, Fitzwilliam to Mr. Sykes, Mar. 1797.

2 All figures, tables and graphs relating to the peers' attendance are based on the lists of members present each day which are printed in the *Journals of the House of Lords*. Attendances were taken for 1785, 1786, 1787, 1794, 1795 and 1796 by three single persons. Intermittent spot checks were made to determine accuracy, but some errors are doubtless incorporated into these figures.

nobility's parliamentary attendance was extraordinarily low. For five of the six sessions for which we have figures, the median frequency of participation was under fifteen times a session, and in 1796 it sank to under ten.

Graph

Incidence of attendance among
active peers at the house of lords

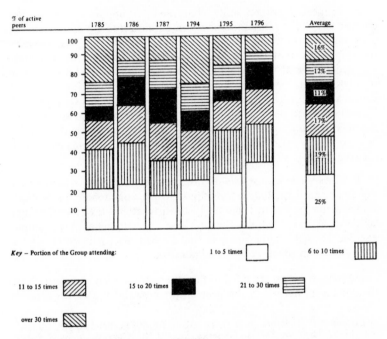

Key – Portion of the Group attending: 1 to 5 times   6 to 10 times

11 to 15 times   15 to 20 times   21 to 30 times

over 30 times

The correspondence of party leaders indicates that the services of ordinary members were only required in special circumstances. Noblemen were regularly informed of the proceedings in the house, and great care was taken by ministers, who regarded their applications as an imposition, to see that peers did not attend unnecessarily. Thus, the duke of Portland wrote to the earl of Hertford in 1783 that he eagerly awaited the end of the session when he would no longer have to 'trespass upon the Patience & Indulgence of those very Respectable Friends whose Support is no less honourable than essential to the existence of Administration'. Fifteen years later Lord Grenville anxiously told the marquis of Bute that he 'should have been much concerned if you had put yourself to the least inconvenience in order to attend, as we have had no occasion to trouble our friends'. [1]

As these communications imply, party leaders called upon their supporters when serious confrontations loomed on the parliamentary horizon, not to participate in the details of business. Daily attendance figures reinforce this conclusion; the greatest number of peers normally came to the house for major divisions. Such events occurred on six of the seven days in 1785 when the number of peers present exceeded seventy-five, and on nine of twelve similar occasions in 1795.

If the peers were primarily concerned to support or oppose the government, it is essential to know how extensively they participated at divisions. In 1785 there were six major party confrontations, at which the opposition mounted serious challenges to government measures: 152 peers (66% of those eligible to vote) attended at least one of these six divisions. In 1795 there were nine divisions of similar importance at which a total of 185 noblemen (74% of those eligible) were present.[2] Table I demonstrates that while a tiny proportion attended all divisions, the majority appeared at less than half. Yet, when viewed in the context of their total parliamentary participation, the peers' attendance at such events appears positively diligent.

Moreover, attendance lists do not provide a complete record of the nobility's participation at divisions. When summoned by Sydney, leader of the house, to come up to town to attend the second reading of the government's India Bill in 1784, Lord Brudenell, for example, excused himself on the grounds that he had placed his proxy in the hands of a firm adherent of the administration.[3]

As long as a peer attended to take the oaths in each new parliament, he could avail himself of this peculiar privilege and express his opinions

---

1 Egerton MS (Hertford Papers), Eg. 3260, fo. 60, Portland to Hertford, 12 July 1783; Harrowby Papers, 1st series, xxi, fo. 40, Grenville to Bute, 9 Oct. 1799.

2 1785: Motion on the payment of the Nabob of Arcot's debts, 1 March; Motion for papers relative to trials of servants of the East India Company, 18 February; Motion to commit Shop Tax, 3 June; Motion for statutes on Ireland, 6 June; Motion to postpone consideration of the Irish propositions, 8 July; Motion that the propositions be passed, 18 July.
1795: Amendment to the address to the king, 30 December 1794; Motion against interference in the internal affairs of France, 6 January; Motion for peace with any French government, 27 January; Approval of the subsidy for Austria, 9 February; Motion for peace, 12 February; Address to the king promising to meet the financial burdens of the war, 27 March; Motion for a committee on the state of the nation, 30 March; Motion for papers relative to Lord Fitzwilliam's dismissal from the Lieutenancy of Ireland, 8 May; Motion for peace, 5 June.

3 Sydney Papers, Box 2, Brudenell to Sydney, 29 July [1784].

Table I

The Peers' Attendance
at Divisions

divisions attended	1785	1795
1	19	23
2	28	24
3	30	22
4	36	27
5	19	19
6	20	15
7		26
8		15
9		14

in absentia by filling out a printed form and returning it to the clerk of the house with a guinea.[1] Critics of the system complained that the outcome of crucial measures often depended upon the votes of men who had not heard any of the arguments for or against, and some lords refused on principle to grant proxies.[2] Still, their use expanded rapidly throughout this period. Between 1785 and 1787 an average of fifty-eight members left proxies each session. From 1794 to 1796 the average increased by 40 per cent to eight-one while the size of the house grew by only 15 per cent.

The circumstances in which peers bestowed their proxies varied enormously. Most left them as a matter of course in the hands of party leaders and even permitted colleagues to fill in the name of the individual to whom the proxy could most conveniently be entrusted. Others sent them to politicians as expressions of confidence, and a few regularly exchanged proxies with close friends or political associates.[3] Occasion-

1 *The Correspondence of George, Prince of Wales, 1770-1812*, ed. A. Aspinall (London, 1965), iv, no. 1457. Proxies could only be used when the house was in full session. No peer was permitted to hold more than two at a time, and bishops were only allowed to take the proxies of their colleagues on the episcopal bench.

2 *The Times*, 21 July 1785; Hardwicke Papers, Add. MS 35391, fos. 96-9, J. Yorke to P. Yorke, 6, 11 May 1786.

3 Holland House Papers, Add. MS 51821, fos. 193-4, Oxford to Holland, 21 Mar. 1799; Harrowby Papers, ix, 1st series, fo. 41, bishop of Bath to Harrowby [no date]; Pitt Papers, PRO 30/8/173, fo. 82, Rolle to Pitt, 26 Mar. 1797; Portland Papers, Pwf. 8862, Vernon to Portland, 18 Nov. 1794; Hardwicke Papers, Add. MS 45030, fo. 17, Portland to Hardwicke, 2 Nov. 1783. The tenth earl of

ally a peer dispatched instructions with his proxy though these ranged widely both in their clarity and scope.[1]

If proxies were called for, peers were obliged to cast those they held on the same side as they, themselves, voted. Recipients thus took some care to ascertain the views of their colleagues when controversial questions came before the house, and some conscientious noblemen, such as the first Viscount Sydney, made it a rule 'to refer to those who do me the honour to trust me with their Proxys' on these occasions. Normally, however, lords trusted their colleagues to represent their views, and only the most fundamental differences of opinion caused them to transfer their votes to more congenial hands.[2]

The proxy system enabled the less active portion of the peerage to exert some influence on the proceedings of the house of lords. In 1785 seventy-four peers left proxies: twenty-one of these men failed to appear at any of the major divisions that session, and thirty-three others attended between one and three. Eighteen of the eighty-one peers who left proxies in 1795 did not take part personally in any of the nine major divisions that year, and thirty-nine others only attended between one and four. Thus, the system insured that a policy passed by the upper house would receive the sanction of the largest possible number of peers.

The low level of the peers' parliamentary attendance combined with their increasing use of proxies suggests that in general they were uninterested in the details of parliamentary business. Most acknowledged an obligation to participate in important divisions, but it was not usually their object to evaluate the merits of those policies whose fate they would decide. Instead, the majority used these occasions to demonstrate their continuing loyalty to the king's government and their willingness to support whatever projects his ministers recommended.

Any administration which found itself suddenly faced with dimished majorities in the house of lords was assumed to be in trouble. Peers

Exeter and the fourth earl of Sandwich annually exchanged proxies between 1784 and 1790 as did the earls of Beaulieu and Coventry.

1 Sydney Papers, Box 1, H. Cowper to Sydney [no date]; *HMC, 13th R.,* iii, *Fortescue MSS,* i, 252; Morley Papers, Add. MS 48218, fos. 69-70, Boringdon to Grantham, 8 Feb. 1785; Holland House Papers, Add. MS 51802, fos. 30-1, Richmond to Holland, 8 June 1806.

2 Dropmore Papers, Add. MS 58989 (unfoliated), Grenville to Effingham, 24 May 1799; Braybrooke Papers (Essex Record Office), D/DBy C9/71, Onslow to Howard, 29 Jan. 1795; Hardwicke Papers, Add. MS 45030, fo. 21, Hardwicke to Portland, 13 Dec. 1783; *Lady Holland's Journal,* i, 181.

were therefore reasonably diligent in attending major divisions or at least in leaving their proxies. Yet, they did not come up in these instances merely to assure the current ministry's numerical superiority over its opponents. In 1795 when the whigs constituted an insignificant threat to Pitt's administration, a larger proportion of the peerage attended at divisions than in 1785 when the opposition still had some force.

The crisis of the 1790s vividly illustrates why the nobility attached such importance to its regular support of government. On the eve of England's entry into the war the earl of Macclesfield announced that 'in the present Situation of things it seems to me to be necessary for everyone who wishes the Continuance of our Constitution to give his utmost support.' Somewhat more emphatically, the duke of St Albans told Pitt that

> at this Critical Juncture of Affairs I think it incumbent upon every Person of Rank & Property to come forward, & profess their Sentiments in Support of the Government, & Constitution of this Kingdom. . . It is my intention to give all the assistance in my Power to Administration, in order to afford that energy so necessary to the executive power, to enable them to guard against the wicked intentions of persons, who wish to subvert this Constitution. . .

The sentiments of these men were shared by many whigs. Lord Spencer, for example, told his mother that

> at present, I feel that the part of an active Politician is not at all suited either to my health or disposition, and I should be very much disposed to give up any interference in public business, if the preservation of all the desirable comforts of life did not at present seem very much to depend on an active exertion in support of that order which alone can secure them to us, & to call for every effort that one is capable of making.[1]

None of these men feared that the ministry would lose its majority. Spencer had talents which were eventually used by the government, but Macclesfield and St Albans never even rose in the house to proclaim their views. Rather, their presence was a symbol of their support for the administration's campaign to eradicate sedition. Along with most of their colleagues they believed that substantial majorities in the house of lords would facilitate and make more effective the exercise of government.

Eighteenth-century administrations depended upon the influence derived from property rather than on a national bureaucracy to implement their mandates. The peerage contained the leading representatives of rank and property, and as the demands for change at home became increasingly radical and the revolution in France more violent, it

---

1 Liverpool Papers, Add. MS 38228, fo. 157, Macclesfield to Hawkesbury, 4 Dec. 1792; Pitt Papers, PRO 30/8/175, fo. 9, St. Albans to Pitt, 5 Dec. 1792; Spencer Papers, Box 12, Spencer to Dowager Countess Spencer, 26 Feb. 1794.

sought to strengthen the forces of law and order by adding the weight of property to the administration. As early as 1792 Portland told the duke of Leeds that he thought it 'highly desirable that everything that could give weight to Govt by uniting Talents, Character, and Property in the Executive Administration of the Country should be exerted.' Somewhat more colourfully the earl of Chesterfield predicted that all attempts to control popular disorders would fail 'unless we have more acres added to our abilities'. Lord Grenville explained to his brother in the spring of 1794 that the time had come for the property of the nation to put aside those partisan distinctions which had divided the advocates of law and order, and as a result of the Portland whigs' accession to the government, Pitt's ministry did secure the virtually unanimous support of large property holders by the fall.[1]

The huge administration majorities in the house of lords symbolized the nobility's determination and ability to uphold the constitution and the king's government in Westminster and throughout the country. In the commons peers contributed substantially to the minister's enlarged following; about half of the MPs who transferred their support to government by 1794 sat for seats controlled by noblemen.[2] In the country members of the peerage proved themselves to be invaluable instruments of ministerial policy. They raised loyal addresses in support of administration measures pending in parliament and encouraged the growth of the loyalist Association.[3] At country meetings they collected subscriptions for the militia from their neighbours[4] and later urged them to contribute one-fifth of their incomes to the government.[5] As lords lieutenant, colonels of the militia or commanders of volunteer regiments raised from their own estates, they laid plans for local defences and used their troops to control unrest both at home and in Ireland.[6] During the food shortages of 1795 and 1800 they directed

---

1 *Political Memoranda of Francis, Fifth Duke of Leeds*, ed. O. Browning (London, 1884), 176, 199; *Memoirs of the Court and Cabinets of George the Third*, ed. Duke of Buckingham and Chandos (London, 1853-5), ii, 256-8.

2 The activities of the peers' members in the house of commons are analysed below in chapter 8.

3 For their addresses see chapter 8, pp. 168-70; Melville Papers, Box 1041, fos. 5-6, Townshend to Dundas, 2 Oct. 1791.

4 *Journals and Correspondence of William, Lord Auckland*, ed., bishop of Bath and Wells (London, 1862), iii, 205-7; *The Times*, 22, 28 Mar., 4, 14, 17, 18, 21, 29 Apr., 12 May 1794.

5 Dundas urged the duke of Buccleuch to encourage his neighbours 'to give a fifth of their Income to the Publick Service as a very moderate Insurance for the remainder *immediately* and of the whole *ultimately*'. Buccleuch Papers, SRO GD 224/30/4, Dundas to Buccleuch, 27 Jan. 1798. See also *HMC, Verulam MSS.* 175-6.

6 Chichester Papers, Add. MS 33108, fos. 180-1, Kinnoul to Pelham, 18 Oct.

programmes to feed the hungry who when left without sustenance often caused serious disorder.[1] Finally, local contacts enabled them to provide the central government with invaluable intelligence,[2] and on the basis of experience derived from dealing with a wide range of problems they were able to give ministers good advice on a variety of topics.[3]

The French Revolution did not create but only accentuated this pattern of behaviour which reflected the peers' deep conservatism and longing for stability. If in quieter times a portion of the nobility ventured into opposition, the majority did not. These men wished for nothing more than the continued operation of the existing political system, and to secure that end they loyally provided successive ministers with the support they needed to survive both in parliament and the country. If they disagreed with specific government proposals, they addressed their criticisms to the appropriate minister and then absented themselves from the house. As Lord Rolle told Grenville, 'any opposition from one who has been & still continues to be a very sincere Friend to the present Government might tend to thwart the Measure & encourage our Enemies & Adversaries.'[4]

Strong administrations testified to the constitution's continuing vitality. Since the majority of peers did not, like the whigs, have a programme which they wished to implement, they were not bound to any one group of politicians. Thus, Lord Sheffield could tell Auckland in 1804 that he did not care who was minister so long as he and his friends did not ruin the country.[5] Any government capable of compet-

1801. Lord Fitzwilliam admitted that the foremost object of the Yorkshire Volunteer Cavalry was to support 'Civil Magistrates in the maintenance of Law and Order'. Wentworth Woodhouse MSS, F44(c)/47, Fitzwilliam to Wilkinson and Tooker, 8 Aug. 1795. For examples of the nobility's use of local military forces to control disorders see Wentworth Woodhouse MSS, F44(d)/55, F45(a)/28, F47(g)/36, Portland to Fitzwilliam, 8 Sept. 1800, 23 Apr. 1801, 3 Mar. 1800; *HMC, Laing MSS*, ii 567, 621-2.

1 Wentworth Woodhouse MSS, F47(a)/3, B. Hall to Fitzwilliam, 20 Dec. 1793; *ibid.*, F47(b)/11, J. Browne to Fitzwilliam, 19 July 1795; Braybrooke Papers (Essex Record Office), D/Dby 0/12, 'Resolutions of the Meeting at Saffron Waldon'; *ibid.*, D/Dby 0/12, Onslow to Howard, 11 Aug. 1795.

2 Both Fitzwilliam and the duke of Buccleuch surveyed the opinions of their countrymen at the request of the home scretary and found the populace to be generally loyal. Portland Papers, Pwf. 8226, Buccleuch to Portland, 4 Dec. 1796; Wentworth Woodhouse MSS, F44(b)/37-44. Other peers, however, reported on the existence of potentially seditious groups, *HMC, Laing MSS*, ii, 603-4, 676-8.

3 For a discussion of the lords' involvement in militia business see chapter 8.

4 Dropmore Papers, Add. Ms 58991 (unfoliated), Rolle to Grenville, 22 Sept. 1799.

5 Auckland Papers, Add. MS 34456, fos. 62-3, Sheffield to Auckland, 21 Apr. 1804.

ently carrying on the king's business was sufficient for most of these men who were obviously the crown's natural allies.

The ultimate test of the house of lords' effectiveness as the balancing agent of the constitution was its members' ability to impose their views on those branches whose conduct seemed dangerous and disruptive, not their capacity to strengthen the king's government through their loyal adherence. Weak as the house may have seemed to some observers, it did upon occasion take decisive action to uphold what the majority felt was the proper equipoise. In 1783-4 and again in 1801 the lords by adhering to the king became a vital instrument in preventing alterations being made to the established political system, and in 1784 they also helped to restore political stability. The peers did so in each case not as the king's creatures but as his allies, and without their support it is unlikely that George III would have overcome his adversaries.

In the aftermath of Lord North's collapse in 1782 the political world fragmented so rapidly that stable government soon became impossible. The first phase of this disintegration was marked by the splintering of the group which had previously opposed the American war. Within three months the alliance between the whigs and the Shelburnites, already strained by their differing plans for settling the American question, collapsed because of the former's justifiable suspicion that Shelburne was conniving with George III to divide the Rockingham administration and block the passage of its reforms.[1] Consequently, Fox and the other Rockingham whigs refused to serve under Shelburne after the death of their leader on 1 July 1782.

Without a clear majority in the house of commons, it was widely expected that Shelbourne would attempt to form an alliance with Lord North who commanded about 120 MPs. However, this union was never accomplished: North disliked Shelburne and found his terms for peace to be unacceptable, while some of the latter's colleagues, including Pitt, Keppel, Richmond, Camden and Grafton, all refused to sanction negotiations with their old opponent.[2] Instead, Fox and North put aside former differences and united to defeat Shelburne's preliminary treaties on 17 February 1783. After a delay of six weeks during which George III tried unsuccessfully to form a more congenial administration, he was reluctantly forced to entrust his government to these men.

[1] J. Cannon, *The Fox-North Coalition*, (Cambridge, 1969), 4-19; L. G. Mitchell, *Charles Fox and the Disintegration of the Whig Party, 1782-1794* (London, 1971), 15-17.

[2] Cannon, *The Coalition*, 28-9, 44, 46-7, 59-64.

Though the Fox-North Coalition was only the most recent of many political marriages of convenience, it was bitterly attacked on account of its apparent opportunism and lack of principled foundation. Even loyal whigs found it distasteful. Shortly after its conclusion Fox's intimate friend, Richard Fitzpatrick, told his brother that *'unless a real good Government* is the consequence of this juncture, nothing can justify it to the public'. Two months later Sheridan found that it was still highly unpopular; 'we must do something', he told the earl of Surrey, 'to convince People that we are not the worse for it'.[1]

Despite the new government's more than adequate majorities Fitzpatrick's and Sheridan's unease was well-founded. No sooner had the ministry been installed than George III wrote to Lord Temple that he expected the Pitts and the Grenvilles to rid him of a ministry he had only accepted under duress. To publicize his dissatisfaction further the king refused to make any new peers on the Coalition's recommendation.[2]

The inner circle of the king's friends viewed the new ministry with the same distaste as George III himself. When news of the Coalition was announced, several peers offered their services to the king in hopes that he might be able to build an alternate administration: Lord Walsingham, for example, implored his sovereign 'to rely on my implicit and unalterable attachment to your Person, Family and Government in every possible situation and extremity of affairs'. Six months later John Robinson told Charles Jenkinson that the government's 'sole View is to *secure the Benefits* [of power], while disgrace is brôt upon the Country, and I am afraid Ruin'. Similarly, the earl of Clarendon complained that the Coalition was 'formed for selfish ends & probably of too little duration to establish any permanent system of government', and he objected particularly to its attempts to 'render Monarchy insignificant'.[3]

Richard Fitzpatrick had been especially concerned in February 1783, by the critical reaction of leading independents. Bishop Watson of Landaff claims that the Coalition destroyed his confidence in public men. Such leading independent lay peers as Abingdon, Ferrers and Radnor also opposed the new government; indeed, Lord Pembroke,

1 *Memorials and Correspondence of Charles James Fox*, ed. Lord J. Russell (London, 1853), ii, 19; *The Letters of Richard Brinsley Sheridan*, ed. C. Price (Oxford, 1966), i, 154.

2 *The Correspondence of King George the Third, 1760-1783*, ed. J. B. Fortescue (London, 1928), vi, no. 4272.

3 *Ibid.*, v, no. 3602; Liverpool Papers, Add. MS 38567, fos. 155-6, Robinson to Jenkinson, 2 Oct. 1783; Clarendon Papers, C347, fo. 592, 'Thoughts on the Situation in 1783 . . . . '.

himself an old Chathamite of some independence, wrote in July that Abingdon had sworn he would have Fox and his cronies out of office within a few months. Friends as well as foes of the new government suspected that Fox's principles and tactics had rendered the Coalition's hold on power extremely tenuous.[1]

The Coalition's adversaries objected primarily to the constitutional credo of Charles Fox, not to his opportunism. In 1783-4 Fox claimed that politicians in control of a parliamentary majority had the sole right to determine the composition of a cabinet and that the crown possessed no faculty of private judgment. According to this interpretation the monarch exercised his powers only through his ministers; the degree to which he possessed confidence in them was immaterial so long as they were able to maintain majorities in both houses of parliament.[2]

Opposition to this novel definition of ministerial authority continued into the autumn, but only gained a powerful momentum after the introduction of the India Bill. In fact, the importance of that measure was that it confirmed the fears of men who already suspected that Fox and his cohorts had challenged traditional constitutional theories and practices in order to enhance their own power.

For ten years politicians had recognized the need to establish some government regulation over the East India Company's empire. Earlier attempts to set up direct government supervision foundered in the face of ministerial hesitation and parliament's unwillingness to augment further the powers of the crown. The Coalition's solution was ingenious and surprisingly modern: Indian affairs would henceforth be directed by seven commissioners, appointed to a term of four years and removable only by the address of one house of parliament. Meanwhile, nine officials selected from among the ranks of the company's stockholders would direct its commercial activities. In effect, the government of India was to be taken out of the hands of the East India Company and placed instead in a board whose members, though appointed by the crown, would enjoy a tenure more comparable to that of judges than ministers responsible to parliament.

---

1 *Memorials and Correspondence,* ii, 16-7; R. Watson, *Anecdotes of the Life of Richard Watson, Bishop of Landaff* (London, 1817), i, 170-3; Leeds Papers, Add. MS 28060, fo. 35, Pembroke to Carmarthen, 20 July 1783. Lord Townshend, master general of the ordnance in the Coalition government, told John Beresford that 'our follies, factions & unprincipled Conduct, are little likely to allow any stability anywhere'. *The Correspondence of the Rt. Hon. John Beresford,* ed. W. Beresford (London, 1854), i, 239-40.

2 Pares, *George III and the Politicians,* 123-4; L. Mitchell, *Fox and the Whigs,* 56, 84-5.

Immediately upon its presentation to parliament this measure, along with another bill that defined the commissioners' powers over the various Indian authorities, encountered bitter opposition. The entire plan was unwieldy: men who would wait months for information to reach them were nevertheless expected to govern India. The bill, it was claimed, also impinged upon the rights of a chartered company. But the principal objections to the bill were political. All seven of the new commissioners came from the ranks of Fox's or North's associates. To their opponents it seemed as if 'Carlo Khan' and his allies wished to buy themselves a permanent majority in the house of commons.

The government did not undertake this great measure lightheartedly. Many ministers had misgivings about its wisdom, and they realistically acknowledged that the opposition would be both violent and numerous. However, as the bill progressed triumphantly through the house of commons, earlier doubts gave way to exuberant confidence. 'It is impossible', Eden told Lord Northington, 'to describe to you the Degree & Opinion of Strength which the Management & Success of this Business has given to Government'. Though the opposition had a formidable array of speakers in the lords and its leaders were 'moving Heaven & Earth (not to say Hell) to get a superiority of strength in the Lords', Sir John Burgoyne reported that Fox expected to carry the bill in the upper house by a majority of two to one, and even the cautious Eden predicted that the government would have a margin of thirty votes.[1] Thus, ministers canvassed potential supporters and rounded up the proxies of absent friends but without any sense of urgency: the battle had been fought, and victory was assured.

Events leading up to and immediately following the defeat of the India Bill are generally familiar to all students of this period. In an interview between the king and Lord Thurlow, the former lord chancellor, on 1 December 1783, the opposition began to prepare the way for George's eventual decisive intervention. Asserting that the India Bill would seriously undercut the prerogative, Thurlow suggested that the king might defeat the measure by making his opposition known to members of the house of lords. Unwilling to move against the Coalition without first finding a successor to it, George opened indirect, secret negotiations with William Pitt in the course of which Pitt agreed to form an administration if in turn the king would publicize his sentiments on

1 Mitchell, *Fox and the Whigs*, 65-7; Cannon, *The Coalition*, 112-3; Pelham Papers, Add. MS 33100, fos. 391-3, 399, Eden to Northington, 10, 17 Nov. [1783]; Manchester Papers, PRO 30/15/11, Fox to Manchester, 17 Nov. 1783; *Auckland Correspondence*, i, 62; Pelham Papers, Add. MS 33100, fos. 446-7, Eden to Northington, 6 Dec. [1783]; *ibid.*, Add. MS 33100, fos. 448-51, J. Burgoyne to Northington, 9 Dec. 1783.

the India Bill. On 11 December, his majesty empowered Pitt's cousin, Lord Temple, to inform peers that the king would no longer consider as his friends those who voted for the bill. Four days later the Coalition was beaten in the house of lords by a vote of 87-79, and after losing again by a slightly larger margin on the seventeenth, ministers were dismissed and replaced by Pitt.[1]

Because they had been confident of victory, the news of the king's interview with Temple struck leading government politicians not as a bomb but as an improbable opposition ruse. Eden told Lord Northington that

> we do not give any Credit to this [rumor] farther than that L^d T is said to have asked an Audience, & probably for the purpose of gaining some Pretext which the loose Conversation of such an Audience might furnish, for holding a language likely to gain five or six Recruits . . . In the Mean Time His Majs Behaviour to Day was remarkably gracious.

Portland, who had also found the king to be unusually cordial, likewise refused to believe the reports, and on 12 December the government agreed not to demand an explanation from the king until after the bill had passed.[2]

More incredibly, ministers made no systematic effort to discover whether rumours about Temple's assignment were true. Lord Loughborough acknowledged on 13 December that the king probably did oppose the India Bill, but he doubted that the opposition would exploit the foolish story of Temple's authorization. Others resorted to the most specious logic to reassure themselves: the rumours could not be true, Windham wrote, since their reputed source, Lord Lothian, had seen Temple before, not after the famous interview and thus could not have known what took place in the meeting.[3]

By ignoring or frivolously discounting reports of events on 11 December, ministers avoided learning the truth for three days. Nor was it possible by 14 December to counteract the effect of the king's action. Last minute efforts were made to round up absentees, but Fox and many of his cohorts remained naively assured that their majority was secure. Thus, a government, which in late November was, according

---

1 *The Later Correspondence of George III,* ed. A. Aspinall (Cambridge, 1966), i, xxii-xxvii; Cannon, *The Coalition,* 124-44.

2 Pelham Papers, Add. MS 33100, fo. 456, Eden to Northington, 12 Dec. [1783]; *ibid.,* Add. MS 33100, fos. 471-2, G. A. North to T. Pelham, 16 Dec. [1783].

3 *Auckland Correspondence,* i, 67-8; Pelham Papers, Add. MS 33100, fos. 522-3, W. Windham to Northington [Dec. 1783].

to Eden, 'taking great Pains to ascertain a considerable support', was defeated in part by its own carelessness and overconfidence.[1]

The king's intervention followed so quickly by the defeats in the house of lords left the whigs in a state of shocked indignation. Nothing short of the lowest treachery could have transformed their position so suddenly. Understandably the coalitionists' reactions were sudden and violent: George III was vilified as the prime mover of a treacherous plot, and the perfidy of the household troops, the bishops and the Scots was loudly denounced.[2] In the midst of their fury the whigs failed to perceive that a number of peers genuinely detested the bills and that Pitt and his allies capitalized on their abhorrence to prepare the ground for the king's intervention.

Among the peers who co-operated with Pitt in plotting his successful coup were some who sincerely detested the India Bill. Upon hearing the first reports of it Lord Thurlow remarked that 'it appears to me so un-principled, irregular, and rash, that I do not impute to them [ministers] so much want of common sense', and he was honestly distressed that so 'scandalous' a measure would pass easily through the house of commons. Likewise, Thurlow's old ally, Lord Gower, opposed the bill because 'he thought that the intention could be no other than to enslave the K., overturn the Constitution & to make himself [Fox] sovereign ruler of these kingdoms'.[3]

By late November the marquis of Carmarthen, assisted by Lord de Ferrars, a Chathamite, was canvassing against the bill. De Ferrars him-self felt that the measure's passage 'would be more fatal to this Country than Anarchy itself', and letters among Carmarthen's papers show that a number of independent peers shared this alarm. The ailing earl of Effingham exclaimed that the bill's unjust and potentially tyrannical provisions and the unseemly haste with which it was being propelled through parliament were enough to 'rouse a man of any Sensibility fro [sic] his Death Bed', and Lord Percy, later the second duke of North-umberland, wrote that it was 'fraught with so much mischief' that he was determined to go up to town on purpose to oppose it. Even Lord

---

1 Cannon, *The Coalition*, 133-4; Northington Papers, Add. MS 38716, fos. 142-4, Burgoyne to Northington, 15 Dec. 1783; Mitchell, *Fox and the Whigs*, 73-4. Fox told Windham at three in the morning of the fifteenth that the Coalition's majority in the lords was still about thirty. Pelham Papers, Add. MS 33100, fos. 473-4, Windham to Northington, 18 Dec. 1783.

2 Fox Papers, Add. MS 47570, fo. 156, Fox to Mrs Armistead [Dec. 1783]; *Memorials and Correspondence*, ii, 220-1; *Auckland Correspondence*, i, 68-9.

3 *HMC, 5th R.*, i, *Sutherland MSS*, 210-11; *Later Correspondence*, i, no.7.

Dacre, who never attended the house, came up specially to take his seat in order that he might leave his proxy against the bill.[1]

The strongest and most forceful independent attack against the India Bill was delivered by the earl of Abingdon on 15 December. This measure, the earl argued, would enchain the king by destroying his prerogative and would enslave the people 'through the medium of a corrupt majority in parliament'. Thus, it was their lordships' duty to 'exercise that function which the constitution hath placed in us; I mean, my lords, that of holding between the king and the people the balance of the state in the scale of its government'. In effect, Abingdon was recommending a course which most independents believed to be the primary purpose of their political activity.

The independent prided himself on the uniformity with which he had endeavoured to uphold the constitution's equipoise. During the American war he had opposed North's attempts to destroy the legislature's autonomy and inflate the powers of the crown. In 1783 he resisted Fox's plan to destroy the monarchy, believing that such action was entirely consistent with his past conduct. Lord Hawke opposed the India Bill, he said, in order that the system of government which he had always defended might be preserved. Acting to protect those branches of the constitution whose independence was threatened, the earl of Harcourt had found himself called a republican for opposing North and a king's friend for voting against the India Bill; like Hawke, however, he believed that his conduct was consistent and honourable.[2]

The numerical strength which the independent peers added to the opposition was almost as important as that which the king produced by proclaiming his sentiments to Temple. Twenty-three peers who had some claim to be classified as independents voted against the India Bill. Two of them subsequently received an office in the new government, and two others were given earldoms. Yet, even if we assume that the latters' conduct was interested, and there is no evidence to support such an assumption, nineteen men with fairly independent credentials did

1 Leeds Papers, Add. MS 28060, fos. 43-4, de Ferrars to Carmarthen, 29 Nov. 1783; *ibid.*, Add. MS 28060, fo. 49, Effingham to Carmarthen, 4 Dec. 1783; *ibid.*, Add. MS 28060, fo. 45, Percy to Carmarthen, 1 Dec. 1783.

2 *PH,* xxiv, 136, 15 Dec. 1783; Leeds Papers, Add. MS 28060, fo. 47, Hawke to Carmarthen [Dec. 1783]; *The Harcourt Papers,* ed. E. Harcourt (Privately Printed), vii, 91-2. For the reactions of four other independent peers – Coventry, King, Radnor and Rawdon see *PH,* xxiv, 175-94, 17 Dec. 1783. Bishop Watson wrote to the duke of Portland: 'It is impossible for me who have, on all occasions, opposed the corrupting influence of the Crown, to support the measure which is pregnant with more seeds of corruption than any one which has taken place since the revolution!' Watson, *Anecdotes,* i, 203. He did not vote on the bill.

oppose the bill.[1] In contrast the government was only able to attract the support of four or five such peers.

The fact that independents were canvassed indicates that the Coalition's adversaries did not rely on the nobility's spontaneous sense of outrage to defeat the bill. Evidence relating to the opposition's organization is sketchy. As noted, de Ferrars and Carmarthen began to canvass former opponents of Lord North in late November, even before Thurlow met with the king to discuss the bill's defeat. Working at the instigation of some higher authority, they successfully recruited supporters without publicizing their efforts. However useful a public meeting would have been in enabling them to gauge the extent of their support, it would also have startled the government.[2]

While de Ferrars and Carmarthen surreptitiously canvassed the more independent peers, the king's friends were left to John Robinson, a man whom North mistakenly counted as his friend until after the bill's defeat. Robinson's recruiting, like that of the independents, was done quietly and in consultation with Charles Jenkinson. Through his son-in-law Robinson solicited the votes of Lord Abergavenny and the duke of Beaufort, the latter being particularly important because other peers were likely to follow his lead. Another trusty messenger was dispatched to Lord Hillsborough in Ireland because he had powerful influence with three of his colleagues. And the effectiveness of these appeals was reinforced when Jenkinson informed Robinson on 5 December that the king was decidedly opposed to the bill.[3]

This energetic, stealthy pursuit of supporters reinforces the impression that the opposition carefully organized its campaign against the India Bill in the house of lords. Friends of George III were surreptitiously proclaiming the king's sentiments six days before the famous interview with Lord Temple. The object of these whispered hints was undoubtedly to prepare the way for George's intervention. On 7 December Robinson was instructed to prepare a state of the house. Because the results of his

---

1 Abergavenny, Abingdon, Beaulieu, Chedworth, Courtenay, Coventry, Dacre, Effingham, Ferrers, Fortescue, Harborough, Harcourt, Hawke, Grantley, King, Middleton, Pembroke, Percy, Rawdon, Romney, Say and Sele, Stanhope and Tankerville. Effingham and Tankerville received offices; Abergavenny and Beaulieu were made earls.

2 Leeds Papers, Add. MS 28060, fos. 43-4, de Ferrars to Carmarthen, 29 Nov. 1783.

3 For a discussion of Robinson's political loyalties, see I. Christie, 'John Robinson, M.P., 1727-1802', *Myth and Reality in Late-Eighteenth Century Politics and Other Papers* (London, 1970), 145-82; Liverpool Papers, Add. MS 38567, fos. 165-6, Robinson to Jenkinson, 3 Dec. 1783; *HMC, 10th R.*, vi, *Abergavenny MSS*, 61.

work have disappeared, it is impossible to determine precisely how he weighted the balance of forces. Robinson himself claimed that he had been slightly cautious, but others who scrutinized his work concluded that 'there was no *manly* ground of apprehension'. The analysis, therefore, must have demonstrated to the king and Pitt that the canvassing activities of the previous ten days had rallied sufficient support to insure that the bill would be defeated once the king's sentiments were publicized.[1]

The final phase of the opposition's campaign commenced after Temple's interview with the king. Once again its success depended on effective organization, for the king's declaration did not produce an immediate shift of noble opinion. Indeed, many peers were initially baffled by the contradictory rumours: Lord Onslow told Lord Sydney that 'having taken a part in favour of the Bill from the beginning, I could not change my Conduct till I know from better *Authority* than vague Report & Opinion, that which alone can & will make me do so'. Obviously neither Pitt nor his closest allies could confirm the truth without implicating themselves in the plot. Instead, several royal favourites were drafted to remove the confusion by clarifying the king's views. Lord Salisbury, who applied for an interview in order to learn the king's opinion, then went out and recruited four supporters for opposition, while the duke of Dorset bragged later of having obtained twelve votes. Even allowing for exaggeration, these two must have influenced many of the peers who at the last moment changed sides.[2]

Of course the India Bill's rejection did not remove the threat which Fox has posed to the traditional constitutional equilibrium. On the contrary, the lords' actions on 17 December and the king's subsequent dismissal of the Coalition precipitated one of the most severe and prolonged political crises of the eighteenth century. By the end of December the crown and the commons were irreconcilable. Fox, claiming absolute sovereignty for the house of commons he controlled, demanded that Pitt's ministry resign. George III vowed never to permit the Coalition's return to power. Pitt as a result was forced to govern for three months in the face of a hostile majority, slowly cutting away at the Coalition's once insurmountable majority. Then, having won the

---

1 Liverpool Papers, Add. MS 38567, fos. 167-70, Robinson to Jenkinson, 7, 9 Dec. 1783; Abergavenny Papers, B.L. Facs. 340(20), fos. 293-5, R. Atkinson to Robinson, 8 Dec. 1783.

2 Sydney Papers, Box 1, Onslow to Sydney, 15 Dec. 1783: *Later Correspondence*, iv, 164, n. 1; Northington Papers, Add. MS 38716, fos. 142-4, Burgoyne to Northington, 15 Dec. 1783; Pitt Papers, PRO 30/8/130, fos. 80-3, Dorset to Pitt, 3 Mar. 1794.

support of public opinion and having carried a few essential bills, he dissolved parliament and trounced his opponents in a carefully prepared election.

What part did the house of lords play in this phase of the crisis? According to Nathaniel Wraxall, the peers, seemingly exhausted by the effort of throwing out the India Bill, 'remained silent and supine spectators of the contest carrying on between the Crown and Commons'.[1] Yet, this statement reflects only on the house itself. It ignores the peers' activities elsewhere.

Like their colleagues in the house of commons many members of the house of lords were initially shocked, baffled and not a little outraged by the course of proceedings in mid-December. The bishop of Ely disliked the royal intrigue and lamented that 'the Country seems to require only the confusion of new elections, and an unbridled demagogue of great abilities driven to extremities, to effectuate its ruin'. The duke of Marlborough, who also disapproved of the king's intervention, was troubled by other disturbing consequences of the turmoil: two of his members in the commons supported Pitt while the rest were coalitionists, and the retiring duke saw no way to re-establish order within his little flock. It was this confusion which so alarmed Marlborough and his colleagues: as Sir Joseph Yorke told the second earl of Hardwicke, 'we quiet men who only think of the general good are ballotted up and down by rival Parties, & are dupes of our Simplicity & integrity, which are banish'd from all political association'.[2]

The alarm created by this political confusion only reinforced the peers' natural inclination to support the king. Between 17 December and the general election of 1784 several peers who had absented themselves during the proceedings on the India Bill came forward to pledge their support to the new government, and sixteen of those who had supported the measure changed sides.[3] At first sight the motives of lords in this last group seem narrowly interested: three of the converts were courtiers, while the bishop of Bristol shortly received a translation

---

1 *The Historical and Posthumous Memoirs of Sir Nathaniel Wraxall*, ed. H.B. Wheatley (London, 1884), iii, 300. See also *Annual Register* (1784), 92-3.

2 Hardwicke·Papers, Add. MS 35391, fos. 60-1, Ely to P. Yorke, 22 Dec. 1783; Auckland Papers, Add. MS 34419, fo. 311, Marlborough to Eden, 18 Dec. 1783; Hardwicke Papers, Add. MS 35372, fos. 346-7, J. Yorke to Hardwicke, 15 Dec. 1783.

3 *Later Correspondence*, i, nos. 5, 6, 10, 14, 15, 16, 22; J. Holland Rose, *Pitt and Napoleon* (London, 1912), 202. Those who changed sides before the general election were: Atholl, Bagot, bishop of Bristol, Fauconberg, Gage, Gordon, Harrington, Harrowby, Eglinton, Marlborough, Onslow, Rosebery, Sandys, Sussex, Westmorland and Willoughby.

to a more lucrative see and the dukes of Atholl and Gorden were granted the British peerages they coveted! Yet many also concluded that in order to restore stability they must stand by the king, even if they disapproved of his actions in bringing down the Coalition.

Superficially, none of these men appeared to be more craven than Henry, second Earl Fauconberg, one of the lords of the bedchamber. Being unaware of George's views, his lordship had permitted his proxy to remain in the hands of a coalitionist, an error he afterwards endeavoured to rectify by composing an abject apology to his sovereign. Yet Fauconberg was not a royal pawn. On the contrary, his political conduct in Yorkshire during these months demonstrates that he was independent, even radical. Throughout the autumn the earl had combated the pretensions of the Yorkshire Association in union with such whigs as Thomas Dundas and Earl Fitzwilliam. Suddenly, however, he reversed course: on 17 December he joined a committee appointed to draft a petition for the reform of parliament, and during the spring of 1784 public affairs so excited him that he worked with the Association to rout the whigs. Fauconberg's conversion preceded the news of the king's intervention, and his conduct thereafter cannot have been altogether pleasing to his majesty. But for the rest of his life he took pride in the steps he had taken to drive from power a clique of politicians who threatened the very existence of orderly government.[2]

Other conversions occurred as a result of fear and principle. The duke of Gordon had entrusted his proxy with the Coalition at the beginning of December because it was still the king's government. In so doing, he chose to disregard an application from Henry Dundas in behalf of the opposition: on the other hand, it was inevitable that

1 Bagot bishop of Bristol was transferred to Norwich in 1785. Fauconberg, Onslow and Willoughby were bedchamber peers. For the Scots' demands for British peerages see Pitt Papers, PRO 30/8/157, fos. 351-4, Dundas to Pitt, 25 Jan. [1784].

2 *Later Correspondence*, i, no. 5; N.C. Phillips, *Yorkshire and English National Politics, 1783-84* (Christchurch, New Zealand, 1961), 55-6. The following ballad, used by the son of another courtier, Lord Waldegrave, at the election of 1784 points out the degree to which the king was perceived to be the protector, the Coalition the violator of the constitution.

> We love the King & we will sing
> God bless great George for ever;
> He fights our Cause & keeps our Laws
> God bless his Heart for ever.

> Fox with his Bill may go to Hell
> with Portland, Byng & Surry,
> Fitzpatrick too, and Powys who,
> Turn'd his Vote in a hurry.

Granville Papers, PRO 30/29/5/1, fo. 34.

this stalwart friend of the king would transfer his allegiance to Pitt as soon as he was installed in power. George III himself solicited the duke of Marlborough's support. At first the duke was ambivalent, but by January he had resolved to exert his 'best endeavours to promote a moderate spirit in these turbulent times': soon afterwards he began to pressure his members in the commons to support Pitt. The earl of Hardwicke, whose dominant political concern was to see that the Yorke family always received its share of patronage, also made his decision independently. By February 1784, his lordship had become so alarmed and confused by events that he begged the duke of Portland to compromise with the king. Rather pathetically, he told the duke that 'People in general do not wish to see Things carried to Extremitys, & when Confusion arises, It is impossible to say wch Side will prevail. Those who have stakes in the Hedge, s^{hd} have *That* always uppermost'.[1]

Nor were these recruits the only peers affected by the mounting political turmoil. The confused and dangerous state of politics induced Carmarthen, Richmond and Gower to accept posts in the cabinet. Each of these men believed that the very existence of the constitution depended upon the prevention of another direct confrontation between Fox and the king. So too did the prolongation of George's reign. Mindful of the king's recurrent threats to abdicate, the duke of Dorset urged ministers to call a general election and thereby gain a parliamentary majority. If instead they resigned and left the king to face the Coalition, his grace feared that a 'national calamity' would ensue.[2]

While the majority of Pitt's noble adherents were unable or unwilling to serve in high office, they performed other important services for him. Throughout the early months of 1784 each side competed for public support. Pitt routed his adversaries in this contest; the more than two hundred addresses raised in support of his administration reflected a genuine popular preference for the king and himself.[3] However, it is

1 *Later Correspondence,* i, no. 14, 22; Auckland Papers, Add. MS 34419, fo. 385, Marlborough to Eden, 4 Apr. 1784; Hardwicke Papers, Add. MS 45030, fo. 26-7, Hardwicke to Portland, 19 Feb. 1784.

2 *Leeds Political Memoranda,* 91, 94-5; Leeds Papers, Add. MS 28060, fo. 75, Dorset to Carmarthen, 19 Jan. 1784.

3 In the face of popular enthusiasm for the Pitt government, whig leaders found it almost impossible to stem the tide of adulatory addresses. Lord Spencer told his mother that 'some of the most violent politicians in the town [of Northampton] . . . took it into their wise heads to send up an Address to his Majesty thanking him for turning out his late Ministers and calling them all the rogues and rascals that ever were. I did all I could with any sort of propriety under hand to prevent people from supporting it or attending the meeting convened for that purpose but in vain, for the address was carried by a large and tumultuous majority. . .' Spencer Papers, Box 5, Spencer to Dowager Countess Spencer, 12 Feb. 1784.

clear that the nobility exerted every bit of its extensive influence to insure that countrymen would turn out in large numbers to express their fulsome support. In some instances, in fact, noble prodding was of decisive importance in securing a favourable address.[1]

Peers loyal to the new government did not limit their activities exclusively to the countryside. From the moment Pitt took office his noble allies endeavoured to buttress his position in the house of commons. Sympathetic lords ordered several MPs who had absented themselves from parliament in the autumn to take their seats on the government side once the house reconvened in January. More importantly they successfully dislodged many MPs from Fox's grasp. Half of those members who, according to Burke, changed sides between December 1783, and the following spring either sat for seats controlled by or were closely related to Pittite peers.[2]

Having rallied support for the new government in the commons and the country, the peers returned to their house and on 4 February, adopted two resolutions condemning the unconstitutional actions of the commons by a decisive vote of 100-53. Lords Thurlow and Gower, both of whom had taken part in the opposition's manoeuvreings prior to the king's intervention in December, wisely confined themselves to condemnations of the commons' intemperate and unconstitutional interference in the affairs of the executive. Lord Fauconberg and the duke of Richmond, however, went further, reviving the arguments which independent peers and royalists had hurled against the ministers in December. Both believed that the coalitionists, driven by their lust for power, endangered the constitution's equipoise. Under these circumstances they claimed it was necessary for the house of lords to step in and condemn such conduct. The house, Richmond argued,

> could not therefore . . . continue silent consistently with its duty as hereditary counsel of the crown, to interfere when either the commons or the Crown, in the exercise of their respective functions, clash with each other. The respectability of their Lordships depended not a little on their acting, in the present crisis, with energy and unanimity.[3]

Opposition peers naturally rejected Richmond's argument. The duke of Manchester and Earl Fitzwilliam contended that the peers would only anger the lower house by adopting the proposed resolutions; more

---

1 Cannon, *The Coalition*, 185-90; Leeds Papers, Add. MS 28060, fo. 93, Rivers to Carmarthen, 8 Feb. 1784; Rose Papers, Add. MS 42774, pt. 1, fos. 43-4, Percy to Rose, 15 Mar. 1784.

2 For a discussion of the influence which the peers exerted over members of the house of commons in 1783-4 see chapter 8.

3 *PH*, xxiv, 502-4, 506-9, 4 Feb. 1784.

seriously they would limit, Loughborough argued, parliament's ability to control the administration, thus permitting the crown to govern virtually at will. Finally, Lord Stormont rejected as absurd the notion that the king had the sole right to appoint his ministers: such power was not only impracticable in a balanced monarchy but also contra- dicted innumerable precedents which clearly established parliament's right to state its opinions on this very question.[1]

Until February the opposition had ignored the house of lords, and even after the debate on the fourth some continued to belittle its importance. Lord Loughborough, for example, told William Eden to treat that episode 'as a weak attempt of a falling Administration to create a disunion which they did not know how to effect'.[2]

Nevertheless, there is evidence to show that the Coalition's leadership was impressed by this demonstration of the lords' steadfast loyalty to the king. On 16 February, the duke of Portland informed Fox of a rumour that Pitt would resign and go into opposition if he did not obtain the supplies necessary to carry on the government. Such a prospect disturbed Portland: being countenanced by the king, the new opposition would 'effectually defeat every measure attempted to be brought forward in the H of Lds., & by that means render Our Administration as inefficient as theirs was by our influence in the H of Coms'. Nor did Portland's letter merely represent the fears of one rather timid politician. Thomas Coutts, the banker, reported to the earl of Stair that Fox would stop supplies on 18 February, but added gloomily that if Fox's party did return to power as a result, 'his measures will stop in the House of Peers, so that neither [Pitt's nor Fox's governments] can go on'.[3]

There is no evidence to show that the obstacles posed by the house of lords in any way affected Fox's decision not to oppose the vote of supplies. Though North was highly disturbed by the prolonged instability, neither he nor Portland spoke for the entire Coalition.[4] Still, we do know that while these politicians were making the most important decision of this phase of the crisis, they and portions of the political community recognized that the house of lords' hostility would make it difficult, if not impossible, for Fox to form an effective administration.

1 *Ibid.,* xxiv, 498-502, 504-6, 509-13, 4 Feb. 1784.

2 *Auckland Correspondence,* i, 75.

3 Fox Papers, Add. MS 47561, fos. 69-70, Portland to Fox, 16 Feb. 1784; E. H. Coleridge, *The Life of Thomas Coutts, Banker* (New York, 1920), i, 174-5.

4 North revealed his concerns in a series of letters to his father written in January and February, 1784. Waldeshare Papers, U471 C23/2, 4-5, 10.

In conclusion, it is clear that the support which Pitt and George III received from the majority of members of the upper house helped them to triumph over the Coalition. The India Bill's rejection, made possible by the surprisingly strong opposition of the independents as well as by the opposition's skillful canvassing and the king's intervention, provided George with an excuse to dismiss the Coalition. In the ensuing weeks the peerage's natural inclination to support the crown was reinforced by the intensification of the political crisis and by a growing feeling that the coalitionists' actions and statements amounted to a full scale attack on the established political system. Possessed of enormous stores of power in the commons and the country, the nobility did not have to act exclusively within the confines of their house to insure that Pitt would remain in power. Instead of passing fulsome resolutions which might have antagonized the lower house, the king's noble allies initially worked with some success to raise addresses and lure MPs from their allegiance to Fox. When they did turn again to their own house on 4 February, it was not without some effect: suddenly Coalition politicians discovered that the lords might render any government they could construct ineffective.

The crisis occasioned by Pitt's determination to introduce a bill for Catholic emancipation in 1801 was far less serious or prolonged than that of 1783-4. Once Pitt recognized the force of the opposition against such a measure, he retreated. Yet, for students of the house of lords this episode is interesting and important. It demonstrates once again that with the support of his nobility the king could thwart the designs of ministers who controlled the lower house.

Pitt made his decision to grant Roman Catholics the full rights of citizenship while preparing the Irish Act of Union. Both Cornwallis, the lord lieutenant, and Castlereagh, the chief secretary, had implied to Catholics that emancipation would come soon after the union was completed. Nor was this merely a cynical attempt to enlist support for a highly controversial measure: along with these men Pitt believed in the justice of emancipation and felt that the union's success would ultimately depend on the government's successful conciliation of the Catholics.[1]

Unfortunately, Pitt's conduct in 1801 contrasted sharply with his deft performance seventeen years earlier. After endless meetings he was unable to convince five cabinet colleagues of the measure's

---

1 J. Steven Watson, *The Reign of George III, 1760-1815* (Oxford, 1960), 399-401; G. C. Boulton, *The Passing of the Irish Act of Union* (Oxford, 1966), 208-14.

necessity,[1] and lesser officeholders such as Auckland also remained unconverted. Their opposition is significant because it prevented Pitt from making emancipation a government measure. But the decisive blow to Pitt's hopes came from George III; on 28 January 1801, the king told Dundas that he would consider anyone who proposed such a measure to be his enemy.

Lord Malmesbury blamed Pitt for this unhappy confrontation. Instead of gradually preparing the king's mind, he apparently assumed that George would accept whatever advice his ministers presented and did not bother to discuss the plan with him. By ignoring the king Pitt left the way open for the measure's opponents — Loughborough, Auckland, Clare, Westmorland and the bishops. These men convinced George by the end of 1800 that emancipation was dangerous, unnecessary and in violation of his coronation oath. In fact, leading ministers were outflanked by a small circle of diehards who gained the ear of their sovereign.[2]

Even without the king's declaration, it is unlikely that the peers, left free to make a choice, would have approved any emancipation bill. The bishops were presumed to be unanimously opposed, and even Pitt's tutor, Tomline of Lincoln, deprecated the measure and believed that it would be rejected by the house. Most of the Irish representative peers who would take their seats for the first time in 1801 were directed by Lord Clare, a notorious anti-catholic, and the courtiers were also generally unsympathetic. Thus, the master of the horse, Lord Chesterfield, told his royal master that

> so long since the period of the recall of the Earl Fitzwilliam from the Government of Ireland [in 1795], I have decidedly formed my opinion on the subject of the repeal of the Test Act & of Catholic Emancipation, and had the question been at that time brought before the consideration of the British Parliament, I should have felt it to be my duty to have opposed it. Nothing has occurred since that period to weaken, many things to strengthen that opinion.[3]

Though of less significance than the king's adamant opposition or

---

1 Chatham, Liverpool, Loughborough, Portland and Westmorland opposed emancipation.

2 *Diaries and Correspondence of James Harris, First Earl of Malmesbury,* ed. Earl of Malmesbury (London, 1845), iv, 2-4; *Auckland Correspondence,* iv, 122-4; *Diaries of Sylvester Douglas, Lord Glenbervie,* ed. F. N. Bladon (London, 1928), i, 168-9; *Memorials and Correspondence,* iii, 319-20; Holland, *Memoirs of the Whig Party,* ed. second Lord Holland (London, 1852), i, 171-2.

3 *Malmesbury Diaries,* iv, 2; *The Diaries and Correspondence of the Right Hon. George Rose,* ed. L. Vernon-Harcourt (London, 1860), i, 359; *Auckland Correspondence,* iv, 111; *Later Correspondence,* iii, no. 2355.

even the division within the cabinet, the nobility's hostility to emancipation was one of the factors which induced Pitt to drop the project. Geoffrey Boulton suggests that the inner cabinet which poisoned the king's mind was prepared to whip up an opposition in the house of lords if Pitt introduced the measure. Notorious Orangemen such as Lord Downshire had been summoned to London, and Lord Darnley's intended motion for an inquiry into the state of the nation provided an ideal ground from which to launch a party of 'king's friends'. Pitt may have wished to avoid this eventuality. He also acknowledged to Lord Castlereagh that any effort to put parliamentary pressure on the king would fail in the house of lords.[1] Because there was so little chance that the lords would approve an emancipation bill, he could not bring the full weight of a hostile parliament to bear against the king even if he had wished to do so. In this instance as in 1783 the upper chamber protected its stubborn sovereign from his ministers and reinforced his determination to oppose political innovation.

The house of lords was, as Lord Stormont correctly noted, the place 'where the great support of Government should naturally lie'. Its members provided ministers with generous majorities in their house. By remaining loyal to the crown, by committing their vast resources so heavily to the government's support, they facilitated the process of administration and contributed to the preservation of stability and the constitution's equipoise.

In fulfilling its duties as the constitution's equipoise, the house of lords was rarely demonstrative or dramatic. Its members' defence of the constitution was normally so discreet and the peers seemed so submissive that many mistakenly dismissed the house as a weak or passive body. Yet the house of lords acting in conjunction with George III was able in 1783–4 and again in 1801 to enforce its conservative will against politicians who commanded majorities in the house of commons. By demonstrating to the politicians that they could not impose themselves and their projects on the monarch so long as his nobility remained firm, the peers helped to prevent the implementation of political and constitutional innovations.

[1] *Correspondence of Charles, First Marquis Cornwallis*, ed. C. Ross (London, 1859), iii, 335-6; Boulton, *Irish Act of Union*, 212-13.

3

THE PEERS AND PUBLIC BUSINESS

Traditionally eighteenth-century governments had existed to maintain order, wage war and conduct foreign relations. Thus, ministers legislated only to provide themselves with the tools and cash needed to fulfill their limited responsibilities. Twenty-nine of the sixty-four public acts passed in the 1785 session were money bills, eight dealt with various branches of the executive administration, four with the military and fifteen with aspects of domestic or foreign commerce. Though the bills in the first four categories were initiated by ministers, a number in the last were proposed by private members.

There were also in 1785 a few attempts to alleviate social or political problems through legislation: two bills to relieve insolvent debtors, another to regulate madhouses and an ultimately unsuccessful measure which would have reformed election procedures. Each of these bills was introduced privately as were all the more important reforms presented to parliament in this period. Eighteenth-century governments were not expected to legislate solutions to pressing social, economic or political problems.[1]

Even as traditional legislative patterns and practices persisted, new elements emerged during the late eighteenth century to complicate the legislative process. Between 1785 and 1805 the number of acts passed by parliament rose from 189 to 353, an increase of 86 per cent. The majority of bills passed in each session dealt with private or local matters: Charles Abbot estimated in 1796 that over the previous ten years 'the Acts of a strictly public nature were about one-third of the whole number',[2] a figure which remains generally valid for the period between 1798 and 1806 if it is assumed that only those statutes in the set entitled 'Public General Acts' were truly public.[3] However, the number of

1 For discussions of eighteenth-century governments' responsibilities and the nature of legislation see Pares, *George III and the Politicians*, 4-5; Ehrman, *Pitt*, 168-9; P. D. G. Thomas, *The House of Commons in the Eighteenth Century* (Oxford, 1971), 45-6.

2 *Diary and Correspondence of Charles Abbot, Lord Colchester*, ed. Lord Colchester (London, 1861), i, 60. It is difficult to make exact estimates of the number of public or private bills because eighteenth-century parliamentarians were unclear themselves of the precise distinction. Until 1798 a public clause was added to many local acts; the system of promulgation which went into effect that year only confused the issue further. S. Lambert, *Bills and Acts, Legislative Procedure in Eighteenth-Century England* (Cambridge, 1971), chapter IX.

3 Between 1798 and 1806 the statutes in the 'Public General Acts' set comprised

public bills more than kept pace with the general increase in legislative business. In 1785 sixty-four bills went through the procedure for public bills in the upper house, but in 1805 there were 129 public acts.

Events were also pushing ministers into assuming a wider legislative role. During the 1780s the Indian empire was brought under the control of the government, the national administration was at least partially reformed and commercial relations with Europe and the empire were readjusted. In the 1790s civil liberties were curbed in order to stifle radical agitation, the military force was enormously increased and re-ordered, an income tax was imposed and cash payments were suspended. With the passage of the Act of Union in 1800, Anglo-Irish relations were set on their final, bitter course: parliament was at once confronted with the demands of its Roman Catholic subjects, and in proposing emancipation Pitt broke with the tradition which had left the introduction of such reforms to private members.

As governments moved to deal with these new, often contentious problems, their policies came increasingly to reflect an explicit political ideology. Much of the controversy over the Coalition's India Bill derived from the whigs' unwillingness to augment the powers of the crown by granting it control over Indian patronage, and the debates in the house of lords on the French Commercial Treaty of 1786 were at their best intelligent confrontations between the disciples of Adam Smith and up-holders of more traditional mercantile theories. During the 1790s the crisis provoked by the French Revolution, the outbreak of the war and the worsening situation in Ireland engendered bitter partisan divisions. While the majority of peers felt that the danger of internal sedition justified a restriction of civil liberties, a small group of whigs argued that the government's draconian legislation was unconstitutional and likely to be ineffective in any case.[1] Thus, as traditional eighteenth-century patterns of legislation persisted into our period, they were being modified by new forces: not only did the volume of legislation increase, but its scope became broader and its tone more explicitly representative of contentious political ideologies.

35.9% of the total legislation passed during these years. The yearly percentages are listed below:

1798 – 37.7%	1803 – 32.9%
1799 – 36.0%	1804 – 40.6%
1800 – 34.5%	1805 – 36.5%
1801 – 28.2%	1806 – 41.8%
1802 – 33.4%	

1 For the French Commercial Treaty the speeches of Watson, bishop of Landaff, Lansdowne and Liverpool are especially good. *PH*, xxvi, 538-50, 553-66, 1 Mar. 1787. For debates on the restrictive legislation of the 1790s see *ibid.*, xxxi, 574-603, 22 May 1794; *ibid.*, xxxii, 244-70, 527-54, 6, 11, 13 Nov., 9, 14 Dec. 1795.

Developments which complicated the legislative process had little impact on the house of lords. Table II demonstrates that only a few public bills were lost or even altered in the upper house. The seemingly dramatic increase in the number of bills amended during the second half of the period (137 as opposed to sixty-four in the first half) proves on closer examination to be less than spectacular. Between 1785 and 1805 the number of public bills passed by the house doubled. There were sessions, particularly that of 1802-3, in which the peers

Table II

Public Bills Amended or Lost in the House of Lords, 1783-1805

Session	no. of bills amended	gov't bills amended	no. of bills dropped or defeated*	gov't bills dropped or defeated
1783-4	2	2	3	1
1785	3	1	4	0
1786	10	4	6	2
1787	2	2	4	0
1787-8	11	1	2	0
1788-9	5	2	11	2
1790	2	0	4	3
1791	7	3	2	0
1792	4	0	3	0
1792-3	9	4	3	0
1794	9	3	3	1
1795	6	3	2	0
1795-6	4	1	4	1
1796-7	12	10	3	0
1797-8	15	10	6	0
1798-9	17	14	5	1
1799-1800	19	5	3	0
1800-1	11	4	3	0
1801-2	7	5	6	0
1802-3	25	14	6	0
1803-4	9	3	4	0
1804-5	12	6	9	4

Note: The material for this table is drawn from the *Journals of the House of Lords.*

* Bills are counted only once. If an amended bill was later dropped or rejected by the lords it is included only in the latter category.

were abnormally active, but overall the proportion of amended bills merely kept pace with the growing volume of business. And the proportion of public bills which were dropped or rejected was slightly lower in the early years of the nineteenth century than it had been in the 1780s.

It is clear from the figures in Table II that the lords eschewed the role of an active legislative critic. In fact, even they inflate the extent of the upper chamber's critical interventions. A small but significant portion of the bills in the dropped/rejected category were voluntarily withdrawn by their sponsors. Some proved to be no longer necessary or suitable for their stated purposes,[1] and sponsors occasionally preferred to introduce new, redrafted measures rather than amend imperfect ones or accept alterations made in one of the two houses.[2] A few measures lapsed at the end of the session for lack of time.[3] And among those bills that were rejected only a small portion were of the first importance. Most, while useful, were of limited scope and significance.[4]

Nor is the number of amended bills a very accurate measure of their lordships' impact on the legislative process. A large portion of the measures which were revised received only one or two minor alterations: ten of the fifteen bills amended in 1797-8, for example, and seven of the twelve in 1805. Moreover, few peers evinced much interest in this aspect of parliamentary business. On some occasions bills of considerable importance received extensive amendments in a house which consisted of only three or four members.[5]

Several factors influenced the lords' performance of its legislative duties. As a second chamber the house was subjected to certain temptations and impediments which restricted its ability to participate actively in the formulation of public policy. Most legislation originated in the commons where it was discussed and, if necessary, amended before

1 *LJ*, xxviii, 671, 9 May 1787; *The Times*, 14 July 1789.

2 *LJ*, xlii, 232, 316, 27 May, 4 July 1799; *ibid.*, xlii, 505, 16 May 1800; *ibid.*, xliii, 112, 12 Apr. 1801.

3 The Scotch Protestant Oath Bill was, for example, reported from the committee on 23 Mar. 1784. Parliament was dissolved the following day. *LJ*, xxxvii, 69, 23 Mar. 1784. See also, *ibid.*, xxxviii, 671, 8 June 1791. However, peers merely used the lateness of the session in some instances to provide themselves with another excuse for rejecting legislation they disliked on ideological grounds. *PH*, xxvi, 178-9, 29 June 1786; *Hansard*, ii, 926-32, 3 July 1804.

4 Appendix A contains a list of the bills dropped or rejected in the house of lords from December, 1783 to the end of 1805.

5 *LJ*, xlii, 43-5, 7 Jan. 1799.

being sent up to the lords.[1] Inevitably, the commons' labours tempted some noblemen to relax their own scrutiny. Lord Sydney, the rather inadequate leader of the house from 1783-9, periodically referred critics of pending measures to pertinent debates in the commons as a means of cutting short discussions in the lords. In the last weeks of the 1805 session a bill which would allow the duke of Atholl additional compensation for his hereditary rights over the Isle of Man provoked extensive opposition: in particular, peers wished to know why the duke should receive a sum of more than £300,000 after an earlier government had made substantial grants to his uncle for the same purpose. However, the earl of Carlisle claimed that the commons' recent inquiry made such questions irrelevant: the lower house, after having examined the problem intensively, had decided in Atholl's favour, and it only remained for their lordships to approve the measure as expeditiously as possible.[2]

Careful scrutiny and debate were luxuries which the lords could not in any case always afford. Throughout the century peers compained that the commons waited until the last moment before sending up the bulk of the session's public legislation. In 1786 twenty-four bills were passed before 1 June, thirty-two during that month and thirty-one more between 1 July and the end of the session eleven days later. Similarly, in 1796 the house passed thirty-five public bills before 1 May and forty more by the time parliament was prorogued on the nineteenth of the month. As George III told Lord Eldon, this last minute flood of business meant that there was 'too little decent deliberation in the House of Lords'.[3]

Even when it had the time and inclination, the house of lords was not always free to shape legislation as it wished. The commons jealously guarded its prerogative to vote monies to the crown and since the late seventeenth century had refused to accept amendments which the peers made in those bills. Noble opponents of individual money bills naturally protested against this restriction on their freedom; in June 1783, for example, the duke of Chandos 'reprobated the idea of that House not being competent to make alterations in any bill that should

1 Tradition dictated that acts of grace be introduced in the house of lords. Thomas, *The House of Commons,* 47. Most other public legislation originated in the commons unless it was initiated by a peer. Among the few important pieces of legislation to be introduced in the house of lords during our period were the Aliens Act (33 Geo. 3, c. 4), the Treasonable Practices Act (36 Geo. 3, c. 7), and the act to abolish the slave trade (47 Geo. 3, c. 37).

2 *The Times,* 22 May 1787; *Hansard,* v, 783, 8 July 1805.

3 Lambert, *Bills and Acts,* 75; H. Twiss, *The Public and Private Life of Lord Chancellor Eldon* (London, 1844), i, 458-9.

be sent up from the other House, provided their Lordships found such alterations were necessary. . .' He was warmly supported by Lorde Ferrars who rejected the commons' claim that it possessed the sole prerogative to frame revenue bills

> which they [the peers] were to give their assent to as a matter of course, without being at liberty to judge whether they were proper and equitable, or partial and unjust, or to make an alteration, which might be of the greatest advantage to the nation at large. He thought their Lordships were as capable, from their education and experience to amend and frame taxes as this wise House of Commons. . .

Several years later Lord Chancellor Thurlow took a similar position, and even Charles James Fox, the champion of the commons' supposed supremacy, claimed when it suited him that the privileges of the lower house were often 'too strictly construed'.[1]

These periodic criticisms of the commons' special privileges were generally provoked by practical political considerations. Just as their opponents decried the power of the lower house, supporters of disputed money bills welcomed the limitations it imposed. Lord Sydney, who defended the right of the house to scrutinize all legislation while he was in opposition, claimed as leader of the house that disputed money bills should pass unaltered.[2] It seems evident, in fact, that the limit on their legislative independence did not engender any deep sense of grievance in the minds of most noble lords. When they thought about the restriction at all, it was usually because their immediate political interests led them to do so.[3]

In any case, the nobility continued throughout our period to alter money bills. Though such amendments were sufficiently remarkable to attract the attention of the press, Hatsell with his usual thoroughness demonstrates that they were far from rare. The house of commons accepted changes that corrected literal or verbal errors, noting in their Journals their reasons for so doing. Bills which received more substantial modifications in the upper house were invariably rejected, but afterwards the commons often introduced new bills which embodied many or all of the lords' amendments.[4]

1 *Parl. Reg.*, xi, 237, 18 June 1783; *The Times*, 30, 31 July, 1 Aug. 1789; Earl Stanhope, *Life of the Rt. Honourable William Pitt* (London, 1879), i, 87.

2 Parl. Reg., xi, 236-7, 18 June 1783; *The Times, 30 July 1785.*

3 Problems did arise when a peer introduced legislation in his own house. If any of the clauses in such bills related to the grant or disposition of money, they had to be added by an ally when the bill reached the commons. See, for example, Dropmore Papers, Add. MS 58907, fo. 116, Grenville to Pitt, 17 June 1798 (copy).

4 *Ibid.*, 4 June 1790; J. Hatsell, *Precedents of Proceedings in the House of Com-*

Ultimately, however, the legislative personality of the house was determined by its members, not by these various institutional restraints on its legislative freedom. Many noble lords were uninterested in the business of legislation: summoned by the government to attend parliament in 1782, the ninth duke of Somerset apologetically replied that after his long absence from the house he could not revive any interest in parliamentary affairs.[1] Many, too, disliked the rigours of parliamentary life. Thus Earl Spencer explained to his mother:

> I was very glad to get a little respite from London, as the perpetual Battle of Life there added to the effect of two very hot & long days in the House had discomposed me not a little. I don't know whether custom & practice will reconcile me more to it, but at present, I feel that the part of an active Politician is not at all suited to my health or disposition. . .[2]

Their responsibilities in the countryside also interfered with the peers' participation in the house of lords. During the war years many wondered like the first marquis of Buckingham whether they would be more useful as government supporters in Westminster or by performing their militia duties at home. Lord Boringdon, on the other hand, had no doubt that 'by remaining here [in Devonshire] I am enabled to discharge at the same time my duties of citizen (wch lead me to reside on my own estate) & those of commanding officer of battalion; either of which duties but certainly the latter, I conceive in the present moment

mons (London, 1818), iii, 136ff; Thomas, *The House of Commons,* 64-8. Normally the house of commons accepted the few amendments which the lords made in other bills with apparent equanimity. On the rare occasions that the two houses failed to agree, they endeavoured to settle their differences in conference. Usually the lords dropped alterations that they earlier insisted were essential at these sessions. In 1802 they gave up four of their amendments in the Militia Bill while the commons agreed to accept one it had earlier opposed. Two years later the house dropped all nine of its contested changes in the Volunteers Consolidation Bill after Lord Hawkesbury, the leader of the house, insisted that this vital legislation would not otherwise pass in the current session. *LJ,* xliii, 701, 711-12, 722, 18, 21, 22 June 1802; *ibid.,* xliv, 550-3, 24, 28 May, 1804; *Hansard,* ii, 433-8, 28 May 1804.

1 *Correspondence of George III,* v, no. 3512. The monumentally lethargic fifth duke of Devonshire and his painfully shy fellow, the fourth duke of Marlborough, were temperamentally incapable of taking part in the lords' business. Chatsworth Papers, fifth duke's group, no. 508, duchess of Devonshire to Lady E. Foster, 18 June; A.L. Rowse, *The Churchills from the Death of Marlborough to the Present* (New York, 1958), 102-8. The duke of Gordon remained in Scotland rather than reveal his poverty to the great world in London, and the earl of Northampton was forced to retire to Switzerland in order to recover from a fantastically expensive election at Northampton. Melville Papers, Box 5, fos. 1-5, Gordon to Dundas, 6 Dec. 1783. Northampton was joined on the continent by several peers including Horace Walpole's 'Count-Bishop', the wildly eccentric seventh earl of Bristol. Europe's innumerable Bristol Hotels attest to the extent and lavishness of that peer's meanderings.

2 Spencer Papers, Box 12, Spencer to Dowager Countess Spencer, 26 Feb. 1794.

to be paramount to the duty of a Senator in ye upper House'. A number of his colleagues shared Boringdon's priorities, for Auckland told a friend in the autumn of 1803 that the government did not plan to introduce any legislation of importance until the following February since so many members were attending to their militia or volunteer duties!

The business of their estates and their various social obligations also diverted the noble lords' attention from the house of lords. 'As I am very critically going over my Estates & affairs here', Lord Kinnoul told the duke of Portland, '& have a gentleman from England who has been with me some time for his Advice in those Particulars It would have been very Inconvenient for me to Have left this Place at present. . .' to attend parliament. The responsibilities of an estate owner were many and time consuming: the fifth duke of Bedford, a keen farmer, was unable to attend important debates in 1801 because he was in the midst of sheep-shearing at Woburn, and Lord Walpole, though he did not share the duke's enthusiasm for agricultural experimentation, felt that he could best occupy his time '. . .in maintaining & supporting that Edifice & spot of ground the building & ornamenting of which afforded my late worthy father so much satisfaction'.2 No less pressing than the management of an estate or the refurbishing of the ancestral homestead were the social obligations imposed on England's greatest proprietors. A duke of Devonshire or Northumberland, an earl of Derby or Fitzwilliam entertained literally hundreds of their neighbours and tenants at a time. Both in the country and in London the peers were society's leaders, the companions most fit for royalty. Thus, the prospect of a royal ball alarmed government leaders, many of whose supporters were lured from their seats even for less momentous social occasions.3

In most instances the conduct of public business was left to the politicians and a small number of men of business. Other peers might

1 Grenville Papers, Add. MS 42058, fos. 34-5, Buckingham to T. Grenville, 4 Sept.; Harewood Papers, Bundle 66, Boringdon to Canning, 9 Sept. 1796; Auckland Papers, Add. MS 33456, fos. 37-9, Auckland to Rosslyn, 20 Nov. 1803. Peers were also active in other aspects of local government. Viscount Midleton told Pelham, for example, that he had to try forty-one larceny cases. Chichester Papers, Add. MS 33130, fo. 240, Midleton to Pelham, 19 July 1801.

2 Portland Papers, Pwf. 4958, Kinnoul to Portland, 1 Nov. 1795; Holland House Papers, Add. MS 51533, fo. 41, Moira to Holland, 13 June 1801; Hardwicke Papers, Add. MS 35621, fo. 113, Walpole to Hardwicke, 15 Sept. 1783.

3 For accounts of truly princely noble hospitality see Lady Holland's Journal, i, 197; The Francis Letters, ed. C. F. Keary (London, 1901), ii, 429-32. Pitt Papers, PRO 30/8/153, fo. 32, C. Long to Pitt, 18 Apr.; Life and Letters of Sir Gilbert Elliot, First Earl of Minto, ed. Countess of Minto (London, 1874), iii, 320-1.

occasionally appear at debates on controversial issues, but (as we shall see below, pp. 71-4), they did not usually take part in them. Their low level of attendance and their increasingly frequent use of proxies also indicate that most of these men were uninterested in the details of highly complicated questions. When they attended it was to vote for or against bills on the basis of their well-established political affiliations. Since ministers invariably received the majority's support, they were able to dominate the lords' legislative proceedings.

This consistent willingness to advance the projects of the king's government is probably the most important of the various factors which combined to shape the lords' legislative personality. Governments had a serious stake in only fifteen of the ninety-six bills rejected or dropped in the upper house. They had a major stake in a far higher percentage of the bills amended: 98 of 201. Numbers reveal in the first instance that it was all but impossible to defeat measures to which ministers were strongly committed. While it was somewhat easier to amend public bills, this does not mean that ministerial control over the amendment process was weak. By and large ministers dominated all stages of the proceedings on their bills. In some instances they might be forced to negotiate with powerful groups in the house. On a few occasions they accepted alterations proposed from the floor by their adversaries. However, only the Coalition lost a measure of the first importance, its East India Bill, to a hostile majority in the house of lords.

When the house of lords intervened to amend or defeat public bills, it was often because ministers themselves initiated such proceedings. Three times the house rejected public bills introduced by leading members of the opposition: in each case the measure would have reversed some important government policy, and ministers understandably oversaw its speedy rejection.[1] Government politicians were also prepared voluntarily to withdraw bills which time had proved to be unnecessary or which seemed unsuitable for their declared purposes, [2] and in 1789 and 1790 they introduced motions for the rejection of money bills which were drafted in a manner that violated the lords' standing orders.[3] Because Forster, the Irish chancellor of the exchequer, failed to consult the lord lieutenant, Lord Hawkesbury

1 *PH*, xxx, 1424-37, 21 Feb. 1794; *LJ*, xl, 750, 17 May 1796; *ibid.*, xlv, 47, 15 Feb. 1805.

2 *The Times*, 8 July 1786; *ibid.*, 14 July 1789.

3 *Ibid.*, 5, 7 Aug. 1789; *LJ*, xxxviii, 664, 3 June 1790.

had to withdraw two Irish revenue bills in 1805,[1] and on three occasions the government intervened to halt the progress of measures which their lordships' had extensively altered. However, they also re-submitted only slightly modified versions which then passed without further discussion.[2]

Ministers were also responsible in a number of instances for the alterations made in government bills. Controversial proposals initiated in the upper house were almost bound to be modified, and government politicians took a lead in adding the necessary revisions.[3] Many of these were minor readjustments of detail. Indeed, one of the lords more important legislative tasks was to make such revisions. A number of bills were poorly drafted and were likely to contain errors even after passing through the house of commons. When possible, their lordships made the necessary alterations: they revised dates at which measures would take effect, extended or limited the terms during which their penalities would apply and added words or phrases which would clarify the intention of certain clauses. However, some bills including those introduced by the government, were dropped because no amount of alteration could overcome their initially sloppy preparation.[4]

The lawyers in particular relished this aspect of the lords' legislative business. They delighted in pointing out the inaccuracies or incon-sistencies in the commons' work, and they endeavoured through their 'clarifying' or 'corrective' amendments to bring poorly drafted bills into accord with established legal precedents.[5] Where the lawyers led, the lay peers eagerly followed: nothing delighted the house more than the chance to compare its own diligent attention to detail with the commons' sloppy negligence. Thus, at the third reading of the amended Public Offices Bill Lord Stormont treated his colleagues to the type of harangue they adored.

> The causing this bill to be altered, and not suffering it to pass as it
> had been presented by the Lower House for their [the lords'] con-

1 *Colchester Diaries*, ii, 7, 13.

2 Lottery Duty Bill: *LJ*, xxxviii, 659, 664, 31 May, 3 June 1790; Tobacco Duty Bill: *ibid.*, xxxviii, 665, 667, 3, 7 June 1790; Militia Reduction Bill: *ibid.*, xlii, 232, 316, 27 May, 4 July 1799.

3 Aliens Bill: *ibid.*, xxxix, 503, 506, 22, 24 Dec. 1793; Safety of His Majesty's Person Bill: *ibid.*, xl, 531-2, 11, 12 Nov. 1795; Habeas Corpus Suspension Bill: *ibid.*, xli, 543, 20 Apr. 1798.

4 *The Times*, 1 July 1786; *ibid.*, 12 May 1790. Despite their vaunted editorial skills the lords permitted many ill-constructed measures to pass through their house. Thus, it was not uncommon for ministers to introduce legislation to correct, clarify or make more effective acts whose passage they had secured in the same session.

5 See chapter 7.

currence, was in his opinion, an instance of their regard and jealousy of that honourable station which they possess in the Government of their country. The sending the bill back to the other House with the amendments, would convince the authors of the bill, that their [sic] existed in their Lordships not only a power but a disposition to correct either their negligence or their ignorance, in whatever bills they might thus produce for their acquiescence. This he therefore trusted, would cause them to be more careful and circumspect in the future. He hoped they would not again present bills in which the framers of them appeared to have an entire ignorance of the object and principle for which the bill was formed.[1]

Not surprisingly the whigs were most successful in carrying amendments in government bills when they too could point out glaring errors in the commons' text. The government's Lottery Bill of 1787, which permitted holders of tickets to insure their gambling investment, remained substantially unaltered until Lord Loughborough sensibly pointed out that there was nothing to prevent the holder from insuring in several places and thereby deriving all the advantages of multiple insurance. In 1799 Loughborough, who was by this time lord chancellor, agreed to drop a clause from the Tanners Bill when the duke of Bedford pointed out that it contradicted established legal precedents. Again in 1803 Lord Grenville demonstrated a number of instances in which the Volunteer Exemption Bill was so unclear as to be unenforceable. Though his objections were belittled by Hobart, the secretary of state for war, Lord Chancellor Eldon on the following night presented several revisions 'with a view to remove the objections stated by Lord Grenville'.[2]

The whigs were also able from time to time to convince the majority that justice in a specific instance lay on their side. Despite the fact that he was the member of a tiny minority the duke of Leeds persuaded ministers in the committee on the Seditious Meetings Bill that since there were degrees of treason, there should also be appropriate punishments for each degree. Lord Lauderdale also claimed that he and his friends were able to establish that spoken words would not be construed as treason and that penalties for second offenders under the act would be slightly relaxed. In 1799 Grenville agreed to the suggestion of Lord Holland that all persons who were not journeymen should be exempted from the Workman's Combination Bill, a measure which Holland called 'unjust' and 'oppressive'. In the same year the duke of Norfolk, after failing to defeat the Seditious Societies Bill, at least was able to carry an amendment stating that the act would remain in force only for one year.[3]

1 *The Times*, 13 Apr. 1785.
2 *PH*, xxvi, 617-9, 9 Feb. 1787; *The Times*, 12 June 1798; *Hansard*, i, 1878-82, 1884, 16, 17 Dec. 1803.
3 *PH*, xxxii, 257, 11 Nov. 1795; Grafton Papers, 423/734, Lauderdale to Graf-

On very rare occasions the whigs were even able to force concessions from the ministers. The amendments which Lord Sydney moved in the Anglo-Irish commercial resolutions were designed to pacify the manu-facturing interest and its whig allies in parliament. The house of lords was the opportune forum in which to make these concessions. The angry denunciations of industrial tycoons and the indignant protests of William Eden or Lord Sheffield did not penetrate the upper house. There government retained its firm control over a majority that was quite unmoved by the great issues at stake. There Sydney could move his amendments without seeming to bow to superior force. In a house where its majority was firm, ministerial concessions seemed more like voluntary and magnanimous acts of conciliation than admissions of political weakness.[1]

Of course the peers did not always permit ministers to retreat so gracefully. Pitt's cabinet always remained divided on the wisdom of demanding that Russian troops withdraw from Ochakev in 1791. But it was the persistent opposition of the whigs in both houses of parliament and the defection of such key supporters as the duke of Grafton and his members which finally caused ministers to reverse themselves.[2]

While Pitt recovered immediately from this unfortunate episode, Addington demonstrated less resilience in April, 1804. A powerful, growing opposition chose to attack his Volunteers Consolidation Bill during March and April as a means of demonstrating its own strength. The target was wisely chosen, for the bill was poorly drafted and unpopular.[3] By exploiting these weaknesses, Lord Grenville was able to prolong the committee proceedings on the bill for eight days, and in the process he and his allies forced the government to accept many of their amendments.[4] Indeed, the plight of Addington's colleagues in the house of lords during these proceedings is almost without parallel in the years between 1783-1806. A weak government proved itself incapable of fending off the onslaught against a rather poor piece of legislation. Within a month the government resigned.

Aside from their support for or opposition to controversial govern-ment measures, the rank and file among the lords' membership proved

ton, 12 Nov. 1795; *The Times*, 10, 11 July 1799.

1 *Parl. Reg.*, xvii, 98, 13 July 1785.

2 *Leeds Political Memoranda*, 154-5.

3 Liverpool Papers, Add. MS 38240, fos. 266-7, Dynevor to Yorke, 24 Mar. 1804.

4 *Hansard*, ii, 26, 38, 68, 106-7, 140, 9, 10, 11, 12, 17 Apr. 1804. For a more detailed discussion of Addington's position in the house of lords during the final weeks of his administration see chapter 4.

to be intermittent participants in the legislative process. Only those measures which affected their professional or territorial interests, or offended their conservative instincts attracted their critical attention. Even in these relatively rare instances, however, the number of noble lords who played a direct part in the legislative process of the house was small. As we shall see in chapter 8, most preferred to influence the shape of policy indirectly by appealing to sympathetic ministers or by directing the activities of members in the commons. Active participation in the lords was for many a last resort.

There were at least three groups with distinct, professional affiliations in the house of lords. The most important of these was the lawyers whose legislative role will be discussed separately in chapter 6. Though no other body of peers possessed the same degree of influence as the law lords, the bishops and militia officers did in very different ways make a notable imprint on legislation which directly affected their respective interests.[1]

Subsequent generations, along with many of their contemporaries, have found little of the inspirational in the lives of eighteenth-century prelates. Whigs and Pittites alike regarded them as the government's toadies, and few historians have challenged this view. More often in London than in their sees, they left the administration of their dioceses in the hands of lesser officials, and to the intense annoyance of Wilberforce they only slowly rallied to the great moral crusade of the period — abolition. Moreover, when the revolutionary upheavals threatened to shatter the harmony of eighteenth-century society, the bishops clung obstinately to traditional theories: striving to convince the poor of the inevitability of their lot; fulminating against illusory conspiracies and generally refraining from appreciating the realities of their changing environment.[2]

Whatever their shortcomings eighteenth-century bishops constituted a formidable legislative bloc. In 1783 and in 1804 their conduct helped

1 Because so many members took such interest in their passage, ecclesiastical and militia bills were more likely to be amended in the upper house than other types of measures. Ten of the twenty-five bills amended in 1803 dealt with military affairs, four with the English or Irish church. Clearly, the growing volume of militia and church related legislation is itself an explanation for the greater number of bills amended in the upper house after 1795.

2 For examples of contemporary attitudes towards the bishops see *Courts and Cabinets,* ii, 14-16; *Lady Bessborough and Her Family Circle,* ed. Earl of Bessborough in collaboration with A. Aspinall (London, 1940), 87-8. For modern studies of the eighteenth-century episcopacy see N. Sykes, *Church and State in the XVIIIth Century* (Cambridge, 1934), chapters 2 – 4; R.A. Soloway, *Prelates and People: Ecclesiastical Social Thought in England, 1783-1852* (London, 1969), 1-84.

to drive ministers from office. Ultimately they joined ranks with the abolitionists, a factor which facilitated the eventual passage of that great reform through the upper house. On several occasions their united support was also sufficient to carry measures, such as Auckland's bill to prevent marriage between partners in adultery, which might not have gained a majority in a house composed exclusively of lay peers.[1] And of course the prelates took a lead in shaping ecclesiastical legislation.

In order to summarize the bishops' legislative role, we must briefly trace the progress of the bill to enforce clerical residence. This measure initially sprang from two sources: from a widely shared belief that the effective propagation of religion was essential to the preservation of social order, and more immediately, as a result of a startling report from the diocese of Lincoln which revealed that less than a third of the people surveyed had any contact with the church. The report itself, while offering a variety of explanations for this alarming discovery, suggested that the church's survival depended on an active ministry. Thus, in the autumn of 1799 and the early months of 1800 Pitt and Lord Grenville, in consultation with their episcopal allies of Lincoln and Chester, began to prepare a bill enforcing stricter clerical residence. By March the heads of a bill were ready for submission to the entire body of bishops, who while assenting to the general purpose of the proposal, were apprehensive about a myriad of details. Indeed, the project seems to have languished in a sea of apprehension and confusion until 1802 when Sir William Scott introduced a Clerical Residence Bill which was ultimately put off to the following session on the advice of Lord Grenville. Noting the absence of many bishops, Grenville argued that 'it would be highly improper in that House to pass the Bill he alluded to, unless they [the bishops] were present to give it the sanction of their approbation'.[2]

Ironically when it was reintroduced in the next session and the bishops were present in force, they had a generally negative effect on the proceedings. *The Times* only records the speeches of six bishops. One made a minor point of detail, and two others introduced amendments which weakened the bill by exempting certain clergy from its penalties. Only Horsley, bishop of St Asaph, and Barrington of Durham presented alterations designed to extend the bill's competence. Otherwise, the members who pressed most adamantly for compulsory

1 For discussion of the bishops' role in 1783 see Cannon, *The Coalition,* 134-5; in 1804, see chapter 4, 86–8. For their activities in support of Auckland's Adultery Prevention Bill see *PH*, xxxv, 229-30, 273-4, 283-99, 4 Apr., 16, 23 May 1800.

2 Soloway, *Prelates and People,* 50-2; *HMC, 13thR.,* iii, *Fortescue MSS,* vi, 5-8, 20-1, 160, 181, 197; *The Times,* 3 June 1802.

residence and who criticized the innumerable exemptions were lay-men.[1]

The history of this bill's passage illustrates several points about the bishops' legislative role. There were active, zealous prelates who pressed eagerly for the reform of the church: Barrington, Horsley, Porteous of London, Tomline, Pitt's crony, Watson of Landaff and several others. [2] Most were wary of reform, unwilling to disturb vested ecclesiastical interests. It is not surprising, therefore, that much of the more import-ant and certainly the most radical ecclesiastical legislation was introduced and sponsored by laymen.

Yet, even the most powerful lay reformer found it difficult to circumvent the episcopal bench. The earl of Aylesford, who was neither formidable nor progressive, still complained that when church business came before the house, the bishops treated their lay colleagues with highhanded condescension. They demanded and were generally accorded the right to present their views on all measures relating to the church or religion. Recognizing the prelates' testiness, Pitt and his successors took care to consult directly with one or two episcopal intimates before dealing with church affairs. These bishops helped to draft legislation; they explained it to their colleagues; they served generally as the government's spokesmen at all episcopal conclaves.[3] Even so, ministers along with such reformers as Earl Stanhope or William Wilberforce found themselves repeatedly thwarted by conservative prelates who were able invariably to veto unpalatable legislation or at least to modify it to their tastes.[4]

In contrast to the prelacy the militia officers rarely as a body dis-turbed the calm atmosphere of the house or offended the egos of their

1 *Ibid.*, 8, 11, 15, 17, 18, 20, 23, 25 June 1803.

2 R. Hodgson, *The Life of the Rt. Reverend Beilby Porteous, D.D.* (London, 1811), 76-82; Dacres Adam Papers, PRO 30/58/3, Porteous to Pitt, 16 May, 2 July 1805; Pitt Papers, PRO 30/8/168, fo. 91, Porteous to Pitt, 27 May 1805; R. Watson, *Anecdotes*, i, 145-6, 156-61, ii, 126-31.

3 *HMC, 15th R.*, i, *Dartmouth MSS*, iii, 275-6. For examples of the manner in which Pitt used his colleagues on the episcopal bench to help draft and pass ecclesiastical legislation see Lord Ashbourne, *Pitt: Some Chapters of His Life and Times* (London, 1898), 340; Pretyman-Tomline Papers, HA/119 T108/42, Pitt to Tomline, 24 Oct. 1798, 10 Feb. 1799; *ibid.*, HA/119 T108/45, Tomline to Mrs. Tomline [Feb. 1799].

4 For their opposition to Stanhope's various bills see *PH*, xxvi, 125-8, 14 June 1786; Stockdale, *Parliamentary Debates*, iii, 218-24, 9 June 1789. For opposition to Wilberforce's bill to permit Catholics to serve in the militia see R.I. and S. Wilberforce, *The Life of William Wilberforce* (London, 1838), ii, 222-3. According-ing to Watson Pitt made his support for a bill which would repeal the Test Act as it applied to dissenters conditional on the bishops' support; they, of course, strongly opposed such a measure. Watson, *Anecdotes*, i, 261-2.

fellow members. With any militia legislation, Grenville told Henry Dundas, success depended on the lords lieutenant and the militia colonels. 'Whatever scheme they favoured ought to be adopted. A measure which they refused to support would be futile, even if it could be carried in parliament'.[1] In order to insure their support, militia officers were summoned to meet with ministers to go over pending legislation: details were arranged at these conferences, and differences were composed. Consequently, militia bills only provoked prolonged discussion in the house under very special circumstances.

Trouble arose in the first place when a potentially controversial measure was introduced without prior consultation between the government and the militia leadership. In 1798 a bill permitting the government to appoint officers to fill vacancies left open by lords lieutenant provoked criticism even from members who were normally loyal ministerialists. The complaints of the earls of Carnarvon and Radnor, both of whom were relatively independent and jealous of the militia's prerogatives, might perhaps have been expected, but criticisms from Grenville's brother-in-law, Earl Fortescue, and such stalwarts as Sydney and Powis forced the administration to remove the offensive clauses, thereby destroying the bill's effectiveness.[2]

There was also a small group of diehard officers who refused to be bound by the agreements reached in meetings with ministers. Including the earls of Carnarvon, Radnor, Fitzwilliam and Romney this group spoke for a substantial number of country gentlemen. The militia, they believed, was a force raised and officered by local men of property, a force designed to protect the lives and possessions of local inhabitants. They regarded any attempt on the part of the government to break this local connection — whether by appointing officers itself, recruiting men from the militia for the regular army or dispatching certain regiments to Ireland — as violations of the militia's constitution and subversive of its order and efficiency. They also regarded most government bills as affronts to their personal dignity: the effect of recent legislation was to reduce them from the exalted position of commanding officers to the demeaning status of recruiting serjeants.[3]

While the great majority of their colleagues accepted changes which

1   J. R. Western, *The English Militia in the Eighteenth Century; The Story of a Political Issue, 1660-1802* (London, 1965), 228.

2   *Ibid.,* 230-1; *The Times,* 19 May 1798. Hobart, the secretary of state for war, faced similar difficulties in 1803. See, for example, Chichester Papers, Add. MS 33111, fos. 216-7, Sheffield to Pelham, 12 June 1803.

3   Western, *The English Militia,* 233-6. The attitudes of the militia diehards are summarized in their protest against the Militia Bill of 1799. *LJ,* xlii, 349, 4 Oct. 1799.

seemed justified by pressing national needs, the diehards were incapable of setting aside their parochial, old-fashioned concepts of what the militia should be. Normally they constituted a noisy source of obstruction in the house of lords. But because they spoke for many officers, their objections could not be summarily dismissed. Particularly when the more moderate colonels indicated some sympathy for their position, the diehards were able to modify legislation.[1]

Years at the command of a regiment gave lords lieutenant or militia colonels extensive experience and distinct views on what constituted proper militia policy. Within this group there were some, such as the diehards, who were petty, petulant and obstructive, but almost all derived from their experience an intimate knowledge of the problems confronting these forces. Because few secretaries of state for war had a similar familiarity, it was essential for them to consult with leading militia officers before embarking on new legislation. As will become apparent in chapter 8, the militia peers offered good advice on so many occasions that the advantages derived from their powerful presence more than offset their sporadic lapses into narrow self-interest.

While the professional obligations of a bishop or a militia officer stimulated only a portion of the house to activity, regional or more personal interests inspired many peers to take a direct part in the legislative process. Despite sharp partisan differences the Scottish peers, for example, were able to unite in order to pass local legislation and to protect national interests in the hostile or indifferent atmosphere of the Westminster parliament. When in 1784 Lord Chancellor Thurlow attempted to postpone the popular Forfeited Estates Bill, he was successfully opposed by a phalanx of Scots led by the earls of Balcarres and Dunmore. Between 1784 and 1786 several peers played a leading role in modifying what they considered to be the discriminatory treatment of Scottish distillers, and in 1789 the proponents of the Highland Society Bill, a measure designed to release certain government funds for the economic development of the highlands, waged a long and eventually triumphant campaign against Thurlow's obstructive opposition.[2]

Of course, these Scots were not able in all instances to shape legislation to their tastes. The earl of Hopetoun only carried minor amendments to the Hawkers and Pedlars Bill, a measure which he claimed would be especially harmful to small Scottish towns which depended on these merchants. Likewise, several Scots failed in 1788 to make

1 *The Times*, 10 July 1799; *ibid.*, 4 June 1802.
2 *PH*, xxiv, 1363-73, 16 Aug. 1784; *The Times*, 9, 16 June 1789.

any alterations in a bill that restricted the right of Scottish distillers to sell their products in the south. The important point, however, is that these men as well as many English peers felt obliged for a variety of reasons to fight actively for the advancement of local rights and interests.[1]

Among the most interesting members of the late eighteenth-century English nobility was Granville, Earl Gower, elevated in 1786 to the marquisate of Stafford. A politician of some note, owner of extensive properties in Staffordshire and proprietor of mines and iron works in Shropshire, Gower built up an extensive and varied clientage. Many of those clients were actual or potential political supporters of the earl's interest. In 1775, for example, Gower arranged a compromise between Staffordshire potters and a Richard Champion who wished to take out a patent for making porcelain which would have impinged on the activities of the former group. A year later Josiah Wedgwood, who was anxious to settle the duties on Meissen porcelain as quickly as possible, appealed to the earl and got the speedy response he desired. Some of his clients were also Gower's business partners: in 1784, for example, Richard Reynolds, the earl's tenant at his Donnington Wood iron works, relied on Gower to get Pitt to drop an unpopular tax on coals.[2]

Equally successful as lobbyists for their localities were those Cornish peers who were owners of copper mines. Throughout the 1780s they worked with such Birmingham manufacturers as Boulton or Garbett to open markets in India or the Far East to Cornish copper. When the price of copper soared and Birmingham demanded that its export be prohibited in 1798, a county meeting voted special thanks to Lord de Dunstanville and four other peers and MPs who had taken a lead in opposing such a plan.[3]

The activities of the Scots, the Cornish copper proprietors or Lord Stafford were by no means unique. The age expected great landed proprietors to undertake such services in behalf of their communities, and, as will be seen in chapter 9, a very large number did. Indeed, the largest number of peers only took an active part in the legislative

1 *Ibid.*, 23, 30 July 1785; Stockdale, *Parliamentary Debates,* iii, 246-7, 18 Feb. 1788.

2 *The Selected Letters of Josiah Wedgwood,* ed. A. Finer and G. Savage (New York, 1965), 55-6, 177-8, 180, 199.

3 Boulton Papers, Garbett to Boulton, 9, 24 Oct. 1787; *The Banks Letters,* ed. W. R. Dawson (London, 1958), 131-3; Pitt Papers, PRO 30/8/134, fo. 44, Falmouth to Pitt, 13 Mar. 1789; *ibid.,* PRO 30/8/314, fos. 57-8, 'Resolutions of a Special Committee of the Lieutenancy and Magistracy of the County of Cornwall'; J. R. Harris, *The Copper King: A Biography of Thomas Williams of Llanidan* (Toronto, 1964), 117-30.

proceedings of the house of lords in order to advance the causes of their neighbours or associates, causes in which they often happened to have a direct stake themselves.

The limits of a legislative system in which members regularly inter- vened to protect or further specific interests are obvious. Yet, this system had distinct advantages. The Birmingham proposal to limit the export of copper, for example, would not have reduced its price for domestic consumers; in opposing it de Dunstanville and others protected a vital local industry as well as their own financial interests.[1] Peers, in fact, often succeeded in calling local needs to the attention of politicians who might otherwise have ignored them when framing pertinent bills. In this way they helped to accommodate the process of legislation to the circumstances and needs of a variety of groups and regions.

The third impulse which induced noblemen to become active legis- lators was their hostility to reform. The peers amended but eventually passed in 1788 a bill to regulate conditions on slaving vessels after Pitt threatened to dismiss those of his colleagues who continued to resist it.[2] For the next nineteen years, however, the house refused to take any action against the slave trade. Its members insisted on con- ducting their own inquiry into the trade in 1792 and 1793, thereby postponing proceedings on a bill for gradual abolition until after the hysteria bred by revolution, war and slave revolts destroyed all chances of success. Five years later they rejected Henry Thornton's bill which would have enjoined slave traders from conducting their business on certain portions of the African coast, and in 1804 a general abolition bill was defeated.[3] Success came only in 1807 when by deft manoeuvreing and assiduous canvassing, Lord Grenville was able to assemble a majority in favour of abolition.[4]

Despite the length of the campaign for abolition the arguments of its opponents remained inflexible and unvaried. Most often the anti- abolitionists cited the commercial value of the trade; abolition would

1 The primary cause for the rising cost of copper was the heavy domestic demand; exports to India, cited as an important cause by Boulton and Liverpool, were in fact declining during the 1790s. J. Harris, *The Copper King*, 132-5.

2 *LJ*, xxxviii, 252-5, 2 July 1788; *HMC, 13th R.*, iii, *Fortescue MSS*, i, 342; Ehrman, *Pitt*, 394-5.

3 *PH*, xxix, 1350-5, 8 May 1792; *ibid.*, xxx, 652-60, 11 Apr. 1793; *ibid.*, xxxi, 467-70, 2 May 1794; *ibid.*, xxxiv, 1092-1139,,5 July 1799. For the division lists for Thornton's Bill see *Later Correspondence*, iii, 226-8. *Hansard*, ii, 926-33, 3 July 1804.

4 R.Anstey, *The Atlantic Slave Trade and British Abolition, 1760-1810 (Atlantic Highlands, N.J., 1975), 364-402.

58

diminish England's wealth while leaving other nations, unencumbered by any exaggerated humanitarianism, to reap additional profits. Peers who were sensitive to the rights of private property complained that abolition or even regulation constituted an unwarranted invasion of a right that should be absolute. The duke of Chandos claimed in 1788 that even the most modest regulation would lead to slave revolts in the West Indies, and a number of peers reversed the abolitionists' moral arguments to their own advantage. The duke of Clarence asserted that slavers performed a humanitarian service in removing Africans from the primitive violence of their wild continent into the hands of planters whose character was, according to his highness, notoriously of the highest repute. Nor were the evils of the middle passage excessive in the eyes of the hero of the seige of Gibraltar, Lord Heathfield: the general protested in 1788 that conditions on slaving vessels were superior to those on his majesty's troop transports.[1]

The anti-abolitionists drew their strength from all segments of the peerage. The most obvious recruits included noblemen such as the duke of Chandos or Lord Harewood who owned extensive plantations in the West Indies. Thurlow, Eldon and several other judges were unwilling to place restrictions on private property or business practices. Another group whose most prominent representative was the first earl of Liverpool spoke for the merchants of the trade and warned repeatedly of the dire economic consequences which would accompany hasty abolition.[2] The court was also an important center of opposition, particularly in 1799. However, it is unlikely that the king determined the conduct of his friends, as many of them had nothing but scorn for the 'do-gooders' among whom Wilberforce was, of course, the most detested and ridiculed.[3]

Proceedings on the slave trade question are further instructive because they demonstrate the myriad of snags that any reformer acting independently of the king's ministers might encounter in the upper house. First, he had to beware of offending their lordships' institutional

1 *The Times*, 24 June 1788; *PH*, xxvii, 638-48, 25 June 1788; *ibid.*, xxix, 1353-4, 8 May 1792; *ibid.*, xxx, 652-8, 11 Apr. 1793; *ibid.*, xxxiv, 1092-1105, 1109-17, 1138-9, 5 July 1799.

2 Charles Jenkinson was elevated to the peerage as Baron Hawkesbury in 1786. In 1796 he was created earl of Liverpool, and his son was called to the house by right of his father's barony in 1803. In order to avoid confusion the father will be referred to throughout as Liverpool, the son as Hawkesbury.

3 Anstey, *Atlantic Slave Trade*, 289; Wraxall, *Memoirs*, v, 144; *The Farington Diary*, ed. J. Greig (London, 1922), i, 100-1. For examples of Thurlow's opposition see *PH*, xxvii, 643-4, 25 June 1788; *ibid.*, xxix, 1354-5, 8 May 1792. For Eldon's opposition see *Hansard*, ii, 931-2, 3 July 1804. Liverpool argued in 1792 that the trade was a bulwark of England's commercial system. *PH*, xxix, 1353-4, 8 May 1792.

pride. In 1792 several members demanded that the house make its own inquiry into the slave trade before passing a bill for gradual abolition: to accept the commons' recommendations without an independent examination would, they argued, undermine the separate identity of the house of lords. Not surprisingly the inquiry proved itself almost immediately to be a farce, but Grenville, recognizing the peers' sensitivity on matters of privilege, refused to interrupt the proceedings. Another tactic adopted by the opponents of abolition was to move for the postponement of bills on the grounds that their lordships lacked the time to examine such measures adequately: though this ploy proved unsuccessful in 1788, its advocates triumphed in 1804 primarily because they received support from several of Pitt's closest associates in the upper house.[1]

Because the slave question was an 'open' one, members were free to vote according to their inclinations and did not have to follow the course adopted by Pitt or Fox. A number of peers, however, were strongly influenced by the opposition of such powerful members as Eldon, Portland or Thurlow. These steadfast opponents of abolition were able to drag less prominent members in their wakes, particularly when they seemed to be speaking for the court. Thus, their conduct and that of other hostile cabinet ministers enormously complicated the process of regulating or abolishing the trade.[2]

Dolben's Bill foundered because cabinet ministers in the lords were virtually unanimous in their opposition. Nor did Pitt's demand that his colleagues support the measure or resign soften their attitudes: if anything, Sydney, Thurlow and Liverpool became more determined in their opposition as a result of this incident. In 1789 the latter complained about Pitt's strange support of the abolitionists, and he correctly predicted that further action would be defeated in the house of lords.[3] Though Grenville warmly advocated emancipation in the early 1790s, he received little support from his colleagues, and in 1799 as in 1804

1 *PH,* xxix, 1350-5, 8 May 1792; *ibid.,* xxx, 652-60, 11 Apr. 1793; S. and R. I. Wilberforce, *Life of Wilberforce,* i, 351-2, ii, 18, 50-1; *PH,* xxvii, 638-47, 25 June 1788; *Hansard,* ii, 926-33, 3 July 1804.

2 For the extent of Thurlow's influence in the lords see *Auckland Correspondence,* ii, 414-7; Granville Papers, PRO 30/29/6/1, fo. 248, E. Legge to G. Leveson-Gower, 13 Aug. 1792. Even so minor a politician as the second earl of Chichester had four or five followers in the upper house. Buckinghamshire Papers, D/MH C504, Hobart to Hawkesbury, 1 Oct. 1803 (copy). For the court's role against the slave bill of 1799 see Stanhope, *Pitt,* ii, 322-3.

3 Granville Papers, PRO 30/29/4/6, fos. 808-10. A.Macdonald to Lady Stafford, 25 July, 1788; Liverpool Papers, Add. MS 38223, fo. 96, Sydney to Hawkesbury, 29 June 1788; Sackville Family Papers, U269/C182, Hawkesbury to Dorset, 4 July 1788, 18 May 1789.

the majority of cabinet ministers opposed abolition measures presented to the house.[1] The fact that ten of the twelve members of the 'Talents' supported abolition in 1807 was thus not simply a reversal of past practices; the government's nearly unanimous support undoubtedly was an important factor in carrying the measure.

Most of the remaining measures dropped or rejected in the house of lords fall into one of seven categories. The nobility continued with extraordinary consistency to oppose the abolition of imprisonment for debt: fourteen bills which would have modified the penalties imposed on various categories of debtors or readjusted the process of settling debts were thrown out in the house of lords.[2] Their lordships rejected six minor attempts to alter established election procedures and four other measures which would have reformed certain aspects of the system of poor relief. Nine measures designed to encourage a trade or regulate its operation and labour force failed to secure passage. More surprisingly, the house threw out six bills relating to agriculture, in particular the General Enclosure Bill of 1801.[3] Finally, nine measures designed to amend some aspect of the legal code or judicial procedure were lost or dropped: two, however, were subsequently reintroduced and passed.

The nobility's reaction to bills which might affect the religious constitution of the realm was particularly complex. The Catholic Relief Bill of 1791 and some of the measures to enforce clerical residence and improve the position of curates passed through the lords. At the same time the house quite laudably rejected a bill which would have prevented the further immigration of members of Roman Catholic teaching orders.[4] In each instance these victories depended in large part on the combined actions of leading ministers and bishops. Where the latter stood aside or actively opposed, reforms floundered. Thus, Wilberforce

1   No minister supported Grenville's efforts to proceed with the bill for gradual abolition in 1792-3; Liverpool and Thurlow both insisted on the necessity of the house of lords conducting its own inquiry. *PH*, xxix, 1350-1, 1353-5, 8 May 1792. In 1799 Liverpool, Portland and Westmorland opposed Thornton's Bill. Stanhope, *Pitt*, ii, 322-3; Liverpool Papers, Add. MS. 38191, fo. 245, Portland to Liverpool, 12 July 1799. In 1804 all five ministers who spoke on the Abolition Bill opposed carrying it through the house that session. *Hansard*, ii, 926, 929-32, 3 July 1804.

2   The leading sponsors of these measures in the house of lords were the duke of Norfolk, the third earl of Effingham and the earl of Moira. *PH*, xxvi, 1199-1207, 22 May 1787; *ibid.*, xxvii, 547-53, 23 May 1788; *The Times*, 1 June 1793; *ibid.*, 28 Mar. 1797.

3   For discussions on the General Enclosure Bill see chapter 7 and R. Mitichison, 'The Old Board of Agriculture (1793-1822)', *EHR*, lxxiv (1959), 53-9.

4   *PH*, xxix, 664-83, 31 May, 1791; *The Times*, 4, 8 June 1791; *ibid.*, 8, 23 June 1803; *Hansard*, v, 243-5, 703-5, 10 June, 1 July 1805; *PH*, xxxv, 368-86, 10 June 1800.

attributed the failure of his bill to enable Roman Catholics to hold commissions in the militia to the lack of government support and to the opposition of the bishops of Bristol and Rochester.[1]

Bishops were particularly formidable opponents of religious reform. They defeated Lord Stanhope's various bills to restrict the jurisdiction of ecclesiastical courts, remove archaic ecclesiastical penalties and eliminate certain harassing aspects of tithe collection. In 1796 a Quaker Relief Bill was dropped because of their strong oppostion.[2] Moreover, bishops joined with a substantial number of lay peers to oppose Catholic emancipation. Though the house never directly rejected an emancipation bill before 1806, its sentiments on the issue were well known.[3]

As their treatment of various ecclesiastical legislation demonstrates, the peers did not pose an insurmountable barrier to change during these years.[4]   The house accepted Pitt's major legislation, some of which substantially altered traditional administrative, military, imperial or taxation policies. Likewise, it approved many of the reforming measures which were introduced without the sanction of the administration. As a means of regaining control of their own peerage elections, Scottish peers introduced a resolution which barred members of the British peerage from sitting among the sixteen or even voting for eligible candidates. Despite the opposition of ministers, the house accepted this resolution. In 1792 the lords enthusiastically removed penalties which had bound Scottish episcopal ministers for generations. Though they approved amendments which limited the right of Roman Catholics to teach Protestant children in their schools, the peers still accepted the Catholic Relief Bill of 1791 and refused to permit Thurlow and his episcopal cronies to add a host of restrictive amendments. Similarly, they put aside the objections which the lawyers raised against Fox's Libel Bill

---

1   *Life of Wilberforce*, ii, 222-3.

2   *PH*, xxvi, 125-8, 14 June 1786; Stockdale, *Parliamentary Debates*, iii, 218-24, 9 June 1789; *The Times*, 17 May 1796.

3   Both houses rejected the petition of Roman Catholics in 1805, but the issue of Catholic relief was not presented to the lords either in 1801 or 1807.

4   North and George III looked to the upper house to oppose legislation which governments could or did not wish to defeat in the house of commons. Pares, *George III and the Politicians*, 40-1; *Later Correspondence*, V, xiv-v. Pitt does not appear to have adopted such a course. In 1788 he did make his support for the repeal of the Test Act as it applied to dissenters contingent on the approval of the bishops. Watson, *Anecdotes*, i, 261-2. But there is no indication that he wished the prelates to respond in the negative manner they did, and his application to them may only have reflected the widely held belief that bishops should be consulted on all matters pertaining to religion. In 1788 and 1799 Pitt applied direct pressure on the lords in favour of two slave bills; in so doing he enraged his noble cabinet colleagues and in the latter instance his conduct diminished his standing with the king.

and passed that important measure in 1792 at a time when it was most urgently needed.[1] Most significantly, they reversed their opposition of the previous two decades and voted to abolish the slave trade.

This is not to say that the house of lords encouraged change. Its members steadily thwarted the abolitionists along with those who wished to reform the laws relating to the treatment of debtors. They refused to consider the most minor alterations in the electoral structure and even rejected legislation that would have made the process of enclosure cheaper and easier. Obviously the nobility disliked substantial change and was wary of measures which threatened to disrupt or to invade established property rights. Yet, the house of lords was not, during these years, the scourge of reformers.

Thus, it is important not to overstress the negative consequences of their lordships' very real conservatism. With the exception of the slave bills, the reform legislation which the upper house rejected was relatively minor. Some bills were certainly useful and humane, but their defeat in one session was not irreversible. Fox's Libel Juries Bill passed in 1792 after having been rejected a year earlier, and if the peers refused to end the practice of imprisoning debtors, they did ameliorate the latters' condition. Moreover, not all reforms were good or useful. Parts of Wilberforce's Criminals Bill of 1786, for example, were brutally inhumane, and the measure deserved to be thrown out. Finally, their lordships' suspicion of change served to stimulate scrutiny and debate of important issues in some instances. The house of lords did eventually agree to set aside those Elizabethan statutes which had protected working men, but only after considerable hesitation. While the peers hesitated, parliament was forced to examine and discuss the question thoroughly.[2]

Viewed from a legislative as well as a constitutional perspective the dominant trait of the house of lords was its conservatism. The history of the abolition movement offers an example of the peers at their most rigid. However, their behaviour in this instance was atypical rather than the reverse. In a period when the range of public policy was expanding and its context took on a more ideological hue, in a period of war, unrest and revolutionary economic transformation, the house of lords

[1] *PH*, xxvi, 1158-67, 18 May 1787; *ibid.*, xxix, 1341-9, 2 May 1792; *The Times*, 4, 8 June 1791; *PH*, xxix, 1404-31, 1534-7, 16, 21 May, 1, 11 June 1792.

[2] *PH*, xxvi, 195-202, 5 July 1786. For a discussion of the lords' role in the struggle to repeal the ancient corpus of legislation that regulated wages and the conditions of labor in the woollen industry see J.H. Ramage, 'The English Woollen Industry and Parliament, 1750-1830: A Study in Economic Attitudes and Political Pressures', Unpublished Ph,D. Dissertation (Yale, 1970).

was more likely to do 'nothing in particular' than to stand forth as an obstructive obstacle to reform. Quiescence is more truly indicative of the peers' approach to the business of legislation than their summary treatment of various reforms. Placing as they did primary emphasis on stability, identifying stability with political calm in Westminster, the majority of peers were unwilling and unlikely to adopt a critical and potentially disruptive legislative posture.

Like any second chamber the house corrected and updated texts of bills. Ministers found it to be a convenient place in which to modify legislation to their tastes or to make discreet bows to their opponents — bows which were less offensive in that friendly environment because they appeared more as magnanimous efforts at conciliation than unwanted concessions. The whigs did not often force amendments from ministers, and in some cases their triumphs had deleterious repercussions: more often, however, their intermittent successes removed glaring errors from bills and provided some protection for individual rights of which Pitt and his colleagues became increasingly careless in the 1790s.

The legislative contribution of the great body of peers, though narrowly circumscribed, had positive as well as negative aspects. The bishops impeded the process which might have revitalized their church; militia officers were sometimes incapable of distinguishing national requirements from their own self-interest; and the nobility as a group translated its political conservatism into obstruction or outright opposition to necessary social and political reforms. Yet, the house of lords did not stand forth in our period as the nemesis of all reform, and its members were able through their interventions to improve legislation on topics ranging from the militia to the regulation of hawkers and pedlars. By calling attention to circumstances unknown to ministers, peers enriched the legislative process: they provided information on the basis of which measures could be framed to reflect more accurately the needs of a diverse and complex national community.

4

ACCOUNTABILITY: THE LORDS AND THE KING'S MINISTERS

The triumphant achievement of parliament during the seventeenth and early eighteenth centuries was to secure for itself a voice in deciding upon the fate and the composition of the king's government. This right was vested equally in the lords and the commons. Thus, in February 1784, Lord Loughborough explicitly contradicted the views of his ally, the duke of Manchester, when the latter questioned whether the lords should have a voice in the appointment of ministers: precedent clearly established, Loughborough maintained, that the lords and the commons each possessed the authority to advise the king on the composition of his cabinet.[1]

Individual peers continued throughout the eighteenth century to call upon their colleagues to remove ministers. Having seen the opposition to the American war crumble in the house of commons, Lord Shelburne urged the peers in 1778 to do what the lower house had been unable to accomplish — reject Lord North. Sixteen years later the duke of Grafton, critic of another war, asserted that 'it was the especial duty of that House to watch that in the executive government there was neither delinquincy nor want of ability'. Again in the last years of the century Lord Suffolk and the duke of Bedford introduced a series of motions calling for the dismissal of the government; while many peers challenged the wisdom of this course of action and the grounds on which the opposition rested its arguments, none of them questioned the right of their house to take such action.[2]

As the movers of hostile motions implied, the nobility's obligation to hold ministers accountable for their conduct of the king's business was an essential part of its legislative responsibilities. Members of administration formulated public policy. They also shaped much of the public legislation which came before parliament. Where their policies and legislation were sound, it was the duty of the peers to support them. On the other hand, parliament could not tolerate a consistent record of ministerial failure. Where such a pattern existed, the needs of the nation compelled peers to reject those ministers who had proved themselves incompetent for their tasks.

1 *PH*, xxiv, 504, 509-13, 4 Feb. 1784.

2 *Ibid.*, xix, 1048, 8 Apr. 1778; *ibid.*, xxxi, 1451-2, 30 Mar. 1795; *ibid.*, xxxiii, 183-95, 735-66, 1313-52, 27 Mar., 30 May 1797, 22 Mar. 1798.

Opposition leaders repeatedly complained that ministers denied the house of lords the time and the information needed to deal effectively with the complex questions which came before it. Occasionally standing orders were brushed aside, and the house rushed to pass controversial legislation over the objections of opposition members.[1] Ministers sometimes refused to budge from their narrowly limited discussion of important topics or to give reasons why the house should support their policies.[2] In 1791, during a debate in which the foreign secretary, Leeds, admitted privately that his colleagues were 'gagged', the earl of Carlisle bitterly summarized the frustrations of an opposition forced to endure such highhandedness.

> It had been the plan of the present ministers to treat that House with less respect, than had been the practice of their predecessors; they came down, therefore, and without offering any explanation of the measures they proposed, called upon their lordships to give them implicit confidence, and vote whatever they desired.[3]

Yet, if ministers sometimes gave their opponents cause for complaint, it is also evident that the whigs' protests were frequently disingenuous or exaggerated. In many instances oppositions adopted this line of criticism for lack of any better argument. Attacks on ministerial highhandedness also served an opposition's tactical purposes: such a cry enabled the whigs to obstruct the progress of business and, more rarely, to arouse the sympathy of undecided or independent peers.[4] Most important, these outraged politicians carefully ignored the fact that the house of lords possessed a variety of devices which, if properly exploited, might permit them to secure much of the information they required.

By our period, for example, the direct interrogation of ministers had become a well-established procedure. Questions were posed on every possible topic: the ability of the nation to raise financial resources to fight wars, the health of the king, the future grants under Queen Anne's bounty or even the size of the government's subsidy to the Caledonian Canal.[5]

Of course, interrogators did not in every instance receive satisfactory replies to their questions. Some were simply too obscure or detailed

1 *LJ*, xli, 649-50, 19 June 1798; *ibid.*, xlii, 243, 3 June 1799; *ibid.*, xliv, 311, 4 July 1803.

2 For examples of narrowly focused debates see *Hansard*, i, 1760-80, 12 Dec. 1803; *ibid.*, v, 461-82, 20 June 1805.

3 *Leeds Political Memoranda*, 159-160; *PH*, xxix, 35-6, 29 Mar. 1791.

4 See, for example, *ibid.*, xxxvi, 1132-7, 13, 15 Dec. 1802.

5 *The Times*, 29 Mar. 1791; *Hansard*, i, 634-42, 1 Mar. 1804; *ibid.*, i, 1760, 12 Dec. 1803; *ibid.*, ii, 33-4, 10 Apr. 1804.

to be answered at once. Lord Hawkesbury, while leader of the house, also refused to respond to questions which were posed for tactical rather than informational purposes. Generally, however, the ministers' refusal was based on their sense of the national interest. In 1791 Lord Chancellor Thurlow reprobated the opposition's contention that ministers were disrespectful of the house if they failed to answer all questions put to them; any challenge whose answer required the publication of information potentially damaging to the king's service could be ignored. The duke of Bedford's attempt to force the government to reveal the proposals it would offer to mutinous sailors in 1797 provoked a similar response from Lord Grenville; words he might utter in response to a question so 'invidiously and irregularly put' would be subjected to the grossest misrepresentations by the whigs and others who encouraged disorders.[1]

Oppositions were never deterred by such fulsome protestations. Thus, when Lord Eldon ruled that the duke of Clarence's persistent questioning was 'inconsistent with the order and regularity of their lordships proceedings', the duke refused to be cowed: no peer, he argued, could rely on the government to supply him with the information needed to evaluate its policies, and therefore, the practice ought to continue.[2] In fact, ministers were bombarded with questions, and in a surprising number of instances they gave direct, explicit answers.

A more traditional source of information was the official state papers. Various laws required that data be annually transmitted to parliament, and when an administration demanded the co-operation of parliament, for example at the declaration of war or the conclusion of peace, pertinent documents were delivered to both houses. The peers themselves could request information on current topics, though where such requests impinged on the prerogative, an address had to be moved to the king.

The actual release of state papers again depended upon the acquiescence of the king's ministers. Those men expected oppositions to give some prior notice of what materials they desired,[3] but they did supply

1 *Ibid.*, ii, 338, 30 Apr. 1804; *PH*, xxix, 45-6, 29 Mar. 1791; *ibid.*, xxxiii, 492, 9 May 1797. Disputes could be avoided by giving notice to the appropriate minister. If the question was an important or controversial one, prior notice was expected. See Dropmore Papers, Add. MS 58993 (unfoliated), Bristol to Grenville, 22 Feb. 1806.

2 *Hansard*, iii, 478-80, 15 Feb. 1805.

3 *Ibid.*, iii, 721-2, 6 Mar. 1805. Normally the opposition took care to give notice of its motions for papers. Yet, it was under no obligation to do so; on 11 Feb. 1805, Lord Albemarle's motion for one document was carried without

many papers which the whigs and other groups subsequently used as the basis for attacks on the government. The requested documents were often unobjectionable in themselves, and to deny access to them would only permit an opposition to assert that the house of lords was being asked to legislate without adequate information.[1]

Ministers did, of course, withhold certain documents from their opponents. Grenville told Pitt on one occasion that Lord Holland's application for the instructions sent to Lord Keith about Kleber's army had to be resisted because they related to a pending military action. More frequently the government's motives for opposing opposition applications were political: Hawkesbury, for example, refused to hand over certain Irish papers on the grounds that the information contained therein might be misconstrued to the disadvantage of certain officials. Backed by their large majorities, ministers could easily reject motions for papers whose publication might prove embarrassing to them. In fact, the whigs often moved for documents which they knew they would not receive simply as a means of provoking a potentially damaging debate.[2]

Where the state papers contained especially confidential information or where the house required additional materials, the lords could appoint a select committee to investigate the facts of a problem.[3] Select committees were rarely used before 1790, and most of those that were established merely collected precedents to justify a course of action which the house wished to adopt.[4] After 1790, however, the lords relied more heavily on these bodies; an increasing number were appointed to investigate an ever wider range of problems.

objection despite the fact that he had given no notice. *Ibid.*, iii, 336-7, 11 Feb. 1805.

1 For instances in which government leaders readily accepted opposition requests for papers see *LJ*, xl, 284, 29 Jan. 1795; *Hansard*, i, 1017-8, 1176-7, 29 Feb., 26 Mar. 1804; *ibid.*, iii, 45-6, 22 Jan. 1805; *ibid.*, iv, 18-24, 14 Mar. 1805.

2 Dacres Adam Papers, PRO 30/58/3, Grenville to Pitt, 4 July 1800; *Hansard*, iii, 581-2, 21 Feb. 1805. Motions for papers which constituted direct attacks on ministerial policy include that of Lord Carlisle on 18 Feb. 1785 and the duke of Norfolk's motion for papers relative to the Portuguese trade in 1787. *The Times*, 18 Feb. 1785; *PH*, xxvi, 514-34, 23 Feb. 1787.

3 In certain instances the house of lords called upon the commons to forward evidence which it had collected during its own investigations. To the peers' intense annoyance the lower house generally refused to send up information pertaining to money bills, though Hatsell notes that on some occasions such information was dispatched in apparent violation of the commons' orders. Hatsell, *Precedents*, iii, 143-5. For an example of the peers' angry reaction to the commons' assertion of its privileges see, *Hansard*, v, 764-5, 5 July 1805.

4 Between 1784 and 1790 the house of lords appointed select committees to examine precedents for receiving petitions against bills which would repeal duties, to examine the king's physicians and to examine precedents for establishing a regency. *LJ*, xxxvii, 528; *ibid.*, xxxviii, 269-70, 274.

Though the opposition called repeatedly in these years for the establishment of select committees to delve into the latest ministerial failure, most such bodies were organized to suit the purposes of the government. The report of the committee, appointed in 1794 to examine the evidence on domestic sedition, prepared the way for setting aside Habeas Corpus. In February 1797, a committee was named to determine whether the government's order suspending cash payments should be renewed. On the very day that this body delivered its favourable report another was established to investigate the causes for such a restriction and concluded that the suspension was occasioned by factors which were beyond the control of the administration. Again in 1800, ministers used the report of a select committee inquiring into food shortages to discredit the more extensive relief proposals presented by independent and opposition peers.[1]

In view of their function it is hardly surprising to discover that great care was taken to choose the committees' members. Shortly after the king was stricken in 1788, political leaders on both sides of the house presented their followers with a list of those peers who would sit on a select committee to examine the royal physicians. The committee appointed to study papers pertaining to Irish conspiracies in 1799 included four cabinet ministers – Camden, Grenville, Portland and Westmorland and three government men of business – Auckland, Hobart and Minto. When in 1800 the house established a committee to propose means for dealing with food shortages, Lord Grenville, the leader of the house, chose its members.[2]

The peers were also able to collect valuable information while reviewing private citizens' responses to pending legislation.[3] The house

1 *LJ*, x1, 199, 202, 20, 21 Mar. 1794; *ibid.*, x1i, 109-11, 6 Mar. 1797; *ibid.*, x1i, 186-262, 28 Apr. 1797; *The Times*, 20, 22 Dec. 1800, 30 Mar. 1801. The last committee was mere window dressing. Lord Grenville told his brother prior to the opening of the 1800-1 session that parliament had been called early in the fall not to do anything useful but rather to satisfy the public that government was working to relieve the food shortages. Grenville Papers, Add. MS 41852, fo. 66, Grenville to T. Grenville, 10 Oct. 1800.

2 *Leeds Political Memoranda*, 133; *LJ*, x1ii, 177-8, 1 May, 1799; Hardwicke Papers, Add. MS 35664, fo. 31, Grenville to Hardwicke, 13 Nov. 1800.

3 The house of lords refused to accept petitions which did not conform to established forms, nor would its members consider those which came from individuals or groups that only had an indirect interest in a bill. *Hansard*, ii, 925-6, 3 July 1804; *The Times*, 24 July 1789; *Hansard*, ii, 1056-7, 17 July 1804. There was considerable confusion as to whether the house could receive petitions on money bills: Lords Fitzwilliam in 1783 and Cathcart in 1789 argued that to do so would violate their lordships' orders. On the other hand a committee investigating the subject in 1786 demonstrated that there were precedents for such action, and Thurlow quickly overruled Cathcart's objections in 1789. *Parl. Reg.*, 11, 236, 18 June 1783; *The Times*, 22 July 1789; *LJ*, xxxvii, 533, 22 June 1786.

admitted the right of citizens to present their arguments for and against specific measures by means of a petition. It could, if it chose, ignore these petitions by leaving them unread on the table. It could read them and then set them aside. Or having read them, it could permit the parties, either directly or through counsel, to present evidence in support of their cases, and it could even summon witnesses to testify at the bar.

During our period the most successful effort to influence the outcome of parliamentary proceedings by means of the petitioning process was organized by Josiah Wedgwood as part of the Chamber of Manufacturers' campaign against Pitt's Anglo-Irish commercial resolutions.[1] The importance which Wedgwood attached to this method of lobbying is vividly illustrated in his correspondence with Matthew Boulton. Even while the resolutions were still in the house of commons, Wedgwood was worrying about the lords. Thus, he urged Boulton to rally the various Birmingham trades: 'every petition has its weight, & will have its influence too even in the H of Lords − I mean those presented to the H of Commons'. Though Boulton received assurances from Lord Sheffield, a leading whig in the lower house, that the manufacturers' efforts had been of the 'most essential consequence', Wedgwood was unrelenting. Thus, when Boulton promised to send up a petition, the latter complained that it was inadequate.

> You omit saying anything of Evidences along with your petitions, but I hope they will not be forgot − Nobody knows better than yourself the difference between a Petition heard by themselves [sic], or Counsel, & a simple one without Accompaniments. Simple petitions are, to be sure, better than none, but if we must not expect the *best things* from Birmingham & its Environs, from whence must we expect them? − Many good and Able Lords have promis'd to support the Manufacturing interest in their House, if the Manufacturers will only supply them with the means of doing so.

In the end Birmingham came forward with the desired evidence and upheld its honor.[2]

As Wedgwood expected, the petitioning process had a demonstrable impact on individual peers. The majority did not bother to attend sessions at which counsel for various parties were heard. Nevertheless,

1 For studies of the Chamber of Manufacturers' campaign against the Irish commercial resolutions see W. Bowden, 'The Influence of the Manufacturers on Some of the Early Policies of William Pitt', *AHR*, xxix (1924), 655-74; J. Norris, 'Samuel Garbett and the Early Development of Industrial Lobbying in Great Britain', *EcHR*, 2nd ser., x (1958), 450-60.

2 Boulton Papers, Wedgwood to Boulton, 27, 31 May 1785; *ibid.*, Sheffield to Boulton, 28 May 1785; *ibid.*, S. Garbett to Boulton, 8 June 1785.

evidence was usually printed by the house. After taking copious notes on the testimony of witnesses against the Anglo-Irish commercial resolutions, Earl Fitzwilliam incorporated them into the draft of the speech he prepared on that subject. In 1788 the information presented by supporters of Dolben's Slave Regulation Bill convinced Lord Cathcart of the measure's necessity, and he was appointed by the bill's agents to prepare a speech which would summarize the case they had presented at the bar. Similarly, arguments used by merchants opposing the Tobacco Bill of 1789 were repeatedly cited by the whig opponents of that controversial piece of legislation.[1] In fact, speakers were regularly assigned the responsibility of presenting to the house information which had been collected at such proceedings.

Ministers were able in almost every instance to control the lords' access to vital information. They answered questions as they saw fit; papers were made available at their discretion; and committees of inquiry were appointed and staffed to suit their purposes. If it was more difficult to control the testimony of hostile petitioners, they could at least consign petitions to limbo by leaving them unread; in June 1785, Thurlow and Camden even tried to bar the testimony of the various counsel for the petitioners against the Anglo-Irish resolutions.[2] Yet it would be erroneous and misleading to conclude that leading government politicians treated the house of lords contemptuously.

Throughout our period the house was kept adequately informed on the state of the nation's business. Questions were posed and often answered directly, and the whigs frequently received the state papers they requested. If ministers relied upon select committees to support their point of view and usually rejected the opposition's demands for such bodies, that was their legitimate political prerogative. Even their enormous power was insufficient to stifle the voice of public opinion: in 1785 opponents of Pitt's Anglo-Irish commercial resolutions effectively destroyed that measure by bringing immense pressure to bear in both houses of parliament against it.

Members of the house of lords in fact received far more information than most of them cared to read or consider. A few such as the first Lord Harrowby might pore over papers or testimony on matters which particularly interested them.[3] The great majority, however, remained

1 Wentworth Woodhouse MSS, F65/33-7, 40, 42; Lynedock MSS, Box 3593, fos. 15-18, Cathcart to T. Graham, 25 July 1788; *The Times*, 30 July 1789.
2 *Ibid.*, 4 June 1785.
3 Harrowby MSS, cdxxxv, Documents 52, 54, 'Later Diaries of the first Lord Harrowby'.

quite indifferent to the details of policy or legislation: they ignored sessions at which materials pertinent to important pending questions were presented to the house, and there is little evidence in their papers to show that they studied testimony which the house ordered to be printed. Normally they limited their parliamentary participation to those occasions when major divisions were likely to occur: instead of weighing the merits of policies or legislation, they were generally content to vote according to their well-established political ties.[1]

The lords' debates provided its members with the opportunity to apply their knowledge and understanding to the evaluation of specific measures and the conduct of ministers. By and large these events were dominated by politicians, judges and men of business. Some were very bad, but because the house possessed a number of able, informed men, many were instructive and interesting. Individual debates probably had little impact on the attitudes of peers, but their cumulative effect on the balance of forces within the house is demonstrably evident. At its best the house was in fact a forum for the intelligent discussion of leading national questions.

As might be expected, the lords' performance at debates was often leisurely and restrained.[2] Their lordships normally adjourned before midnight, and when they remained in session into the early hours of the morning, as they did during the debates on Shelburne's peace preliminaries, for example, observers made special note.[3] Custom and good manners apparently dictated the postponement of debates when prominent members were inadvertently absent, and the leadership, unwilling to seem overly highhanded, occasionally bowed to the opposition's requests and deferred proceedings for several days.[4] For their

1 The house of lords devoted fourteen sessions to hearing the testimony of counsel for and against the Anglo-Irish commercial resolutions: attendance at those sessions steadily declined and averaged over the period forty-four. It then went into committee for four days to consider the resolutions in detail along with the various amendments put forward by the government and the whigs: an average of fifty-nine peers attended these sessions. Throughout these proceedings there were four major debates in the full house at which an average of ninety-two peers were present.

2 The lords' standing orders required that peers speak only to motions before the house, and then but once. Despite the intermittent efforts of Lord Chancellor Eldon and a few ministers, these orders were rarely enforced save against the most unruly members.

3 *The Last Journals of Horace Walpole during the Reign of George III, 1771-1783*, ed. A. F. Steuart (New York, 1910), ii, 482-3.

4 *Hansard*, iii, 306, 7 Feb. 1805; *ibid.*, iv, 599, 6 May 1805. Thurlow, who was notoriously rude, refused in 1784 to heed the opposition's request that debate on

part, opposition or independent speakers usually informed ministers if they intended to introduce critical motions.[1]

These well-mannered proceedings were dominated by a small number of members. In 1783 the house of lords contained 238 members. Pitt created ninety-two new peers before 1801, and the Irish Union added thirty-two additional lay and ecclesiastical members.[2] The figures in Table III reveal that only a tiny portion of this growing membership — never more than 18 per cent — spoke in debates even during the most tumultuous sessions. Many of those who spoke on one occasion made the briefest statements of opinion. The number of peers capable or willing to participate in serious, detailed discussions was far smaller; indeed, this group was composed almost exclusively of the professional members of the house.[3]

Obviously the great majority of noblemen felt no compulsion to take part in highly contentious political discussions. In some instances their reticence reflected a lack of interest in or understanding of great political topics. But the peerage as a whole was not indifferent to questions of state. Rather, its members left discussion of those issues to politicians and men of business. If the rank and file spoke at all, it was likely to be on some measure which touched directly on territorial, economic or professional interests.

It is also apparent that many peers were prevented from speaking by a sense of personal inadequacy. Lord Harrington hesitated to accept Lord Sydney's invitation to move the address because he felt that he was too 'little conversant in business, totally unaccustomed to public speaking, & fearful (from an embarrassment which I have never yet been able to conquer) I should probably on such an occasion find myself so much confused as to very ill acquit myself for the task. . .' In the

Pitt's Indian Regulation Bill be postponed due to the absence of Loughborough, thereby earning the ill-will of Portland. *PH*, xxiv, 1302-8, 2 Aug. 1784; Portland Papers, Pwf. 9214, Portland to Loughborough, 6 Aug. 1784. Lord Hawkesbury, however, agreed to postpone the second reading of the Volunteer Consolidation Bill when Lord Spencer claimed that the original date did not allow peers sufficient time to study that measure. *Hansard*, i, 1004-8, 23 Mar. 1804.

1 Sydney Papers, Box 2, Manchester to Sydney [no date]; *HMC, 13th R.*, iii, *Fortescue MSS*, iii, 11.

2 Turberville, *The House of Lords in the Age of Reform*, 42-3.

3 P.D.G. Thomas estimates that 44 per cent of the members returned to the parliament of 1768 spoke at least once during their tenure. Equally thorough research into the lords' proceedings would undoubtedly reveal that the peerage, as a body, was less active. However, Thomas's figures reveal that debates in the commons, like those in the lords, were dominated by a very small group. P. Thomas, 'Check List of M.P.s Speaking in the House of Commons, 1768 to 1774'. *BIHR*, xxxv (1962), 220-6.

Table III

The Peerage's participation
at debates
1784—1803

year	number of peers speaking	number speaking more than once	% of latter who are pols., judges, men of business
1783-4	33	17	82.4
1785	16	6	100.0
1786	17	12	58.3
1787	32	20	70.0
1787-8	35	19	68.4
1788-9	46	23	65.2
1790	9	3	100.0
1791	35	20	70.0
1792	33	20	65.0
1792-3	27	19	73.2
1794	34	28	67.9
1795	47	20	80.0
1795-6	26	14	78.6
1796-7	37	22	59.1
1797-8	35	14	85.7
1798-9	26	12	75.0
1799-1800	38	21	61.9
1800-1	41	25	68.0
1801-2	35	15	86.7
1802-3	36	21	76.2

Note: Figures come from reports of debates in the *Parliamentary History* (superseded in the 1803-4 session by *Hansard).* Though the *Parliamentary History* reports are incomplete and though the thoroughness of its reporting varies, it is the one work that was at the same time accessible and reasonably complete for the period.

end Harrington relented, but for the young Earl Spencer the process of overcoming his sense of inadequacy was more prolonged and difficult, as can be surmised from the following passage in a letter to his mother.

> I should several times have been very glad to have felt myself able to speak, but I scarce think I shall now ever bring myself to it! I think if I could have possessed myself I could have treated the argument in a rather different manner from anyone that spoke on our side; & as I think in a clearer light, but all that clearness, if I had made the attempt, would most probably have been lost in my embarrassment, & I should only have exposed myself without convincing a single person.[1]

Given the rank and file's erratic participation and normal reticence, the quality of the lords' debates was bound to depend almost entirely upon the abilities and diligence of its leading members. Pitt's first cabinet was undeniably mediocre, but even in the mid 1780s there were talented men such as Thurlow and Camden in the upper house. Moreover, the lords continued to receive fresh accessions of talent throughout the period. Liverpool, Auckland and Spencer were able administrators who spoke authoritatively on a range of issues. Eldon was the greatest lawyer of the age and became the leading spokesman for the very conservative segment of the peerage, while Grenville and Hawkesbury, both of them future prime ministers, were so efficient as leaders of the house and of such political importance that their parliamentary statements often carried a weight only slightly less than those of Pitt himself. These, however, are only the most notable members of that talented and experienced group of peers which dominated the house of lords after 1790; most statesmen of any importance ended their careers in that institution.

Opposition, too, had its share of talented speakers. Loughborough was an especially skillful debater, and in the mid 1780s he was ably seconded by Lord Stormont and the earl of Carlisle. The able if pompous Rawdon, who succeeded his father as earl of Moira in 1793, emerged in the late 1780s as the leading spokesman for the Carlton House party at the same time as Pitt's brilliantly erratic cousin, the third Earl Stanhope, moved closer to the whigs. In the mid 1790s Fox believed that Lauderdale, Bedford, Albemarle and Guildford, all recent acquisitions, would make the house of lords 'a very troublesome place to Ministers',[2] and Lords Holland and King, who took their seats at the very end of the century, were both men of recognized ability. Finally, their union with Grenvilles in 1804 gained for the whigs Grenville and Spencer, two of the most formidable figures in the house of lords.

In spite of the many talented members in the upper house, contemporary letters, journals and periodicals are filled with criticisms of the

---

1 Sydney Papers, Box 2, Harrington to Spencer, 9 Nov. 1787; Spencer Papers, Box 9, Spencer to Dowager Countess Spencer, 27 Dec. 1788.

2 *Memorials and Correspondence,* iii, 67.

lords' debates. Wraxall repeatedly commented on their poor quality during the 1780s, and the *Morning Chronicle,* in a passage for which its editors were imprisoned, noted scathingly that

> the House of Lords must now be admitted to be highly important as a political assembly, notwithstanding it has of late appeared to be nothing more than a chamber where the ministers edicts are registered for form's sake. Some of their Lordships are determined to vindicate their importance. It is there that the dresses of Opera dancers are regulated! One of the Roman Emperors recommended to the Senate, when they were good for nothing else, to discuss what was the best sauce for turbot. To regulate the length of a petticoat is a much more genteel employment.[1]

Early in the nineteenth century Lord King complained that nothing was being done at all in the lords, and Fox wrote despondently in 1803 that with the exception of Lord Grenville's there were no good speeches there at all.[2]

Certainly, their lordships' discussions never covered the range of subjects that were taken up in the lower house. In 1785 the *Parliamentary History* and *The Times* only contain the reports of debates on six public bills, the Anglo-Irish commercial resolutions and two motions for Indian papers.[3] Ten years later the house held seven major debates on the war but only discussed five bills in full session. In fact, the nobility made little attempt to discuss fully every major public question; during the 1780s, for example, India received disproportionate attention while many of Pitt's financial programmes passed almost unnoticed.

Moreover, some of the lords' debates were undoubtedly frivolous or outlandish. In the midst of severe food shortages in 1800 a proposal was presented to prevent oats from being fed to pleasure animals. Lord Grenville, in normal times the most sensible of men, opposed this plan for fear that if it were implemented, servants would be transformed into informers; such a reversal of roles, he argued, might jeopardize the established social hierarchy. The lord chancellor's objections were even more outrageous: the proposal, he declared sententiously, was an unjust attack on private property 'because many horses would suffer great injury if deprived of their ordinary food; and it was well known

---

1 Wraxall, *Memoirs,* iv, 4-5; *Morning Chronicle,* 19 Mar. 1798.

2 Holland House Papers, Add. MS 51572, fos. 31-2, 53, King to Holland, 3 Apr. [?], 4 Apr. 1800; *Memorials and Correspondence,* iii, 223-4.

3 The *Parliamentary History* for 1785 contained reports of the commons' debates on eleven bills, three motions relative to India, the Irish commercial resolutions, the report of the committee of public accounts, the status of the fortifications of Plymouth and Portsmouth, Pitt's motion for the reform of parliament, Sawbridge's motion for shortening the duration of parliaments, Fox's motion on the state of the revenue and the budget.

that horses of two or three years old would not thrive, or grow to complete maturity, if they were not fed upon oats'.[1]

An equally obvious flaw in the proceedings of the house was their lordships' habit of wandering far from the main point under consideration. For the first eight years of our period the whig opposition seemed incapable of mounting effective attacks against Pitt's economic policies. Only once did they question his great effort to consolidate the customs duties, and then it was to attack the bill for violating, in their opinion, the privileges of the house of lords. Similarly they attacked with tired, irrelevant clichés the Wine Duty Bill of 1786 and the Tobacco Duty Bills of 1789 and 1790, measures which embodied the government's endeavour to limit smuggling by transferring the responsibility for warehousing and inspection of imported goods to the excise office. Any expansion of the power of the excise office, the whigs charged, constituted a grave threat to the liberties of Englishmen and violated the right of wine and tobacco merchants to preserve their trade secrets?[2]

Of course the whigs did not monopolize this shortcoming. During the debate at the second reading of Addington's Volunteer Consolidation Bill in 1804 ministerial spokesmen raised a host of peripheral issues: they defended the king's prerogative to call out these forces, praised their loyalty and remarked on the speed with which so many men had been enlisted into these regiments. They did not, however, question the ability of this amateur force to repulse an invading French army. Only Grenville and his allies raised this question; only he and Lord Spencer suggested that the government's plan would divert men from England's main line of defence, the regular army. Yet, their remarks were misconstrued or ignored by the ministers who answered them.[3]

This preoccupation with the peripheral arose in some instances from the lords' inability to assimilate the details of highly technical and complex legislation. Following the first major debate on the Anglo-Irish commercial resolutions in the house of lords, John Beresford complained to the Irish chief secretary, Thomas Orde, that 'nobody, I believe, on either side, understood a Sentence of the resolutions, and therefore no one spoke to the merits'. William Eden agreed that 'because they were overpower'd by the complicated extent of so great a Question' the peers' first debate was languid; he hoped, however, that they would fare better when discussing the details in committee.[4]

1 *The Times*, 20 Dec. 1800.

2 *PH*, xxvi, 908-13, 19 Apr. 1787; *ibid.*, xxvi, 169-78, 26 June 1786; *The Times*, 30 July 1789.

3 *Hansard*, i, 1022-47, 27 Mar. 1804.
Ashbourne, *Pitt*, 132-4; Auckland Papers, Add. MS 45728, fo. 44, Eden to

Unfortunately, the first debate set the pattern for future discussions. After the resolutions emerged from committee Eden told Lord Sheffield:

> it was curious to observe that among all the Ministerial Peers there was not one except Ld Thurlow who appear'd to have used common Industry to collect even the superficial Sense & general Purport of the Propositions: — Government however derived some Benefit from the peculiar Idleness & Ignorance of its supporters: for as Men are most apt to be timid in total Darkness, & to be alarm'd by what is utterly incomprehensible, it was quite a vain attempt to reason them into any Amendments. . . .

Only Lords Derby and Thurlow among the leading politicians came out with their reputations intact; according to Eden most of Pitt's cabinet colleagues had shown themselves to be unfit for 'efficient situations'.[1]

The government's stable majorities throughout the proceedings on this question demonstrate that slovenly ministerial performances were not so offensive to the peers as they were to the efficient Eden. Some peers were, as Eden himself noted, idle or ignorant: the earl of Harcourt admitted to his wife that he was too inattentive and impatient to listen to long speeches, and George Tierney was shocked to find in the house 'a palsied indifference in the hearers that checks all spirit'. On highly complicated issues many peers followed their leaders blindly regardless of the merits of the question under consideration.[2]

This loyal, sometimes uncritical adherence bred a security among ministers which inevitably affected their performance at debates. Eden, who was raised to the house of lords as Baron Auckland in 1794, reported to Lord Sheffield in 1797 that

> Ld Grenville made a long & able Speech on the rupture of the Lisle Negotiation. It was evident however that He felt the disadvantage of having no opponents: it is impossible to debate without debaters; and when a Man speaks as free from the fear of Contradiction as the Parson in the Pulpit, the Speech ressembles a Sermon, & has pretty much the same effect on the hearers.[3]

Even more indicative of their paramount authority were the occasional ministerial silences which greeted fierce opposition attacks. A more critical audience would not have permitted Lord Sydney, the government's leader in the house of lords, to decline discussing the Anglo-

Sheffield [July 1785].

1 *Ibid.*, Add. MS 45728, fos. 46, 48-9, Eden to Sheffield, 16, 30 July [1785]; *HMC, 14th R.*, i, *Rutland MSS*, iii, 226-7, 229-30.

2 *Harcourt Papers*, ii, 31-2; *Lady Holland's Journal*, ii,76.

3 Auckland Papers, Add. MS 45728, fos. 292-3, Auckland to Sheffield, 12 Nov. 1797.

Irish commercial resolutions on the grounds that his remarks might be misinterpreted. Like modern politicians ministers sometimes eschewed open discussion, claiming that it might jeopardize the national security, but they also adopted this policy of silence to demonstrate the disdain in which they held their adversaries.[1]

The shortcomings which we have noted did not, however, mar all of the lords' discussions. Some debates were thorough if uninspired, and many were interesting and informative. The duke of Grafton was impressed by the quality of discussion on Shelburne's peace preliminaries and commented in particular on the brilliant performances of Thurlow, Shelburne and Loughborough. Bishop Watson of Landaff, Lansdowne and Liverpool not only scrutinized the details of the French Commercial Treaty in 1787 but skillfully debated the merits of conflicting commercial theories. Four years later, in debating the wisdom of Pitt's ultimatum to the Empress Catherine, ministers found themselves hard pressed to answer the sensible, well-taken criticisms of their whig opponents.[2] On the other hand Pitt praised the performances of several ministerial defenders in the final deliberations on the Aliens Bill in 1793: 'Lord Hawkesbury made a very good short speech; Lord Carlisle a very fair and explicit one. . .; and Lord Loughborough made one of the best speeches I have ever heard. . .' Likewise, Lord Spencer was impressed by the final debate on the resolutions for an Irish Union — a debate, he noted, which 'was conducted by six ex Ld Lieutenants, 3 ex Secretaries, & the rest all Irish peers but one'.[3] Even on such highly technical subjects as monetary policy, the lords were able to distinguish themselves: in 1797, 1803 and 1804 they conducted a series of interesting and informative discussions on the merits of the government's suspension of cash payments, a subject on which several peers including Lords Liverpool, Grenville and King had expert knowledge.[4]

Debates in the house of lords were especially likely to take on incisive qualities when leading peers divided in principle on questions of major importance. India was one of the issues which created such divisions during the 1780s, and the early debates on Indian questions

---

1 *PH*, xxv, 821, 7 June 1785; *ibid.*, xxxiii, 490-2, 9 May 1797; *The Times*. 14 Apr. 1796.

2 *The Autobiography and Political Correspondence of Augustus Henry, Third Duke of Grafton*, ed. W. R. Anson (London, 1898), 361-2; *PH*, xxvi, 514-34, 534-67, 23 Feb., 1 Mar. 1787; *ibid.*, xxix, 33-52, 79-96, 434-49, 29 Mar., 1 Apr., 9 May 1791.

3 *HMC, 13th R.*, iii, *Fortescue MSS*, ii, 360-1; Grenville Papers, Add. MS 41854, fos. 178-80, Spencer to T. Grenville, 22 Mar. 1799.

4 *PH*, xxxiii, 517-40, 15 May 1797; *ibid.*, xxxvi, 1156-62, 1247-58, 22 Feb., 3, 13 May 1803; *Hansard*, i, 697-713, 5 Mar. 1804.

were of a higher quality than the rest.[1] During the 1790s the increasing violence of the French Revolution, the rising tide of discontent at home and finally the outbreak of war seemed to most peers to threaten the survival of the existing order. Yet, the whig opposition was equally convinced that the war was unnecessary and poorly conducted, that the dangers of sedition were exaggerated and that Pitt was accumulating a dangerous degree of power. Turberville has argued that the hopelessness of their task made the whigs shrill debaters and eventually indifferent to their legislative duties.[2] For a few years, however, the intense division of opinion rendered the house of lords a more stirring and interesting forum than it had been earlier. Though the opinions expressed there never encompassed the range of national attitudes, the premises on which policy was founded, the purposes of that policy and its potential for success were thoroughly and intelligently discussed.[3]

What impact did these proceedings have on the division of forces within the house of lords? Examples of sudden conversion were very rare, for the members, as well as being inattentive, tended to stand by their political allies.[4] Certainly, the instances in which the whigs triumphed over their opponents did little to erode a government's majorities. Leading ministerial spokesmen undoubtedly failed to comprehend Pitt's Anglo-Irish commercial resolutions, but the few peers who changed sides on this issue had made up their minds even before the debates commenced.[5] In 1791 the whigs developed a compelling case against the government's Russian policy and ably presented it to both houses; though they were able to muster colleagues whose enthusiasm for opposition had waned after the party's failures during the regency crisis, the only government supporter clearly to be won over to their position was the duke of Grafton.[6] Four years later the whigs, in the

---

1   See debates on the East Indian Declaratory Bill, *PH*, xxvii, 219-59, 17, 18, 19 Mar. 1788.

2   Turberville, *The House of Lords in the Age of Reform*, 89-90.

3   For good examples of these wartime debates see *PH*, xxxi, 962-94, 30 Dec. 1794; *ibid.*, xxxii, 244-70, 6, 11, 13 Nov. 1795; *ibid.*, xxxii, 527-54, 9, 14 Dec. 1795. The two-day discussion of the Catholic petition of 1805 summarizes the peers' attitudes on the emancipation question. *Hansard*, iv, 651-729, 742-843, 10, 13 May 1805.

4   *Ibid.*, ii, 161, 19 Apr. 1804.

5   According to Lord Sydney Lord Dudley voted against the resolutions to please his neighbours, Lord Grey de Wilton because he had been knight of the shire for Lancashire, Lords Radnor and Sackville because they favoured a union. *HMC, 14th R.*, i, *Rutland MSS*, iii, 229-30.

6   For debates on Pitt's Russian policy see *PH*, xxix, 32-54, 79-96, 434-49, 29 Mar., 1 Apr., 9 May 1791. Leeds discusses the importance of Grafton's defection in *Political Memoranda*, 154.

course of their prolonged campaign against the Seditious Meetings Bill, enlisted the support of seven or eight independent peers and thereby increased the size of their normally tiny minority by about one-third.[1] However, as long as a cabinet was united and confident of its ability to remain in power, this modest accession was about the most which the whigs could realistically look for.

It was government which derived the most obvious political advantages from debates. Among the factors which combined to give it substantial majorities in the house of lords two of not inconsiderable importance were the talents of leading government spokesmen and the frequent deficiencies of the whigs. The ministers' superior knowledge and understanding of the intricacies of government enabled them to dominate the lords' debates for much of this period, and some peers were impressed by their ability to handle complex questions effectively. On the other hand, the whigs weakened their position by sometimes adopting frivolous or seemingly dangerous arguments; their performance during the regency crisis and at other important occasions strengthened the resolve of some peers to stand by the administration.[2]

Debates were only likely to drive some of its supporters into opposition when an administration was very weak. During the last six weeks of Addington's administration, for example, leading spokesmen for all segments of the opposition launched a prolonged and effective attack first against the Volunteer Consolidation Bill and then against the Militia Augmentation Bill. Ministers lost all control over these proceedings, and, partially as a result of the opposition's campaign, the government majority evaporated.[3]

At no point during the late eighteenth century was the nobility's attachment to government so strong as to preclude critical independence among at least a portion of its members. Opposition in their neighbourhoods forced Lords Dudley and Grey de Wilton to oppose the Anglo-Irish commercial resolutions, and Radnor and Sackville condemned that proposal because they believed the problem of Anglo-Irish relations demanded a more radical solution.[4] Lord Hopetoun tried repeatedly to

1 *PH*, xxxii, 527-54, 9, 14 Dec. 1795. Among the independent peers who joined the whigs on this issue were Abingdon, Bessborough, Chedworth, Leeds, Moira, Say and Sele, Suffolk and Thurlow.

2 These points are discussed in chapter 6.

3 *Hansard*, i, 1022-47, 27 Mar. 1804; *ibid.*, ii, 18-20, 149-63, 7, 19 Apr. 1804. A discussion of the fall of Addington's government follows.

4 *HMC, 14th R.*, i, *Rutland MSS*, iii, 229-30; *PH*, xxv, 873-7, 18 July 1785;

amend the government's Hawkers and Pedlars Bill, a measure which raised considerable opposition in Scotland; and the duke of Atholl along with the earls of Stair, Galloway and Kinnoul, though normally loyal supporters of Pitt's administration, protested against the passage of the government-supported Small Notes Duty Bill in 1799.[1] The die-hards among the militia officers opposed every attempt to increase the size of the regular army at the expense of the militia even while they pressed for victory against the French, and other advocates of the war and Pitt's attempts to control sedition voted with the whigs against the government's Irish policies.[2] In these and innumerable other cases men who backed the major policies of the king's government and who eschewed all formal ties with the whig opposition were willing to proclaim publicly their opposition to measures presented by their avowed political leaders.

Moreover, disagreement on major public questions sometimes became so fundamental that peers found themselves forced to break with their former political leaders. In the last years of the 1780s nine peers joined the 'third party', a group which eventually merged with the whigs. These men were induced to take such a step partly out of personal ambition, partly because of sharp differences with ministers on issues including Lord Howe's controversial naval promotions in 1788, the India Declaratory Bill of the same year, the question of 'free' peerage elections in Scotland and the proposed limitations on the Prince of Wales' regency.[3] While Fox's radicalism and his opposition to the war drove many of his associates into the ranks of the government, Pitt's war policies forced several old allies, the dukes of Leeds and Richmond and the marquess of Abercorn, for example, into independent opposition.[4] Moreover, by 1796 many peers had tired of the war and desired

Sackville Family Papers, U269/C192, Sackville to Dorset [1785]; Wraxall, *Memoirs*, iv, 161.

1 *The Times*, 30 July 1785. For references to the Scots' dependence on hawkers and pedlars see Auckland Papers, Add. MS 34419, fo. 33, Sheffield to Eden, 9 July 1785; *LJ*, xlii, 325, 9 July 1799.

2 Western, *The English Militia*, 233-6. The attitudes of the diehards are summarized in their protest against the Militia Bill of 1799. *LJ*, xlii, 349, 4 Oct. 1799.

3 Braybrooke Papers, Essex Record Office, D/DBy C9/44, 'Third Party Circular'; *Courts and Cabinets*, ii, 79-80. Hawke and Rawdon, two of the members of this group, were disturbed by Howe's naval promotions and the India Declaratory Act of 1788. *PH*, xxvii, 12-3, 15, 225, 247, 20 Feb., 17, 19 Mar. 1788. For a discussion of the Scottish members of this group see McCahill, 'The Scottish Peerage and the House of Lords', *SHR*, li (1972), 191.

4 Abercorn, the earl of Clarendon and Leeds were the only peers aside from members of the whig opposition to support the duke of Bedford's motion for peace on 27 Jan. 1795. Leeds Papers, Add. MS 27918, fos. 315-6, 321, 'Political Memorandums'. The duke of Richmond opposed Pitt's policy of establishing extensive continental connections. *PH*, xxxi, 1449-50, 30 Mar. 1795.

peace;[1] a smaller number had further become totally disillusioned by the ministers' direction of military activities. Thus, the earl of Carnarvon, who had left the whig party because of his sharp differences with Fox, told Earl Fitzwilliam that

> the Original Object of the War had been totally lost by the mis-management of those who conducted it; & the inability of continuing even a defensive War has been nearly produced by their useless profusion.

Fitzwilliam, who had opposed the opening of negotiations in 1797, told the house in 1801 that prospects for military success were hopeless; in any case, the re-establishment of order in France had removed the original justification for the war. At the same debate the earl of Fife withdrew his support from ministers who had abused their lordships' confidence, ruined Europe and nearly destroyed the British empire.[2]

Members of the peerage were not, in fact, inalterably attached to the king's government. Individuals could respond critically to specific issues without attaching themselves to the opposition, and political allegiances were fluid during our period. A number of noble lords were driven into opposition because they differed with ministers on matters of principle. The political impact of such defections was normally marginal because so few peers were involved; but very weak governments had reason to be concerned about their positions in the house of lords.

Lord Shelburne's doom was sealed in the house of commons where his peace preliminaries were rejected. But his showing in the lords revealed the full extent of his weakness. After what Lord Grantham, the foreign secretary, described as a 'hard run', the preliminaries were carried there by a vote of 72-59. News of this narrow victory disturbed George III: it was the smallest majority he could remember in so full a house, and he recognized that the results boded ill for the government's future.[3]

The reasons for Shelburne's small majority in the lords are clear. His inability to form an alliance with either Fox or North prevented his

1 Camden Papers, U840/C97, Carrington to Camden [no date]; Pitt Papers, PRO 30/8/121, fos. 23-4, Carlisle to Pitt, 31 May, 1797. According to Leeds a number of peers including the marquess of Bath and Lords Dundas, Bradford, Thurlow and Yarborough wished for peace, but before 1796 they did not publicly oppose the government on the issue. Leeds Papers, Add. MS 27918, fos. 310, 312-3, 'Political Memorandums'.

2 Fitzwilliam Papers, Box 59, Carnarvon to Fitzwilliam [no date]; *PH*, xxxv, 871-4, 885, 2 Feb. 1801.

3 *Malmesbury Diaries*, i, 500-1; *Correspondence of George III*, vi, no. 4122.

government from achieving a solid political foundation. The resignation of four ministers within one month further weakened his position in both houses. Ironically, the final blow was delivered by some of the king's friends. Half of the bishops stayed away from the debate, and six or seven of those who did appear voted against the government. Such behaviour indicates that Shelburne had much the same difficulties in the upper house as in the lower where about half of the courtiers deserted to their old leader, Lord North.[1]

Aside from their rejection of the India Bill, the peers' most decisive attack on the king's ministers occurred in 1804. During the spring of the previous year Addington, recognizing the weakness of his position, had endeavoured to secure additional political support. His failure, followed shortly by the renewal of the war, left the administration in a most vulnerable position. Addington's own colleagues began grumbling privately that their leader was weak or worse.[2] More ominously, a formidable opposition gradually took shape in parliament. Animated by his concern to hold his party together, Fox coalesced with the Grenvilles — hitherto Addington's most vociferous opponents — in January 1804. The object of the coalition was to drive the government from power, but this objective remained remote until the following March when William Pitt belatedly resolved to challenge Addington.[3] Within a month of Pitt's accession the opposition had driven the government from office.

Traditionally credit for this achievement has been awarded to the administration's opponents in the house of commons.[4] Charles Yorke, the home secretary, admitted as early as March 16, that Addington's majority in the commons was too fragile to last for long. However, he was either prescient or overly pessimistic. Other observers, including Charles Fox, found the situation far more confusing. Periodically Fox would report to his followers that Addington's doom was sealed, but these predictions were invariably withdrawn within a few days. Not until late April was he convinced that there would in fact be a change of government.[5] And by then the administration's majorities were not

1 E. Fitzmaurice, *Life of William, Earl of Shelburne* (London, 1912), ii, 245; Walpole, *Last Journals*, 483; J. Cannon, *The Coalition*, 55; J. Norris, *Shelburne and Reform* (London, 1963), 267-8.

2 *Later Correspondence*, IV, xv-xvi; Hardwicke Papers, Add. MS 35705, fos. 143-4, 246-7, Hardwicke to C. Yorke, 2 Mar., 20 Apr. 1804.

3 *Later Correspondence*, IV, xii-xxi; R. E. Willis, 'Fox, Grenville, and the Recovery of Opposition, 1801-1804', *Journal of British Studies*, xi (1972), 24-43.

4 *Later Correspondence*, IV, xii-xxi; *Correspondence of the Prince of Wales*, v, 2-4.

5 Hardwicke Papers, Add. MS 35705, fos. 172-3, C. Yorke to Hardwicke, 16

only declining disastrously in the house of commons; a surprisingly powerful opposition had also emerged in the house of lords.

From the opening of the session in the previous autumn, ministers had been uneasy about the lords. Hobart, for example, pressed Lord Hawkesbury to find some foreign employment for the recently retired home secretary, Lord Pelham. Otherwise, he feared that Pelham would be 'driven into opposition — with four or five noble lords in his suite — which in addition to the Grenville & Pitt Party in the House of Lords, & those who may be induced to speculate upon their strength may be productive of inconvenience'.[1]

Events of the following spring proved that these apprehensions were justified. Unlike their counterparts in the commons, opposition peers were united and effectively led from the start.[2] During these weeks Lord Grenville organized an effective campaign against the administration's Volunteer Consolidation Bill, raising in the course of his attack criticisms which Fox later took up in the commons.[3] While Grenville did not succeed in defeating the bill, his attack forced the government into a defensive position which vividly illustrated its weakness. Hawkesbury was obviously unable to resist him, and the burden of defense fell upon Eldon who already had begun discussing with Pitt the possibility of a transferral of power.[4] Aided by a number of able speakers and a respectable body of support, Grenville carried many of his amendments to the bill and, perhaps more importantly, extended proceedings on the measure long beyond the date by which ministers had hoped to have it passed.[5] Indeed, the proceedings on this bill revealed that the government was unable, as strong governments usually were, to induce the lords to enact its important legislation speedily and without significant alterations.

Mar. [1804] ; Fox Papers, Add. MS 47564, fos. 204-6, 207-10, 211-2, Fox to Lauderdale, 15, 25, 30 Mar. 1804; *ibid.,* Add. MS 47575, fos. 116-8, Fox to Holland, [9 Apr. 1804] ; *ibid.,* Add. MS 47565, fos. 120-3, Fox to Grey, 13 Apr. 1804.

1 Buckinghamshire Papers, D/MH C504, Hobart to Hawkesbury, 1 Oct. 1803 (copy).

2 Tom Grenville complained in late March that the differences between Pitt and Fox created 'a distrust in the practicability of any arrangement of measures'. Dropmore Papers, Add. MS 58884, fos. 51-2, T. Grenville to Grenville, 31 Mar. 1804.

3 *Ibid.,* Add. MS 58884, fos. 51-2, T. Grenville to Grenville, 31 Mar. 1804; Grenville Papers, Add. MS 41856, fos. 150, 159-60, 161, Fox to T. Grenville, 2, 30 Mar., 3 Apr. 1804; Fox Papers, Add. MS 47565, fos. 118-9, Fox to Grey, 6 Apr. 1804.

4 *Ibid.,* Add. MS 47575, fos. 116-8, Fox to Holland [9 Apr. 1804].

5 *Hansard,* ii, 26, 38, 68, 106-7, 140, 9, 10, 11, 12, 17 Apr. 1804; Dropmore Papers, Add. MS 58884, fos. 47-50, T. Grenville to Grenville, 17 Mar. 1804.

Nor did the situation improve. On 19 April the government actually lost a minor skirmish in the house of lords and then only carried the second reading of its Irish Militia Bill against a minority of forty-nine, the largest minority on a matter of confidence since the regency debates of 1789. Five days later the opposition forces rose to sixty-one, by which time Lord Minto believed that his side was sufficiently strong to prolong the passage of important legislation indefinitely.[1]

The opposition's onslaught against the administration had, in fact, reached its final decisive phase. Rumours of Addington's imminent resignation were rife. Pitt was by now determined that all possible steps should be taken to force that resignation if the rumours proved to be false.[2] And, as opposition mobilized its forces for the last battle, it finally perceived that as strong an attack might be made in the lords as in the commons. Plans were therefore laid for the marquess of Stafford to introduce a motion demanding an inquiry into the state of the nation, and to make the most of this upcoming test of strength, every possible effort was made to round up potential supporters.[3]

This canvass proved to be remarkably successful. On 18 April for example, Pitt urged Lord Melville to hurry to London, but not before he had obtained the proxies of as many as possible of his Scottish compatriots. When Melville did leave a few days later, it was with the proxies of all those Scottish noblemen who could not attend in person including that of Lord Dalhousie — a peer who had never previously cast his vote *in absentia* because of his disapproval of the proxy system. Moreover, Melville induced the earl of Moray, who had not yet taken his seat and was therefore unable to give a proxy, to journey to London in order to qualify himself to vote.[4]

Nor were the Pittites the only active canvassers. Lord Buckingham assumed at least part of the burden of rallying the Grenville forces. He arranged for one of the family's episcopal nominees to take his seat and leave his proxy. He badgered Lord Bridport, the naval commander, into giving him his proxy, and he passed on to Grenville in London intelligence about other wavering members, adding, of course, extensive advice as to how each could best be secured.[5]

1 *Hansard*, ii, 165, 255, 19, 24 Apr. 1804. According to Lord Minto the minority on the twenty-fourth would have been sixty-two, but Lord Ashburton left just before the division to dress for a ball. *Minto Papers*, iii, 316-7, 320-1.

2 *Fox Papers*, Add. MS 47565, fos. 123-6, Fox to Grey, 18, 19 Apr. 1804.

3 Stanhope, *Pitt*, iii, 209-10.

4 *Ibid.*, iii, 9-10; *Correspondence of the Prince of Wales*. iv, no 1844; Pitt Papers, PRO 30/8/128, fo. 31, Dalhousie to Pitt, 23 Apr. 1804; *ibid.*, PRO 30/8/161, Moray to Pitt, 22 Apr. 1804.

5 *Courts and Cabinets*, iii, 346-7; *HMC, 13th R.*, iii, *Fortescue MSS*, vii, 219-20;

Another measure of the success are the projections of the various opposition leaders. On 22 April Buckingham predicted that between sixty-two and sixty-five peers would vote against the Irish Militia Bill at its second reading: in fact, sixty-one did. On the day this division took place, 24 April, Lord Minto reported that ninety peers were likely to support Stafford's upcoming motion, and the next day he told his wife that the opposition was by then so strong that Addington would be unable to carry any strong measure through parliament. Buckingham, on 26 April, wrote that his lists also indicated that the government's adversaries could reasonably look for eighty to ninety votes at the decisive test, and on 27 April Pitt, perhaps optimistically, told Minto that he expected a minority exceeding 100.[1]

In the meantime government forces began to show the classic symptoms of disintegration. Lord Auckland noted that the bishops were hanging back in large numbers. He also had great difficulty in recruiting his old friend Lord Sheffield.[2] Lord Ellenborough protested that Amherst, a recalcitrant bedchamber peer, 'should be spoken to in *terms not to be misunderstood'*, and Hardwicke, the lord lieutenant of Ireland, reported that Irish members were reluctant to go over to attend parliament.[3]

To compensate for these possible defections or abstentions, Auckland and his colleagues combed the backwoods, even calling upon the crippled and the senile to cast one last vote.[4] The effectiveness of their canvass was hindered, however, by poor organization and poor execution. There is no evidence to show that Hawkesbury, the leader of the house, took any extraordinary measures. The impetus behind the government canvass came from men such as Auckland and Ellenborough who were not members of the cabinet. Lack of central co-ordination and planning resulted inevitably in confusion. Hardwicke, for example, received instructions to secure the proxies of Irish bishops who did not sit in the house, and it was not until 26 April that the government dispatched proxies for him to distribute among the resident peers[5]

Dropmore Papers, Add. MS 58878, fos. 50-3, Buckingham to Grenville, 22 Apr. 1804.

1   *Ibid.,* Add. MS 58878, fo. 53, Buckingham to Grenville, 22 Apr. 1804; *Minto Papers,* iii, 316-7, 320-1; *Courts and Cabinets,* iii, 351.

2   Liverpool Papers, Add. MS 38237, fo. 224, Auckland to Hawkesbury, [Apr. 1804]; Auckland Papers, Add. MS 45729, fos. 158-61, Auckland to Sheffield, 23, 27 Apr. 1804; *ibid.,* Add. MS 34456, fos. 64-5, Sheffield to Auckland, 25, 26 Apr. 1804.

3   *Auckland Correspondence,* iv, 193.

4   *Minto Papers,* iii, 316-7.

5   Hardwicke Papers, Add. MS 35705, fos. 282-3, C. Yorke to Hardwicke, 27 Apr. 1804; *ibid.,* Add. MS 35705, fos. 284-6, Hardwicke to C. Yorke, 28 Apr.

'The House of Peers frightened the wretched Doctor from his seat', Tom Grenville wrote only half facetiously. By 25 April the government's majority in the commons had undoubtedly become unworkable, but it was equally, if not more fragile in the house of lords. The test there on Lord Stafford's motion for a committee on the state of the nation never took place, but all available evidence indicates that the result of this impending confrontation was in doubt. Addington's most recent biographer believes that his majority in the lords had already evaporated, and Cowper, the clerk of the house, calculated that the outcome would have been a tie, 111-111. The opposition was less sanguine: according to Lord Spencer's figures the government would have triumphed 121-99, and Addington believed that his majority would be about ten.[1]

Whether the government would have eventually won or lost in the upper house is unimportant. That the outcome was in doubt at all highlights the appalling weakness of Addington's position, and provides the substantial basis for Grenville's remark. Never during our period did any other minister who enjoyed the confidence of the king find himself confronted by as hostile a house of lords.

Addington claimed that 'it was Mr. Pitt's ascendancy in the House of Lords, through the eighty creations he made, which enabled him to overthrow the government'. The lords did undoubtedly play a vital role in driving that minister from office, but not for the reasons he cites; Pitt's new peers split almost evenly between the government and the opposition.[2] Addington, like Shelburne before him fell because he lost the support of a portion of the king's friends.

Men who had supported Addington while he endeavoured to secure peace were sceptical of his ability to lead the nation once the war was renewed. A series of poorly constructed militia bills had outraged peers who were experts on this subject and raised doubts in their own minds as to the government's abilities.[3] By the opening of 1804 most of

1804. Some Irish peers stayed away at the instigation of Pitt's friends. *Beresford Correspondence*, ii, 288.

1 Spencer Papers, Box 55, T. Grenville to Spencer, 15 May, 1804; Philip Ziegler, *Addington: A Life of Henry Addington, First Viscount Sidmouth* (London 1965), 214; Spencer Papers, Box 57, 'List of Peers who would have voted for Ld Stafford's Motion', 30 Apr. 1804; *Colchester Diaries*, i, 499-500.

2 George Pellew, *The Life and Correspondence of the Right Hon. Henry Addington, First Viscount Sidmouth* (London, 1847), ii, 274. According to Spencer's calculations thirty-two of the peers Pitt created would have opposed the government, and thirty-two others supported it.

3 *Hansard*, ii, 18-9, 6 Apr. 1804; Chichester Papers, Add. MS 33111, fos. 216-7, Sheffield to Pelham, 12 June 1803; *ibid.*, Add. MS 33111, fos. 277-8, Richmond to Pelham, 17 July 1803.

Addington's cabinet colleagues were prepared to resign, and the king, at least according to the ubiquitous Glenbervie, was even reconciled to his favourite's departure.[1]

However, it was Pitt's presence which induced certain of these alarmed peers to risk temporary opposition. Throughout the 1780s and 1790s they had been denied such a course: had they turned their backs on Pitt, they would only have facilitated Fox's return to power? In 1804 the political situation was very different. Not only did most peers believe Pitt to be the only person capable of directing a wartime administration; in him the king and his parliamentary cohorts had a palatable successor to Addington.[3] Thus, Melville was able to inveigle the Scottish peers into opposition. King's friends like the duke of Beaufort, who previously refrained from open opposition, were emboldened to take the leap, and the less daring bishops or Irishmen knew at least that by staying away they were helping to install a safe, competent administration.[4]

Members of the house of lords endeavoured in these years to exercise the prerogative which their ancestors had secured in the constitutional battles of the seventeenth century. The various channels of inquiry were exploited by the opposition, by the independent critics of administration, sometimes even by ministers themselves. National policy and important legislation were scrutinized in debates, often intelligently. It was because the whigs failed for most of this period to recruit followers of the same calibre as leading ministers and men of business that these proceedings tended to strengthen the government's position in the upper house. Nevertheless, the peers did both individually and collectively turn against various administrations. In 1804, in fact, the house of lords drove Addington from office.

In most cases the peers' willingness to criticize a government was tempered by their overriding desire for stable administration and their dread of innovation. Criticism of ministerial policy, inquiry into its details or potential usefulness — these techniques could be used

1 Ziegler, *Addington*, 211; *Glenbervie Diaries*, i, 389-90.

2 Lord Sackville told his nephew, the Duke of Dorset, in 1785 that 'it is surprising how much he [Pitt] owes to the unpopularity of the opposition, for tho' many people dislike Mr Pitt who formerly supported him, yet they by no means incline to change him. . . . .' Sackville Family Papers, U269/C192, Sackville to Dorset, 11 May 1785; *Auckland Correspondence*, iii, 280-2.

3 *Correspondence of the Prince of Wales*, iv, no. 1834; Dacres Adam Papers, PRO 30/58/5, Lyttleton to Pitt, 18 May 1804.

4 According to Spencer's list, seven representative peers would have supported Stafford's motion and only two opposed it. Seven bishops apparently were not likely to participate.

legitimately to enhance the effectiveness of government. Where individuals concluded that a ministry was incompetent to carry on the king's business, they sometimes joined the relatively small group of peers in opposition. The majority, however, was only prepared to move against very weak administrations. For men who put such stress on the need for strong ministries, Shelburne's or Addington's governments were obviously unsatisfactory. But their willingness to reject these ministers depended, particularly in 1804, on the availability of a successor in whose safety and reliability they had confidence.

5

PRIVATE AND LOCAL BUSINESS

Taken together private and local bills comprised two-thirds of parliament's legislative output during the last two decades of the eighteenth century. Individually these measures had only limited significance, but their collective impact was enormous. Men divorced their wives[1] and resolved a myriad of problems associated with estate management by means of private acts. In the second half of the eighteenth century landlords regularly resorted to private acts as a means of enclosing open fields or commons. Of the two categories of local acts, the first permitted the construction of roads, canals and improved harbour facilities out of which emerged that communications network which was a precondition for and a stimulus to further economic growth. The second contained bills which empowered authorities to deal with the range of problems confronting local government: the lighting and paving of streets, sanitation and the provision of water, poor relief and the regulation of wages or even the construction of county, municipal or parochial buildings. In short, private and local bills were at once a part of and a response to forces which were transforming traditional patterns of English life.

Acts of such importance to the nation were also of vital significance to individual peers. Noble lords had a direct interest in a significant portion of the nearly 1200 enclosure bills presented to parliament between 1784 and 1806. Among the fifty-eight bills of this type forwarded from Nottinghamshire between 1787 and 1806 peers were the principal petitioners in fifteen cases. Twenty noble families along with successive bishops of Salisbury enclosed lands in Wiltshire during the eighteenth and early nineteenth centuries: commanding the lead among the eleven families which enclosed over 1,000 acres were the earls of Pembroke with a princely 24,260 acres.[2]

Not only did peers introduce their own enclosure bills; they played a frequently decisive part in shaping the contents of those which others initiated. Agents for the first duke of Northumberland informed projectors of the Tynemouth enclosure that his grace would only support

---

1 Because of the uniqueness of their proceedings, divorce bills will not be discussed in this chapter. The number of bills increased between 1783 and 1806 as did the controversy surrounding their passage.

2 W. E. Tate, *Parliamentary Land Enclosures in the County of Nottingham during the 18th and 19th Centuries (1743-1868)* (Nottingham, Thoroton Society, 1935), v, 68-113; 'Abstracts of Wiltshire Inclosure Awards and Agreements', ed. R. E. Sandell, *Wiltshire Records Society*, xxv (1969), Appendix II.

such a bill in parliament if it incorporated resolutions which he had earlier presented to them. The second duke was equally protective of his interests: thus, he would permit no enclosure of Shire Moor until the Percy rights to the common lands were acknowledged. Nor was the protectiveness of the Percys unusual. Despite the pleadings of his aunt, the marchioness of Rockingham, Earl Fitzwilliam refused to countenance an enclosure of the commons at Hemsworth until such a bill contained provisions recompensing him for the manorial rights which he would forfeit.[1]

The nobility's interest in road bills was hardly less intense than their involvement in the process of enclosure. Many of the road bills presented in these years merely renewed earlier acts or gave the existing trustees power to raise additional funds. The stake of noblemen in such bills was a continuing, even generational one. But they did also work to plan new roads or turnpikes. Lord Harrowby attended meetings to organize the construction of a turnpike from Stone to Uttoxeter; he spent some time preparing the bill for submission to parliament; and in the course of its passage he fended off the violent and misinformed criticisms of his colleague, Earl Ferrers.[2]

By the end of the eighteenth century road bills constituted a familiar, generally uncontroversial mass of business. The canal mania on the other hand reached its controversial height in the early 1790s. Peers participated in the frenzy of new projects with happy and unhappy results. Jackman notes that the construction of one proposed canal was frustrated by a nobleman who complained that the project's promoters had failed to treat him with proper deference. Balanced against such foolishness were the splendid achievements of Francis, third duke of Bridgewater, a daring, successful pioneer in the construction of canals. Other lords, if on a slightly more modest level, were also instrumental in extending this vital new transportation network. Upon discovering that his neighbours at St Albans feared that the Grand Junction Canal would be injurious to the commercial interests

1   Percy Family Papers, liv, fo. 203, H. Selby to R. Grey [1783]; ibid., lvi, fo. 67, W. Charlton to H. Selby and R. Grey, 23 Jan. 1788; Wentworth Woodhouse MSS, F69(a)/10, marchioness of Rockingham to Fitzwilliam, 13 Dec. 1784; ibid., F69(a)/12, Fitzwilliam to Mr. Fenton, 16 Dec. [draft]. The resistance of these peers was important not only because of their political weight; the house of lords refused to consider enclosure bills which were presented without the consent of the lord of the manor affected. Colchester Diaries, ii, 538. See also E. G. K. Gonner, Common Land and Inclosure (London, 1912), 73-74.

2   Fitzwilliam Papers, Box 59, J. Allen to Fitzwilliam, 19 Aug. 1801; Harrowby Papers, S/H Series, cdxxxv, Document 53, fos. 18, 27, Document 54, fos. 5-7; ibid., 1st series, iii, fo. 39, Ferrers to Harrowby, 5 Mar. 1793; ibid., 1st series, vii, fos. 40-1, Ferrers to Harrowby, 7, 19 Mar. 1793.

of the town, Viscount Grimston not only obtained permission from the proprietors of that canal to build a short link from Watford to St Albans. He also initiated the survey of the proposed route and later oversaw the preparation and presentation of the necessary legislation.[1]

The late eighteenth century also witnessed an increase in the number and scope of local improvement acts. Some noble lords intervened in the proceedings on such measures to serve friends: Lord Ailesbury, for example, was pressed by one of his correspondents to insert the latter's name as clerk for the commissioners in a local bill for the recovery of small debts. Other noblemen advanced the causes of boroughs in which they maintained political interests: Lords Grimston and Spencer supported a variety of bills initiated by the corporation and citizens of St Albans, and Harrowby oversaw the passage of the Tiverton Paving Bill, even taking the chair in the committee to which that bill was referred by the house of lords. In all these cases the nobility's participation in the formulation and passage of legislation grew out of their local consequence and their ability to shape events at Westminister. Thus, a number of the groups which considered introducing local bills to make improvements in or around the town of Cambridge applied as a matter of course for the approval and help of the earls of Hardwicke before proceeding too far with their projects.[2]

Both houses of parliament had separate, fairly well-defined procedures for dealing with private and local legislation. In the late seventeenth and early eighteenth centuries the lords enacted orders governing the procedures to be followed by applicants for private bills. These orders, however, were confined in their application mainly to estate bills which were in most cases introduced in the upper house: the various local acts and, after the middle of the century, enclosure bills started their passage through parliament in the commons which consequently set the standards for their scrutiny and forms.[3] Still, sponsors had to con-

---

1 W. T. Jackman, *The Development of Transportation in Modern England* (London, 1962), 403-4. For a discussion of Bridgewater's achievements see H. Malet, *The Canal Duke: A Biography of Francis 3rd Duke of Bridgewater* (London, 1961); Verulam Papers, D/EV F26, *passim; ibid.,* D/EV F34, Grimston's Letter Book, *passim.*

2 Ailesbury Papers, S. Mundy to Ailesbury, 16 Mar. 1779; Spencer Papers, Box 50, J. N. Boys to Spencer, 26 Feb., 10 Dec. 1783; Verulam Papers, D/EV F36, fo. 141, Grimston to T. Kinder, 28 Mar. 1801; *ibid.,* D/EV F28, T. Bucknall to Grimston, 23 Jan. 1797; Hardwicke Papers, Add. MS 35682, fos. 243-4, P. Peckard to Hardwicke, 8 Feb. 1785; *ibid.,* Add. MS 35686, fos. 240-1, J. T. Jordan to Hardwicke, 16 Mar. 1796.

3 These orders are briefly summarized in Lambert, *Bills and Acts,* 85-6.

form their bills to the lords' procedures, if not its orders. To protect property owners from the machinations of wily entrepreneurs or ambitious improvers the lords demanded, for example, that the promoters of enclosure or local bills solicit the opinions of those whose property might be affected. Thus, agents wishing to carry an enclosure bill through committee had to prove that owners of at least 75 per cent of the affected lands had consented to the measure. Frederick Spencer likewise noted that it was a necessary though unwritten rule of parliament, one strictly enforced in the house of lords, that any bill proposing changes in local government be presented with the overwhelming support of those who would pay the increased rates necessary for its implementation.[1]

Promoters of private or local acts commenced their proceedings at Westminster by petitioning the appropriate house for leave to bring in their bills. The lords' orders required that all petitions be referred to the judges, though, in fact, only estate bills received preliminary judicial examination as a matter of course. If thus limited, the judges' role was still important: they altered or redrafted clauses; a number of faulty bills were dropped at this stage; and some petitioners received legal opinion on doubtful points for relatively modest cost.[2]

This preliminary judicial review, as well as insuring that individual property rights would be protected, facilitated the lords' own legislative scrutiny. Not surprisingly, therefore, the house made it as simple as possible for petitioners to secure the judges' rulings. At the beginning of each session the house set a date by which time the judges' reports had to be received: every year this date was extended by several weeks, and even after it had passed, the house accepted late reports upon receiving special petitions from their promoters. By means of a special petition promoters were also able to change the judges on their panel when one of the latter was absent or incapacitated.[3]

Once a bill was brought in or sent up from the house of commons, it required one or more sponsors in the house of lords. The late eighteenth-century parliamentary agent, C.T. Ellis, advised prospective promoters that after a petition for a bill had been accepted by the house, the bill

---

1 W. E. Tate, 'Parliamentary Counter-Petitions during the Enclosures of the Eighteenth and Nineteenth Centuries', *EHR*, lix (1944), 403; Lambert, *Bills and Acts*, 134-5; F. H. Spencer, *Municipal Origins: An Account of English Private Bill Legislation Relating to Local Government* (London, 1911), 7; *LJ*, xvi, 268, 20 Apr. 1698.

2 Lambert, *Bills and Acts*, 112-3.

3 *Ibid.*, 114-5; *LJ*, xliv, 23, 99, 151-2, 158-9, 167, 242-5, 7 Dec. 1803, 23 Mar., 27 Apr., 2, 9 May, 9 June 1804.

itself might be presented the same day by 'applying to a Lord for that purpose, who will move to have it read a first time'. Before 1795 it was fairly common for these noble sponsors to chair committees on bills in which they were interested. However, Ellis recommended that agents only get a nobleman to move the second reading and commitment on a day when they were sure of a good attendance.[1]

Ellis's admonitions were justified, for the committee was the most distinctive and important stage of the lords' private bill procedure. Rather than being referred to committees of the whole house, private and local bills went instead to select committees composed of all peers present at the time a bill was read a second time. Partly because of the pressure of business on the floor of the house, partly because these measures were individually of such limited interest, scrutiny and discussion of them were usually deferred to this stage. In theory the function of the committee was to study the details of bills: its members demanded proof of adherence to the appropriate standing orders, and they then proceeded to go through the measure clause by clause. However, proceedings were extended to consider the principle of the bill as well, for counsel routinely presented proofs to support allegations in the preambles of their measures. The small committees permitted peers to examine all aspects of a bill — a process which would have been impossible on the floor of the house.

As a general rule these committees were presided over by the lord chairman of the committees. Thanks to the painstaking research of Mr J. C. Sainty we know that this post existed for almost a century prior to its official recognition in 1800. Its precise functions, however, remain unclear.[2] The first chairman of our period, Lord Scarsdale, chaired the bulk of committees on private and local as well as public bills but only until the end of May when he usually retired to Kedleston. His successor, the tenth Lord Cathcart, was more assiduous than Scarsdale in attending committees on public bills, but during the

---

1 C. T. Ellis, *Practical Remarks, and Precedents of Proceedings in Parliament* (London, 1802), 33, 41.

2 J. C. Sainty, 'The Origin of the Office of Chairman of Committees in the House of Lords', House of Lords Record Office Memorandum No. 52 (1974), 3-8. Sainty has established that the following peers served as lord chairman.

Third earl of Clarendon (*c.* 1715-23)
Seventh Lord Delawarr (1724-6, 1728-33)
Eighth earl of Warwick (1734-6, 1738-59)
Fifth Lord Willoughby of Parham (1759-65)
Fourth Lord Delamere (1765-70)
First Viscount Wentworth (1770-4)
First Lord Scarsdale (1775-89)
Tenth Lord Cathcart (1789-94)
Second Lord Walsingham (1794-1814)

1792-3 session, the bishop of Bangor, an unofficial deputy lord chairman, chaired 102 of the private committees while Cathcart only presided over fifty-eight.[1]

The chairman's other functions arose naturally from his active participation in the committees. He performed purely mechanical chores for other members: Bangor, for example, took the earl of Hardwicke's Wisbech Canal Bill through its first and second readings, thus enabling his lordship to remain at Wimpole for a few extra days. Agents naturally sought the advice of the chairman on how to proceed with difficult or controversial measures. Of necessity, he was also approached if parties wished to modify the lords' established procedures. Thus, when the agent for the Kennet and Avon Canal Bill discovered that its passage would be impeded by a new standing order, he dispatched the earl of Ailesbury to see Lord Cathcart after having armed him with a memorandum justifying the suspension of the offensive order.[2] However, the degree to which the chairman went beyond the point of giving advice and actually shaped the contents of private and local bills remains unclear.

Only the chairman and two or three other peers regularly followed the progress even of a portion of the private and local legislation. Consequently, parliamentary agents remarked upon the difficulty of obtaining the five peers needed to form a quorum in committees. The lords, for example, had to reconvene the committee on the Essex Shire Hall Bill after only two members turned up for its meeting. Similar situations occurred again and again. As a result the house provided that when fewer than five peers attended at the commitment of a bill or when agents failed to recruit a quorum for the committee, a bill's sponsor merely had to move that the committee open its ranks to all peers who had attended during the session in order to continue proceedings.[3]

1 *Ibid.*, 30-33. During the 1794 session Warren, bishop of Bangor, served as acting chairman while Cathcart was away on active military service. In December, 1794 he offered to resume his activities for the next session. Pitt Papers, PRO 30/8/87, fo. 63, Warren to Pitt, 27 Dec. 1794. A number of other peers chaired committees on an intermittent basis, particularly if the chairman himself was absent or ill. This group included in the 1780s Lords Chedworth, Galloway, Hawke, Morton, Sandys and Walsingham. Some, including Walsingham and Sandys, were interested in the intricacies of parliamentary procedure. C. Vivian, *The Sandys Family History*, revised by T.M. Sandys (London, 1907), 202. Others such as the earl of Morton were simply interested in the business of parliament, especially in his case, the Scottish business. Morton Papers, SRO GD 150/113, Morton to Selkirk, 25 Sept. 1786 (copy).

2 Hardwicke Papers, Add. MS 35686, fo. 160, Creasy to Hardwicke, 21 June 1795; *ibid.*, Add. MS 35392, fos. 348, 350, C. Yorke to Hardwicke, 11, 13 Apr. 1794; Ailesbury Papers, J. Ward to Ailesbury, 3, 5 Feb. 1794.

3 *LJ*, xxxvii, 377, 25 Mar. 1789. The Preston Candover Bill was committed in

Most members only stirred themselves when bills which interested them came before the house. For some peers attendance on private and local bills was a time-consuming occupation: the diary of the first Lord Harrowby reveals that session after session he attended as many as twenty times to oversee the passage of three or four bills. Without comparable records for other members it is impossible to determine whether the range, extent and regularity of Harrowby's annual activities were exceptional. Yet, even if few peers found it necessary to take up bills in each session, it is apparent that many of them did so on a less regular basis. Lord Spencer, who only came six times during the 1785 session, attached such importance to the passage of his South Cave Enclosure Bill that he attended on three of those occasions to be present for its first and second readings and the report stage!

Naturally, committees on contested bills attracted the widest attention. Both friends and foes of the controversial measure took care to see that allies were named to these bodies. Lord Bessborough complained to his wife that his brother-in-law, Earl Fitzwilliam, had kept him at the house from 11.00 in the morning till 7.00 at night on a private bill which encountered some opposition. On the other hand, Lord Euston, one of the members for Cambridge University, requested of the earl of Hardwicke that he be part of a committee in order to insure for the university that walks and paths, which promoters of the Barnwell Enclosure Bill were obliged to construct, would be as wide as possible. Likewise, agents for the Holly Isle Enclosure Bill urged Lord Delaval to attend the committee on that bill and oppose any attempt by the bishop of Bangor to make enclosed lands tithable. In 1801 the Needwood Forest Enclosure Bill only passed through the house of lords because its promoters successfully recruited a sufficiently large body of peers to rout the twenty-one members of the lords' committee who opposed that bill.[2]

In certain instances powerful individuals even called upon ministers to intervene in their behalf. Sir William Lowther, heir to the first earl of Lonsdale, was determined in 1792 to put off the committee on a

1795 when only two peers were present as was the Farnborough Road Bill some months later. In both instances the house ordered that these committees be opened to all peers who had been present during the session. *Ibid.,* x1, 336, 549, 14 Mar., 3 Dec. 1795.

1 Harrowby Papers, S/H Series, Documents 49-55, *passim;* Spencer Papers, Box 6, Spencer to Dowager Countess Spencer, 5, 8 Mar. 1785.

2 *Lady Bessborough and Her Circle,* 89; Hardwicke Papers, Add. MS 35687, fo. 393, Euston to Hardwicke [1807]; Waterford [Delaval] MSS, 2/DE 49/1, D. W. Lockwood to Delaval, 9 June, 1793; Boulton Papers, N. Edwards to Boulton, 13 June, 1801.

harbour bill which was inimical to the family's interests. Since the bill had gone up to the lords, Pitt suggested that he explained his objections to Lord Grenville, the leader to the house. Grenville, in turn, promised to inform Cathcart of Lowther's sentiments.[1]

Given the diversity in their size and composition, it was inevitable that the functioning of committees would vary. Usually measures were left to the chairman, the few peers who regularly participated in this business and the noble lords specially dragooned into attendance. The normal sparsity of attendance did not mean that proceedings were sloppy or casual: on the contrary, an experienced chairman and his aides were likely to be impartial and fairly thorough. It was when the inactive peers attended that impartiality was sometimes jeopardized. Many committees were composed, even chaired by members who had specific interests to protect or advance, and to insure the success of their cause they recruited allies. Thus, large attendances at committees were more likely to indicate intense partisanship than a public-spirited desire to ponder the complexities of difficult or important bills.

Whatever their composition, all committees did share certain characteristics in common. Among the most notable of these was the flexibility with which their lordships enforced their orders. While generally demanding compliance with the standing orders and established practices, members were nevertheless prepared to waive them when sponsors could present valid reasons for so doing. Where the lords were convinced of the benefit to be derived from a local bill, they were inclined to overlook even the most glaring violations of routine procedures.[2] They were also conscious of the expense involved in private bill proceedings and consequently were reluctant to force promoters to bring in new, technically more correct bills if the demands made by the pertinent orders in a particular case seemed arbitrary.[3]

It was the promoters of estate bills who encountered the most persistent difficulties, specifically with standing order ninety-four

1 Dropmore Papers, Add. MS 58989, unfoliated, Sir W. Lowther to Grenville, 10 June 1792; *ibid.*, Grenville to Sir W. Lowther, 12 June 1792.

2 The house accepted the report of the committee on the Southampton Water Bill despite the fact that its sponsors had failed to give proper notice (because the need for the bill only became apparent in September), had failed to include an estimate of expenses (because the town surveyor refused to do any more business for the corporation until he had been paid for earlier work, and the money could not be raised for this purpose until the act was passed) and had failed to secure the consents of those through whose lands cuts would be made. *LJ*, xliv, 158-9, 2 May, 1803. See also report on Ayrshire Roads Bill, *ibid.*, xlv, 138, 9 Apr. 1805.

3 *Hansard*, ii, 1024-5, 12 July 1805.

which required that all parties to such bills deliver their consents in person to the committee. Frequently, those individuals were abroad, and in some instances they had even disappeared.[1] Harried promoters were also plagued by abnormally large numbers of individuals with remote though identifiable interests in an estate or by confusion as to the precise rights of individuals beyond the immediate heirs.[2] Where parties which faced these and other similar impediments could prove that they had endeavoured to collect in some form as many consents as possible, committees waived or at least modified the order's full force and in one instance even enacted that a bill would not go into execution until interested parties, who had not yet consented, concurred.[3]

The committees did not dispense with the standing orders without careful deliberation. As noted above, promoters had to present proof that they had tried and failed to secure the necessary consents. On particularly complicated issues committees commonly sought the advice or approval of the full house before making a decision. They also took care to inform the house when a bill seemed likely to establish new precedents because of the novelty of one or more of its clauses.[4] In both cases, the recommendations for unusual action were presented in special reports which laid out the rationale for the committee's decisions.[5]

During a debate on the Cromford Canal Bill in 1789 Lord Chancellor Thurlow declared 'that private Property should be held sacred. − That no whim, no scheme, no measure what so ever ought to be sanctioned by Parliament, which took away the right of any man without making him full compensation for the loss'.[6] This protective regard for established property rights is another outstanding characteristic of the committees on private and local bills, a characteristic that is best revealed by the manner in which those bodies scrutinized the presentation of consents.

Often this was a simple process. The agent for the Eau Brink Drainage Bill, for example, satisfied the attendant peers by proving that of the 300,000 acres affected by the measure, owners of 213,015 consented, owners of 13,669 opposed and the remainder were either

1 *LJ*, xlii, 71, 1 Mar. 1799; *ibid.*, xliv, 228, 6 June 1803.
2 Committee Books, 26 May 1790; *LJ*, xli, 151-2, 28 Mar. 1797.
3 *Ibid.*, xlii, 220-1, 24 May 1799; *ibid.*, xlv, 242, 6 June 1805.
4 *Ibid.*, xxxvii, 286-7, 31 May 1787, *ibid.*, xxxviii, 626, 10 May 1790; *ibid.*, xli, 279-80, 5 May 1797.
5 *Ibid.*, xxxviii, 648, 26 May 1790; *ibid.*, xli, 131-2, 20 Mar. 1797.
6 *The Times*, 27 June 1789.

neutral, uncertain or out of reach.[1] Yet, routine as this procedure may have been, members never treated it as a formality. Thus, when opposing counsel pointed out that promoters had failed to obtain consents for changes made in the final draft of the Long Sutton Enclosure Bill, the committee adjoined for three months in order to allow the bill to be resubmitted to the community. After the committee resumed, members disallowed sixteen of the consents which had been collected.[2]

While the latter action was unusual, the former was not. Frequently committees adjoined proceedings while agents, acting on their orders, obtained additional consents. In some instances promoters had overlooked groups or individuals who their lordships felt should have been consulted.[3] In others, the committees' members demanded that sponsors make additional efforts to secure the approval of individuals who had hitherto opposed the project under consideration.[4] Where individuals could prove that offensive clauses were added after they had given their consent, those were usually stricken from the bill, and on various occasions committees added clauses preserving the rights of parties to estate bills who were unable at the time of the measure's introduction to give their consent.[5] Anxious to protect property rights, the lords' policy on consents was painstakingly thorough and in most cases strictly implemented.

This rather extreme preoccupation with vested property rights was slightly relaxed when the house was confronted with local improvement acts. In general these received a sympathetic parliamentary reception. The committee sitting on the Leith Harbour Bill agreed to hear counsel for certain pilots who argued that a clause empowering the lord provost of Edinburgh to licence such men would result in their financial loss. Nevertheless, it eventually concurred with the measure's sponsors that such a licencing process was necessary if the quality of Edinburgh's pilots was to be maintained at a high level. Similarly, the house passed the Aberdeen Streets Bill in 1800 after justifiably concluding, despite contrary arguments, that the bill did not constitute an unwarranted invasion of private property because adequate compensation had been made for any property taken to complete the improvements.[6]

1 Committee Books, 15 May 1795.
2 *Ibid.*, 10, 12 Mar., 16 June 1788.
3 *Ibid.*, 27 Apr., 4 May 1790.
4 *Ibid.*, 19, 23 Mar. 1790.
5 *Ibid.*, 23, 26 Feb. 1796; *Hansard*, i, 1100, 20 Feb. 1804; *LJ*, xxxvii, 286-7, 31 May 1785.
6 Committee Books, 5 May 1788; *The Times*, 25, 29 Mar. 1800.

Proceedings on these last two bills point out another aspect of the lords' treatment of private and local bills, namely that the house provided an opportunity for opponents of measures to present and explain their objections. In most instances counsel for the petitioners presented their evidence to the select committees — but to committees which usually had been opened to all active members. If the pending bill was sufficiently controversial, evidence collected in these sessions was printed. Moreover, when opposition persisted, or, contrarily, when it materialized after the report, the lords sometimes recommitted a bill, again to a committee enlarged to include all members who had attended during the session. Because the committees were so often enlarged in this manner, peers who wished to participate in such sessions rarely found themselves excluded, and the lords only occasionally permitted petitioners against private bills to present their arguments to the full house.[1]

Having provided counsel with the opportunity to present the objections of their petitioning clients, committees did upon occasion alter bills in response to the criticisms they had heard. An individual petitioner against the Ashcott Enclosure Bill evidently convinced the committee to which the bill was referred that his complaints had some merit, for it moved to readjust clauses relating to the arbitrators who would make awards. But instances such as this were rare. No matter how strong their case, petitioners were unlikely to make an impact on a committee or on the house itself unless they enlisted the support of one or more peers.[2]

After hearing evidence against such measures as the Stourbridge Canal Bill and the Chelworth and Penge Enclosure Bills, the house rejected them without even sending them to committee. In each case, powerful arguments were raised against passage. The Stourbridge Canal Bill, aside from enraging other canal companies, aroused concern among property and mill owners who feared that water levels of feeding streams and rivers would be lowered to supply the canal; the Chelworth Bill purportedly violated the rights of the poor; and the Penge Enclosure Bill was introduced without proper notice. But in each case the petitioners also received strong support from one or more peers, and, as the agent for the Penge Enclosure Bill told Lord Spencer, the bill's

---

1 For examples of committees on opposed bills being opened to all peers see *LJ*, xxxvii, 113, 115, 8, 12 July 1784; *ibid.*, xxxix, 353-4, 356, 5, 17 Apr. 1792. For recommitted bills see *ibid.*, xxxix, 677, 14 May 1793; *ibid.*, xli, 356, 15 June 1796; G. Bramwell, *The Manner of Proceeding on Bills in the House of Lords* (London, 1831), 63.

2 *LJ*, xli, 263-5, 275-7, 1, 3, 4 May 1797.

most vociferous opponent, 'opposition from any individual member of Parliament clogs a Bill'.[1]

As in the full house, deliberations in the committees were as much affected by diligent spokesmen as by persuasive argument. One source of opposition to the Surgeon's College Bill of 1797 came from the residents of Lincoln's Inn Fields who had been shocked by the college's purchase of a house there to be used for the dissection of executed criminals, but it was due in no small part to Lord Thurlow's forceful intervention that they carried an amendment requiring the College to find suitable facilities nearer to the Old Bailey. Opponents of the Leeds and Liverpool Canal Bill of 1793, among whose number was the earl of Balcarres, raised such strong objections against the measure that the committee at first recommended that the bill be thrown out. Instead, the house recommitted the bill which was then amended to suit its opponents objections.[2]

In this instance the committee served as a forum in which opposing sides could accommodate their differences. Often, however, bills which provoked innumerable petitions were reported without amendment. In some cases the committees properly judged that the objections of the petitioners were groundless. But often opponents of a bill failed because they could not recruit as many adherents as the measure's supporters. Nine petitions, including one from Lord Dudley, were presented against the Birmingham Canal Bill, but the measure's supporters, among whom were Lords Stamford and Harrowby, not only met frequently to plan their strategies, but diligently attended to oversee its passage. Similarly, the Bridgewater interest was able to carry the Rochdale and the Trent and Mersey Canal Bills against the opposition of Lords Derby and Grey de Wilton in the first instance and Moira in the latter. The committee on the Rochdale Bill, for example, turned back opposition challenges by decisive majorities of 18-5 and 16-5.[3]

Where committees failed to resolve disputes, the final decision rested with the full house. The committee on the Aberdeen Streets Bill, for example, was unable to pacify local citizens who complained that the

1 *Parl. Reg.*, xx, 62-70, 8, 9, 10, 11, 12, 18 May 1786; *LJ*, xxxvii, 476, 16 May 1786; *The Times*, 10, 11 July 1789; *LJ*, xxxix, 738, 10 June 1793; Spencer Papers, Box 14, H. Barker to Spencer, 31 May 1793.

2 *The Times*, 28 June 1797; *LJ*, xxxix, 611, 619-20, 655, 677, 755-6, 15, 18 Apr., 7, 14 May, 14 June 1793.

3 *Ibid.*, xxxix, 108, 117, 179-80, 193, 197, 251, 8, 12 Apr., 9, 10, 18, 20 May, 8 June 1791; Harrowby Papers, S/H Series, cdxxxv, Document 52, fos. 7, 11-2, 14; *LJ*, xl, 76, 91, 25 Mar., 2 Apr. 1794; *ibid.*, xli, 59, 125, 20 Dec. 1796' 14 Mar. 1797; Committee Books, 1 Apr. 1794.

bill constituted an attack on private property. Having received the report, the house permitted opposing counsel to present their arguments once again but then voted to pass the measure. Many of the surgeons who would have been licenced to practise by a board established under the Surgeon's College Bill were dissatisfied with that measure even after it emerged from committee with several amendments. Thus, Lord Thurlow and others proceeded to defeat the measure at its third reading. In both of these cases there was some discussion of the very real problems of these bills; many of the peers who took opposing sides had no direct interest in the outcome. There was then a measure of judiciousness to the proceedings.[1]

Often, however, the manner in which the house settled disputes was neither judicious nor disinterested. On the contrary victory again went to the side which recruited the largest number of supporters. Peers unabashedly canvassed for their own bills. Lord Dudley applied in 1776 to the earl of Ailesbury for the latter's attendance at the third reading of the Kent Drainage Bill, and in the course of his note reminded the latter that 'we had like to have lost the Bill on the Report by too great Security'. John Ward, agent for the Kennet and Avon Canal Bill, set up his headquarters in a house on Parliament Street so that he could 'waylay members on the way to the house'. When it appeared that other canal companies would oppose the Kennet and Avon Bill in the lords, Ward immediately pressed Lords Ailesbury and Moira to begin assembling noble supporters in its favour. Similarly, Lord Holland, who protested that 'my whole happiness depends on the success' of the future Lady Holland's divorce, urged his friend Lord Boringdon to secure proxies and an attendance for proceedings on the bill. Holland's concern arose partly from the fact that the government seemed to be exerting its influence against the bill, for in rare instances party leaders did call upon supporters to vote against private bills introduced by particularly important opponents.[2]

Proceedings on these and other bills raise serious questions about the lords' impartiality, particularly with bills in which individual members had a direct interest. There can be no doubt, for example, that friends recruited to help carry a controversial bill through a committee of the house itself frequently paid little attention to the details of those measures. On one occasion Lord Bessborough passed the time in committee by writing to his wife:

1 *The Times*, 25, 29 Mar. 1800; *HMC, 14th R.*, iv, *Kenyon MSS*, 547-8; *LJ*, xli, 348-54, 8, 9, 14 June; *The Times*, 20, 28 June, 14, 18 July 1797.
2 Ailesbury Papers, Dudley to Ailesbury, 4 May 1776; *ibid.*, J. Ward to Ailesbury, 11 Feb., 18 Mar. 1794; Morley Papers, Add. MS 48225, fos. 135-6, Holland to Boringdon [Mar. 1797]; *HMC, Denbigh MSS*, 294.

> you must not be surprized if it [the letter] is not long, as there are
> 2 Committees in the same room & lawyers pleading to each, & I
> set [sic] about the middle between both, by which I get the hearing
> of both at the same time.

Interested peers were sometimes condemned by their colleagues for attempting to smuggle their bills through the house, and some members also objected that noble promoters, apparently supported by officials of the house, seemed to trifle with the standing orders.[1]

Moreover, in its anxiety to accommodate its members the house sometimes trampled on the rights of more humble subjects. To complete the improvements which he had made to Milton Abbey and its park Lord Milton proposed in 1784 to move the ancient abbey school, which stood within thirty yards of his house, to the town of Dorchester ten miles away. Not surprisingly, Milton's proposal provoked opposing petitions from the feoffees of the school and local parents. The lords' committee, however, largely disregarded this opposition; in a special report to the house it revealed its bias by noting that the school 'must be a great Annoyance and Inconvenience to Lord Milton', who had personally begged that body for its removal. In any case, the committee implied that the institution was no longer needed: the town of Milton already had a grammar school, and it did not seem probable to their lordships 'that the Inhabitants, consisting wholly of Labourers and Mechanics, will reap much Benefit from the Foundation, or be likely to send their Children to be educated in the learned Languages, which are chiefly taught in that School'. Indeed, the only impediment to the measure's rapid passage was the refusal of the school's feoffees to give their consent, and after consulting the house, the committee recommended that their opposition be disregarded. By passing this bill the house of lords demonstrated that the rather questionable rights of one of its members took precedence over the claims of his humble opponents.[2]

The proceedings on private and local bills also raise questions about the lords' willingness to impose settlements when bills provoked some controversy. Measures were often sensibly amended, even at the risk of a fight with the commons: the committee on the Sussex Highgate Road Bill, for example, struck a clause which exempted gentlemen

1 *Lady Bessborough and Her Circle*, 90; *The Times*, 3 June 1802; *ibid.*, 12 Mar. 1796.

2 *LJ*, xxxvii, 113, 115, 118-9, 121, 8, 12, 14, 15 July 1784. In the following session Milton introduced another bill to establish the school at Blandford instead of Dorchester. This measure was also opposed by the feoffees, but again the lords decided that the consent of those most directly involved had been secured, and thus, they passed the bill. *Ibid.*, xxxvii, 239, 249, 257, 18, 27 Apr., 3 May 1785.

from tolls, thereby altering a money clause.[1] Committees were also able in many instances to resolve or even impose settlements in disputes arising from enclosure bills which seemed to threaten a vicar's right to suitable tithes or a lord of the manor's claim for just compensation. Moreover, the house remained persistently vigilant where the rights of individuals might be adversely affected by estate bills: in 1785 it ordered the committee on Borrett's Bill to add clauses insuring that the portion of £7,500 for younger children would be secured, and in 1804 Eldon inserted a clause in the Cholmondeley Estate Bill which preserved the rights of the last remainder man until he could give his consent. With these and other cases which involved disputes over details the committees or the full house did impose its judgement.[2]

However, more broad ranging disputes, in so far as they were composed, were normally settled by the parties themselves. Lords Stamford and Middleton along with other individuals met with the promoters of the Trent Canal Bill in 1782 and forced the latter to agree that the bill should not be committed until the country had been consulted and propositions formed 'in order to meet the many and almost insuperable difficulties of the bill'. In March 1794, even while his measure was in the commons, John Ward triumphantly reported to the earl of Ailesbury that disagreements between the sponsors and opponents of the Kennet and Avon Bill had been settled; the measure consequently sailed through the house of lords without a stir. The fifth duke of Devonshire was less fortunate; having arranged through an agent that the second reading of the Shipton Road Bill be deferred until representatives of the duke and other noblemen and gentry of Derbyshire could proffer their suggestions for improvement, he then retired to Chiswick only to be informed that the sponsors had wantonly carried their bill into committee.[3]

Because of navigational problems on the Ouse, the deterioration of Lynn harbour and a continuing inability to control flooding in the region, the Bedford Level Corporation and other groups and individuals

1 *The Times*, 28 May 1791. When the commons refused to consent to the lords' amendments, conferences were held between members of each house. If neither house relented in conference, then the bill failed. Bramwell, *Manner of Proceedings*, 72. Such was the fate of the Warwick Gaol Bill. *LJ*, xxxviii, 652, 667-8, 27 May, 7 June 1790.

2 *Parl. Reg.*, iv, 196-231, 306-18, 30 Mar., 14 June 1781; Leeds Papers, Add. MS 27918, fo. 38, 'Political Memorandums'; Committee Books, 27 Mar., 28 May, 24 June 1789; *LJ*, xxxix, 356, 451, 17 Apr., 30 May 1792; *ibid.*, x1i, 396, 15 July 1797; *ibid.*, xxxvii, 286-7, 31 May 1785; *Hansard*, i, 1100, 20 Feb. 1804.

3 *HMC, Rawdon-Hastings MSS*, iii, 197-8; Ailesbury Papers, J. Ward to Ailesbury, 16 Mar. 1794; Wentworth Woodhouse MSS, F 65(g)/100, J. Heaton to Fitzwilliam, 12 June 1799.

decided in the early 1790s to make a cut on the river at Eau Brink which would run six miles to Lynn. This proposal encountered opposition from every possible source, and consequently its passage was delayed for several years. That it did eventually pass was due in no small part to the labours of the third earl of Hardwicke. Though a warm advocate of the plan, Hardwicke was unwilling to disregard the complaints of its opponents for fear of damaging his electoral interest in Cambridgeshire. Thus, he repeatedly urged the bill's sponsors to avoid precipitate action, preferring instead to accommodate all parties before legislative action commenced. In the summer of 1792 he commissioned a report on the project which converted some former sceptics, but left so many unconvinced that a bill was thrown out in the commons the following year. Nevertheless, Hardwicke continued to work for some compromise: shortly before the bill was again presented in 1795, he opened negotiations with the remaining adversaries and apparently incorporated some of their proposals into the text. Though the opposition never was completely satisfied, the bill was unopposed in the house of lords where its passage proved to be a routine, rather tiresome formality.[1]

That Hardwicke, Stamford or Devonshire should endeavour to compose differences with their adversaries informally was natural. Private compacts settled details in a manner which was more or less satisfactory to all parties. By removing disputes, these agreements also insured the passage of the legislation. Most importantly, perhaps, parties were able through mutual accommodation to avoid costly contests in parliament.

Where the various parties were unable to compose major differences, the house of lords generally proved itself unwilling or incapable of forcing a settlement. The committee to which the Cromford Canal Bill was referred urged at its first session that alterations be made to insure proper supplies of water to opposing canal companies and manufacturing interests. Yet, when the parties proved incapable of reaching agreement, the committee refused to press for a solution and instead reported the bill without amendment to the full house. Following some rather irregular proceedings, it too passed the bill, but only after the Earl Stanhope had assembled the disputing parties at his house and got them to agree 'that a bond should be given for the due performance of the amendments proposed, until the next Session of Parliament when a new bill would be brought in'. Here as in many

1 Hardwicke Papers, Add. MS 35685, fos. 113 ff; *ibid.,* Add. MS 35686, *passim; ibid.,* Add. MS 35392, fos. 255-6, 259-60, C. Yorke to Hardwicke, 23, 27 Nov. 1795; D. Summers, *The Great Ouse, The History of a River Navigation* (Newton Abbot, 1973), 99-112.

other cases the lords' action followed upon private, if rather unusual agreements.[1]

The lords' unwillingness to impose solutions to contentious issues, the ability of peers to shape measures to their own tastes in certain instances — these shortcomings arose from two defects in the private bill procedure of the house — a lack of firm leadership and of orders which were adequate to meet the new complexities of private and local legislation. Between 1792 and 1801 the house moved in two closely related developments to correct these deficiencies. It adopted a series of new orders which at once tightened or more precisely defined existing procedures and made it somewhat easier for legitimate petitioners to secure these acts. More importantly, the 1790s witnessed the transformation of the chairmanship of the committees into a post whose occupant not only presided over but actually supervised the passage of private and local bills.

In most of the instances for which we have information the initiative for the new or amended orders came from individuals. Not until 1801 when it moved to set up a committee to consider orders affecting Ireland and another to examine existing procedures governing enclosure bills did the house as a body move to inspire changes.[2] Yet, in spite of their individual authorship, the lords' new orders all fall within two categories: those designed to facilitate the process for obtaining estate bills and others which reflect the peers' conservative desire to protect propertied interests.

Recognizing the importance of estate acts, the house moved in 1792 to make it easier for Scots to secure those bills. It is not, perhaps, coincidental that while Lord Cathcart, himself a Scot, was lord chairman the house ordered that petitions for bills which affected Scottish estates should be referred to the court of session instead of to the judges in London. Furthermore, Scots judges were permitted to prepare certificates attesting that interested parties, dwelling in Scotland, had delivered their consents to them. Such certificates would be deemed 'to be sufficient Evidence of such Consent and Acceptance' by the committees sitting on the bills for all parties save heirs of entails. Shortly after the Union similar orders were adopted for the Irish[3]

1 Committee Books, 29 June, 1, 2, 7 July 1789. Despite the strong feelings against the bill, the committee was sparsely attended: opposition amendments were defeated on 7 July by votes of 4-3 and 5-2. *The Times,* 20 June, 11, 14 July 1789.

2 *LJ,* xliii, 421, 423, 3, 4 Dec. 1801.

3 *Ibid.,* xxxix, 426, 16 May 1792; *ibid.,* xliii, 424, 427, 7, 9 Dec. 1801.

In 1799 the house approved another series of orders which further facilitated the process for obtaining these acts by simplifying and clarifying its rules governing consents. By the first of these, occupants of a life tenancy, when acting with adult heirs of entail in cases where the two could jointly bar the rights and interests of other persons in remainder, were permitted to proceed with their bills without having to secure the latters' consents for the lords' committee. In two other orders the house established the procedures by which representatives of women and minor children would give their consents, thereby resolving a question which previously had occasioned confusion, delay and additional expense for the promoters of these bills. Finally, the house empowered the court of chancery to fill any vacancy in the ranks of an estate's trustees if the parties to the bill themselves lacked the authority to do so.[1]

Among the most serious obstacles which confronted promoters of the first canal bills was the opposition of landlords who believed like the first earl of Carnarvon that 'a number of privateers took advantage of the occasion and attacked private property'. Indeed, the third Earl Stanhope claimed in justification for the orders on canal bills which he introduced in 1793 'that cuts were to be made through estates, and names obtained to sanction those cuts, when the fact on investigation appeared to be, that those names made but a few partial signatures of the inhabitants'.[2]

To remedy this unsatisfactory system Stanhope's orders demanded first that notices of intended canals be inserted three times in the *Gazette* and also in one paper in each county through which the cuts would be made. These notices, which had to be printed in August or September preceding the opening of the parliamentary session, were also required to contain the names of those parishes through which the proposed line would pass. Before the third reading a map of the line had to be deposited with the clerk of the house along with a list of estimated expenses and another containing the names of the owners of lands through which the canal would pass. Each of these owners had to be applied to for his consent, and if the promoters envisaged any alternate routes, they were obliged to seek out the opinions of owners along those lines as well.[3]

---

1 *Ibid.*, xlii, 171-2, 29 Apr. 1799.

2 *The Times*, 1 May 1793. Carnarvon's complaints were not unusual; similar objections were raised, for example, against the Stourbridge Canal. *Parl. Reg.*, xx, 62-70, 8, 9, 10, 11, 12, 18, 19 May 1786. *The Times*, 12 Mar. 1793.

3 *LJ*, xxxix, 556-7, 11 Mar. 1793. In 1803 the house ordered that these rules should also apply to railroad bills. *Ibid.*, xliv, 146, 26 Apr. 1803.

The conservative desire to tighten procedures and protect established property interests which underlies Stanhope's orders also manifested itself in new orders for estate, enclosure and various local bills. Along with the 1799 orders on estate bills already noted, the house ruled that notice should be given to mortgagees of any property affected by pending estate bills and furthermore, that when petitioners proposed to exchange or sell settled estates, a schedule of the respective rents of all lands involved should be included. To insure compliance with these and other orders, the house moved to establish what already was becoming a regular practice, namely that the chairman of the committee report to what degree the appropriate standing orders on each bill had been complied with.[1] After prolonged deliberation the house also resolved that sums of money intended to be used for the purchase of lands or buildings by promoters of enclosure, road, drainage, paving, dock or canal bills should be placed in the Bank of England until the court of chancery ordered their release. Prior to the issuing of that order, the money, again with the approval of the court, might be invested in the public funds, and any surplus arising from such investments would be applied to the costs of obtaining and implementing the act.[2]

What the lords did in these various orders was to set out new forms and procedures for framing and carrying private and local bills. Provided that promoters adhered to the new regulations, passage of their bills became relatively routine in the upper house. The orders thus helped to obviate many of the difficulties which had hampered earlier proceedings: the strict guidelines for canal builders insured, for example, that those projects would be planned and introduced with the cognizance and general approval of the interests affected. Conflict did not disappear from private bill proceedings as a result of these alterations, but in many instances disputes were narrowed to the specific merits of the contested measures.

That this was the case is due not only to the nature of these orders, but also to the uniformity and strictness with which they were applied. Just as the house set out to redefine its procedures, the office of lord chairman of the committees was substantially transformed and its functions enlarged. From the moment that Lord Walsingham was appointed to this post in the summer of 1794 the chairman's influence over those measures expanded remarkably. To a far greater degree than any of his predecessors Walsingham applied himself to the business of

1 *Ibid.*, xlii, 172, 29 Apr. 1799.
2 *Ibid.*, xlii, 474-5, 7 May 1800.

private bill proceedings: in 1794-5 he presided over 148 out of a total of 190 private bill committees, and between 1796 and 1800 he chaired 801 of 817 such bodies. Given his diligence, it was inevitable that promoters would consult with him when problems arose and attempt to draft their bills in accordance with the standards which he had established.[1]

By every account, Walsingham thoroughly and carefully scrutinized private and local bills. His past experience had given him a taste for the details of business and an invaluable knowledge of the intricacies of parliamentary procedure.[2] Though sometimes hesitant or needlessly rigid, he also dispensed quite freely with standing orders when the occasion warranted such action, and he initiated procedures which further facilitated the manner in which certain bills could be secured.[3]

His vigilance and paramount authority brought about two basic modifications in the lords' private bill procedure. Two years after his appointment a group of lords had attempted unsuccessfully to eliminate the prevalent conflict of interest in these proceedings by ordering that members would be barred from sessions devoted to the consideration of measures in which they had a stake.[4] Where these peers had failed, Walsingham was more successful. After 1794 it was no longer possible for peers to take the chair in committees on their own bills, nor could they prevent alterations simply by stacking those bodies with their friends.

While Walsingham's power was not absolute, he was strong enough to be able to impose changes even in bills sponsored by powerful noblemen. For example, William Hoyle, agent for the Dearne and Dove Canal Bill, reported to Lord Fitzwilliam that:

1   Sainty, 'Lord Chairman', 8.

2   The historian of the eighteenth-century post office says Walsingham was the 'first efficient Postmaster General since 1765', a man who paid an " 'inveterate attention to business and accounts' and was determined to reform the office". K. Ellis, *The Post Office in the Eighteenth Century: A Study in Administrative History* (London, 1958), 111. *The Times* wrote of Walsingham in 1788 that he '. . .ought to be one of the best informed members of the Legislature, his attendance being as constant as the Chancellor in the one house, & the Speaker in the other. When business of importance did not take up the attention of the Peers his Lordship was always to be found in the Gallery of the House of Commons'. *The Times,* 3 July 1788.

3   C. T. Ellis, *The Solicitor's Instructor in Parliament Concerning Estate Bills and Inclosure Bills* (London, 1799), 109-13; Lambert, *Bills and Acts,* 124-5. In 1803 Walsingham accepted certificates from Irish judges attesting to the fact that counsel for Stepney's and Roden's Estate Bills had proved allegations in the preambles of those bills, thus freeing counsel from having to make the journey to perform the same task in London. *LJ,* xliv, 88, 130, 17 Mar., 20 Apr. 1803.

4   *LJ,* xl, 640, 16 Mar. 1796.

Lord Walsingham has objected to some of the clauses, and proposed
others; and I have attended his Lordship upon these, & am to be
with him again soon. . . But I cannot help observing to your Lordship that one of the clauses proposed by Lord Walsingham respecting the reinvestment of purchase monies of Estates of Tenants
for Life &c. goes farther than the direction in our original Canal
Act, and may give unnecessary trouble in making new purchases. . . .

In the end Hoyle accepted the wisdom of Walsingham's suggestions;
even if he had not, it is unlikely that he would have been able to
forestall the lord chairman.[1]

By the end of the eighteenth century Walsingham had established a
second, closely related point: his right to alter private and local bills.
He himself told the earl of Liverpool in 1800 that 'I have seen
& suggested several amendments to the Wapping Dock Bill. — They
have adopted them almost all'. This authority to shape the contents of
private measures extended even into the house of commons. Thus,
while one of his enclosure bills was in that house, C.T. Ellis met several
times with the lord chairman to discuss alterations which the latter
wished to make. In fact, Walsingham told Liverpool that 'they send me
all private Bills whilst they are in the H[e] of Comm., that I may suggest
any alteration I think fit, lest such Alterations should lose the bill in
the Commee of the Lords'.[2]

Walsingham's accomplishments in both respects mark a significant
advance in the degree to which the house of lords acted to legislate on
private and local bills. Before 1794 the house had imposed amendments. Yet, the members' interventions lacked a consistent pattern and
were usually no more than *ad hoc* responses to individual circumstances.
Even with its new orders, the lords' interventions were bound to be
intermittent and sometimes inconsistent, for the memberships' irregular
and interested participation and the earlier chairmen's lack of diligence
inhibited the uniform application of any procedure.

By the 1790s the house of lords recognized the need for attending
more closely to measures that touched so substantial a portion of the
nation's property. One consequence of this concern were the new
standing orders; another was the acceptance of a strong lord chairman.
When the house at last gave the lord chairman formal recognition,
Walsingham congratulated his colleagues for selecting one man

1   Wentworth Woodhouse MSS, F68(b)/4, 5, W. Hoyle to Fitzwilliam, 7, 10
Mar. 1800.
2   Liverpool Papers, Add. MS 38234, fo. 52, Walsingham to Liverpool, 23 May,
1801; Ellis, *Solicitor's Instructor,* 109-13. Ellis advised private bill promoters
'. . .to wait upon the Chairman of the private Committees in the House of Lords a
few days before you go into Committee to know if he approves it'. *Ibid.,* 16-7;
Liverpool Papers, Add. MS 38231, fo. 31, Walsingham to Liverpool, 5 May 1796.

whose duty it shall be to take care that these bills proceed upon one settled and uniform principle, that no innovation shall be made upon the long-established usage and practice of Parliament, and that the property of individuals shall be improved without injury to the public.[1]

Mindful of the rising number of private and local bills, the peers may have concluded that to insure that 'no whim, no scheme' violated established property rights, they required not only stricter orders but also a competent authority to oversee their implementation.[2]

If this was, in fact, their reasoning, their lordships were fortunate to have found a man such as Walsingham to be their chairman. For the transformation of that post was due primarily to his endeavours. Whereas his predecessors were intermittently active, Walsingham was constantly attentive; he had an immense appetite for business and a superb understanding of parliamentary procedure. The lords' prevailing indifference to private business on the one hand, their vague desire to tighten the scrutiny of these bills on the other gave him latitude and a mandate to take strong steps. The willingness of parliamentary agents to accommodate themselves to his forms and practices enabled him in a very short time to impose his own vision of the lord chairman's role and powers. But Walsingham was the dynamic, creative force. Through his constant attendance and forceful initiatives he established the chairman's right to direct the conduct of private business and, within limits, to shape the content of that legislation. Thus, the lords' resolutions of July 1800 were merely a belated and incomplete acknowledgement of the chairman's position.

That they were passed at all was probably due primarily to Walsingham himself. Having enlarged the role of the chairman, he was ready by 1799 to receive official recognition of his achievement. Thus, in a memorandum to Grenville, composed in January 1800, he requested that his income be increased, preferably by levying additional fees on those who brought in private bills. He asked that the house acknowledge that the chairman had the whole responsibility for overseeing private bills, and, in order to protect himself from sudden political fluctuations, he added that the chairman should be removable only by a vote of the whole house. Finally, to enhance the dignity of his post, he

---

1   *Parl. Reg.*, xii, 475-6, 23 July 1800.

2   Lord Westmeath suggested in 1801 that the union of the English and Irish parliaments might necessitate the creation of another chairman to deal with Irish bills. His recommendation was not disinterested, for he nominated himself as a candidate for the post in case it was created. Dropmore Papers, Add. MS 59255 (unfoliated), Westmeath to Grenville, 1 Jan. 1801.

recommended that the chairman be automatically included as a member of the king's commission to pass bills.[1]

The resolutions eventually adopted by the house were more limited than those Walsingham had proposed. Pitt vetoed the idea of levying additional fees, and no mention was made of the chairman's pre-eminent role in private bill proceedings. Grenville and the lord chancellor, Loughborough, did agree to the principle of giving the chairman official recognition, but the initiative behind the introduction of the successful resolutions was again Walsingham's. Two weeks before they were adopted, he was still pressing Grenville to instruct Cowper, the clerk of the house, to prepare the proper address.[2]

In so far as the house of lords dealt with private and local business it was an active, modern legislative body by the end of the eighteenth century. The flexibility it exhibited before 1792 was enhanced by a series of orders as well as by conventions never incorporated into the orders. At the same time the house tightened procedures on a variety of bills to protect property rights. The uniform application of these and other orders was insured by the emergence of a diligent, intelligent lord chairman. Guided by Walsingham, the house scrutinized these bills thoroughly and enhanced the impartiality of its proceedings by limiting the extent to which individual peers could shape their own measures. Finally it demonstrated a more aggressive determination to impose its will on promoters by moving its own amendments to a wide variety of bills. As the number and range of private and local bills expanded, the house of lords was able to deal forcefully, intelligently and efficiently with those measures.

---

1 *Ibid.* Add.MS 58935(unfoliated), Walsingham to Grenville, 19 January, 1800.

2 *Ibid.,* Add. MS 58935 (unfoliated), Walsingham to Grenville, 8 July 1800.

6

THE LORDS' LEADERSHIP: JUDGES, POLITICIANS AND MEN OF BUSINESS

Debrett's *Parliamentary Register,* in describing the lords' proceedings at the committee stage of the Public Offices Bill in 1785, noted that

> in the course of this business, the Chancellor, Lord Loughborough, the Duke of Richmond, and Lord Stormont, were up several times, and the conversation became so often the *pro* and *con* reply, rejoinder and assertion, that it is impossible with any degree of accuracy, to follow their Lordships, or to attempt giving from memory the various amendments, and the many remarks that were made upon them.

Similar scenes occurred again and again throughout our period.[1] In every instance a small group of politicians and judges decided upon the contents of legislation while the rest of the house sat by impassively, unable like the reporter for the *Parliamentary Register* to penetrate the intricacies of their leaders' bargaining.

As long as the house of lords devoted its time to public business, the politicians, judges and senior office holders dominated its proceedings. They attended frequently. They shaped the contents of legislation. As was seen in chapter 4, they directed its debates. To an extent, they determined how the house of lords would function as a legislature. If we are to understand it, we must understand them.

Of Chancellor Thurlow Lord Holland wrote that 'even to the period of his death, the slightest word that dropped from his lips, though but to suggest an adjournment or move a summons, was greeted by a large portion of the House of Lords as an oracle of departing wisdom or a specimen of sarcastick wit unrivalled in any assembly'.[2] In the eyes of his contemporaries Thurlow was a colossus, but to some extent all the law lords seemed larger than life to their lay colleagues.

How are we to explain the unique importance of these men? Undoubtedly their offices inspired awe: lord chancellor of England or Ireland, chief justice of the king's bench or common pleas — these were the nation's senior magistrates[3] and the dignity of the chancellor

---

1   *Parl. Reg.,* xxi, 21, 7 Apr. 1785. For similar proceedings see *The Times,* 4 June 1791, 25 May, 11 July 1799; *Hansard,* ii, 435, 28 May 1804.

2   Holland, *Memoirs,* ii, 5; cf., Wraxall, *Memoirs,* i, 408-10.

3   For a list of the leading judges and office holders during this period see Appendix B.

was further augmented by his position as their lordships' speaker. But the law lords' proximity to majesty was probably of greater significance than their judicial offices. Until 1830 chancellors continued to be the monarch's personal representative in the cabinet. Mansfield, Thurlow, Kenyon and Eldon were at various times George III's close friends and advisers: indeed, Brougham cites Eldon's 'admirable address in smoothing difficulties with princes' as one of his sources of power.[1] In a house where so large a portion of the membership prided itself on its loyalty to the crown, the prestige of the judges was enhanced by the fact that they were thought to speak for the king on certain issues.

It is also evident, as A. S. Turberville contended, that the judges' talents and forceful personalities reinforced their prestige and enhanced their power.[2] Certainly Lord Thurlow compensated for his mediocre judicial capacity by displaying a truly formidable demeanor: 'no man', Fox said, 'was ever so wise as Thurlow looks, for that is impossible'. As a colleague he was often argumentative and untrustworthy, and his old friend Kenyon aptly summarized his career and personality when after one visit he noted that Thurlow was as ever 'splenetick in politics'. Yet, as Fox himself admitted, he was tough, independent and, in his own way, honest.[3] In contrast, contemporaries regarded his successor, Lord Loughborough, with justifiable suspicion. Loughborough's ambition was unbridled, and his dealings with his colleagues were sometimes deceitful. At the same time he was a brilliant orator and so regarded as an invaluable ally in the lords by Portland and Pitt alike.[4] Unlike his two predecessors Lord Eldon was a great

1 A. Aspinall, 'The Cabinet Council, 1783-1835' (London, 1952), 231-2; Campbell, *Lord Chancellors*, vii, 120; R. Gore-Browne, *Chancellor Thurlow: The Life and Times of an Eighteenth Century Lawyer* (London, 1953), 141; G. T. Kenyon, *The Life of Lloyd, First Lord Kenyon* (London, 1873), 385; Twiss, *Eldon*, i, 424-6, 449-50; H. Brougham, *Statesmen of the Reign of George III* (London, 1855-6), ii, 50.

2 Turberville, *The House of Lords in the Age of Reform*, 186-96.

3 Holland, *Memoirs,* ii, 5-13; G. Kenyon, *Kenyon,* 382; Wraxall, *Memoirs,* i, 410-12.

4 Wraxall quotes the following extreme assessment of Loughborough's career. *Memoirs*, ii, 56.

> To mischief trained, e'en from his mother's womb,
> Grown old in fraud, though yet in manhood's bloom,
> Adopting arts by which gay villains rise,
> And reach the heights which honest men despise;
> Mute at the bar, and in the senate loud,
> Dull 'mongst the dullest, proudest of the proud,
> A pert prim prater of the northern race,
> Guilt in his heart, and famine in his face,
> Stept forth.

See also, Brougham, *Statesmen,* i, 167-82; Holland, *Memoirs,* ii, 13-4. For more flattering evaluations of his career, see Portland Papers, Pwf. 9214, Portland to

lawyer; his legal talents alone guaranteed that he would occupy a leading position in the house. Less able as a debator than Loughborough, his amiable pomposity, his occasional forcefulness and his close ties to George III added to his authority.[1] Among the other judges Camden's age and political consistency earned respect as did Kenyon's gruff honesty. With the exception of Eldon Lord Ellenborough was probably the most able lawyer of the period, and his terrible rages may only have made him more redoubtable.[2]

Finally, the judges' power was strengthened by their independence. Rising through the legal hierarchy on the basis of their abilities and connections within the profession and enjoying the special favour of the king, these men rarely allied themselves closely with politicians, who tried, often vainly, to control them. Thurlow and Kenyon at various times openly opposed Pitt's government, while Loughborough in 1801 and Eldon in 1804 helped to displace ministers under whom they served. Such behaviour struck some observers as being disloyal; it also dramatically illustrates the full extent of these autonomous figures' political weight.

The judges' legal talents and expertise qualified them for a leading legislative role. Indeed, they partially made up for the deficiencies of their colleagues by scrutinizing most legislation and moving those amendments which they believed to be necessary. More than other peers, for example, the law lords delighted in pointing out examples of the commons' sloppy draftmanship. In 1791 Lord Thurlow condemned the Catholic Relief Bill as a 'MASS OF NONSENSE put together by some person who pretended to know law, but who in fact seemed to be totally unacquainted with it'. The Tobacco Bill of 1789, strewn as it was with errors, was in his eyes an even more miserable concoction.

> This arose from want of due attention in those whose business it
> was to draw up and superintend the clauses; but such was the
> slovenly manner in which Bills were framed, and such the blunders
> that almost the whole of the Revenue Bills which lately came from
> the other House, were liable to the objections which lay against the
> present one. Many days had been wasted; and much oratory
> thrown away by those who opposed it in the other House, where, if
> one quarter of the time spent on proper declamation had been
> applied to serious and sensible investigation, those errors which now
> so fully stand their Lordships in the face, would have been recti-
> fied. . . .

Loughborough, 6 Aug. 1784; *HMC, 13th R.,* iii, *Fortescue MSS,* ii, 360-1.

1 Campbell, *Lord Chancellors,* ix, 404-20; Brougham, *Statesmen,* ii, 50-66.
2 Campbell, *Lord Chancellors,* vi, 403-4; Holland, *Memoirs,* i, 169; Brougham, *Statesmen,* ii, 174-94.

Such an impression did this diatribe make upon the house that the peers accepted Thurlow's amendments even though the measure was a money bill introduced by the government.[1]

However, judicial peers were much more than legislative editors. Even before bills were submitted to the house, their promoters — government ministers as well as private individuals — solicited the opinion of one or more of the law lords. In fact, the judges frequently had the last voice in determining the legal propriety of measures which came before the house. Thus, Eldon halted proceedings on a bill to increase the salaries of London curates until he had assured himself that the grounds on which it was founded were legally sound. In 1805 the peers agreed at his suggestion to reject amendments to a minor government bill and later deleted the portions of Trotter's Indemnity Bill for which Eldon could find no precedents.[2]

Through such interventions the law lords were able to improve some legislation. They added or reframed clauses to insure that the original intent of proposed legislation would be realized and also altered some arbitrary or ill-constructed bills. *The Times* noted in 1790, for example, that Loughborough's amendments to the Lottery Bill had corrected a measure which in its former state 'was most certainly drawn up in a very loose and inaccurate manner'. On another occasion, when the house amended a private estate bill at the behest of Lord Eldon, another judge, Lord Alvanley, 'took occasion to applaud the care and attention which had usually been paid by the noble lords who sat upon the woolsack to such proceedings as that in question'.[3] Sometimes the house balked at the lawyers' recommendations, but in most instances members apparently expected, even welcomed the participation of men who made the legislation which came from their house more precise and accurate.[4]

Yet, the house of lords also paid a price for this precision. Again and again their lordships' proceedings were delayed while the learned

1   *The Times,* 7 June 1791; *ibid.,* 31 July 1789.

2   *HMC, 14th R.,* iv, *Kenyon MSS,* 534-7; *Hansard,* ii, 1029, 1071, 1106-7, 13, 19, 23 July 1804; *ibid.,* v, 623, 812-17, 27 June, 10 July 1805.

3   *The Times,* 31 May 1790; *Hansard,* i, 1100, 20 Feb. 1804.

4   Thurlow was unable to remove a clause from the Catholic Relief Bill of 1791 permitting Roman Catholics to become lawyers. *The Times,* 8 June 1791. While he and Loughborough were able to postpone the passage of Fox's Libel Bill for a year, it was eventually passed over the objections of most of the law lords. *PH,* xxix, 726-8, 732-6, 8 June 1791; *ibid.,* xxix, 1293-4, 1297-9, 1425-8, 27 Apr., 21 May 1792; *LJ,* xxxix, 483, 11 June 1792. In 1804 Eldon and Ellenborough were unable to convince the house that the Aylesbury Election Bill should be rejected. *Hansard,* ii, 517, 681-2, 6, 15 June 1804.

lords pondered: Charles Abbot records in detail how Loughborough's dilatory behaviour and repeated changes of heart impeded the progress and modified the contents of his Census Bill. Moreover, the judges sometimes permitted their legalism to be carried to absurd and destructive extremes. In the wake of severe food shortages the Board of Agriculture introduced a general enclosure bill in 1801. The main difficulty with this proposal related to the commutation of tithes, an issue which particularly excited the bishops and lawyers. In hopes of pacifying their opponents, the sponsors submitted their bill to Lord Eldon before presenting it to parliament and later accepted all the amendments which he proposed. Nevertheless, this tactic failed to stem the opposition: in a spirit of 'riotous irrelevance' the lawyers descended on the measure and moved over 200 alterations on points of detail, leaving it, according to Lord Thurlow, 'confused and absurd'. When, after all this they joined with the bishops in demanding that ecclesiastics have the right to veto any plans for tithe commutation, the bill was dropped by its supporters.[1] However unscrupulous, ponderous or trivial the judges' behaviour may have been, this last incident demonstrates that other members of the house found it difficult to restrain such knowledgeable, influential men.[2]

In any case, the peers were often unwilling to challenge the law lords who effectively expressed their own political attitudes. Even in the house of lords the lawyers were a conservative force. None proposed and in most instances they actively discouraged attempts to reform the judicial process or mitigate the severity of the penal code. Thurlow and Eldon opposed the imposition of any restrictions on the slave trade,[3] and the law lords particularly detested the idea of Catholic emancipation. As early as 1791 Thurlow impeded the passage of the Catholic Relief Bill, and Loughborough's machinations helped to topple Pitt when he proposed emancipation in 1801. Eldon and Ellenborough shared

---

1 *Colchester Diaries*, i, 212-5; R. Mitchison, 'The Old Board of Agriculture (1793-1822)', *EHR*, lxxiv (1959), 53, 57-8; Buckinghamshire Papers, D/MH 191, Eldon to Hobart [no date]; *ibid.*, D/MH C337, Hobart to Eldon, 23 May 1801 (copy).

2 Some peers found it difficult to contain their dislike of the lawyers. Sackville complained that 'when there are more than one Lawyer in Council they always differ, and by their Ability puzzle and perplex, create delay, and prevent decision'. Sackville Family Papers, U269/C192, Sackville to Dorset, 8 Dec. 1784. See also A. Olson, *The Radical Duke: The Career and Correspondence of Charles Lennox, Third Duke of Richmond* (Oxford, 1961), 200-2 and Lord Abingdon's protest against the Judges' Salary Bill of 1799, *LJ*, lxii, 320, 8 July 1799.

3 Campbell, *Lord Chancellors*, vii, 158-9, 522-4, ix, 436-8. For examples of their support of the slave trade see *PH*, xxvii, 643-4, 25 June 1788; *ibid.*, xxxiv, 1138-9, 5 July, 1799; *Hansard*, ii, 931-2, 3 July 1804.

Loughborough's sentiments, and the first two Irish chancellors to sit in the united parliament — Clare and Redesdale — were if possible more vitriolic on this question than their counterparts.[1] Among the law lords of this era only Camden exhibited the slightest trace of liberalism, and in this respect he was probably less typical of his profession than the diehard Eldon.

The roots of the judges' conservatism lay in their exalted positions and their attitudes towards the law. Naturally, they were suspicious of any measure which might circumscribe their authority; Loughborough attacked a bill which modified punishments for treason and other crimes on the grounds that it would limit judicial prerogatives. Fox's Libel Bill was designed, Thurlow growled, for nothing more than 'mobbing the Judges', and even Lansdowne, a proponent of that measure, expected the judges to oppose this limitation on their freedom.[2]

In addition to being jealous defenders of their powers the judges were skeptical of any bills which challenged established legal conventions. Thurlow disliked Dundas's Forfeited Estates Bill because in altering the traditional treatment accorded to traitors and their heirs it violated the 'wisdom of former times'. Similarly, Kenyon attacked Fox's Libel Bill because it directly contradicted 'the practice of a long series of years. . . . It tended to alter the established law of the realm, and, considered in that light, was a new and dangerous innovation upon the Constitution.'[3]

The conservatism inspired by their reverence for precedent was reinforced by the judges' belief in the sanctity of established property rights. These peers were unprepared to accept any limit on the free use of property unless the consent of the owners concerned was secured. Such a stance had significant political implications, for men of the eighteenth century still regarded parliamentary interests and, in some instances, even the vote itself as forms of property. For example, both Eldon and Ellenborough attacked a bill, designed to expand the electorate in the venal borough of Aylesbury, on the grounds that such an expansion would lessen the value of the current voters' property.[4] Their belief in the sanctity of property provided these men with grounds for opposing any modification in the decadent political structure of the late eighteenth century.

1 *The Times,* 6, 8 June 1791; *Malmesbury Diaries,* iv, 3; *Memorials and Correspondence,* iii, 319-20; *Colchester Diaries,* i, 406-9, 436; *Hansard,* iv, 711-19, 783-5, 804-16, 10, 13 May 1804.

2 *PH,* xxvi, 195-202, 5 July 1787; G. Kenyon, *Kenyon,* 230, 245-6.

3 *PH,* xxiv, 1363-9, 16 Aug. 1784; G. Kenyon, *Kenyon,* 225-6.

4 *Hansard,* ii, 1029, 13 July 1804; *ibid.,* ii, 513-7, 681-2, 6, 15 June 1804.

The importance of the judges' impact on the house of lords cannot be overstressed. While the house did not invariably follow their lead, it usually found it difficult to ignore their advice completely. Thus, these enormously powerful figures were able to shape much of the legislation which emerged from the house of lords. Often their interventions left bills clearer, more accurate, even fairer, but they also destroyed a number of potentially beneficial measures. In a conservative house the law lords were a conservative force: on some issues, such as abolition or Catholic emancipation, they merely helped to justify the majority's unenlightened opposition, but against other measures, including the innumerable bills to relieve imprisoned debtors, they invariably took the lead. Nor did they only thwart humanitarian reformers; a house composed almost exclusively of landlords was unable to prevent them from destroying a bill for general enclosure.

The weight of forces arrayed against them did not preclude the whigs from exercising some influence in the house of lords. The opposition had heroic moments — the prolonged campaign against Pitt's Russian policy in 1791 and the final onslaught against Addington in 1804. But between these majestic peaks came long dreary troughs of hesitation and failure. For much of the time the whigs were superficial in their arguments, haphazard in their timing, content to raise their standard without pressing the attack to its conclusion.

The uncritical, frequently shallow proceedings of the house of lords derive in part from the repeated failures of the whig opposition and more particularly from its inadequate leadership. The party's leading spokesmen suffered from personal shortcomings and a circumscribed, dilettantish perception of public questions. Hesitant and sometimes indifferent, they permitted, even encouraged individuals to embark on campaigns which in some instances left the party open to ridicule. While debates may have had little impact on the balance of forces within the lords, the whigs' perfunctory or controversial performances gave rise to serious doubts about their capacity to govern.

The hopelessness of the party's position in this period sapped much of the energy within its ranks. A dejected Eden wrote to Lord Sheffield in the fall of 1785:

> if the Dead could be awakened you would resusticate them: but L[d] N[orth] & Mr Fox are more dead than the People: you are the only Man alive — I was alive too when there was a Nail to drive; but I have neither Turn nor Talents nor Spirit enough to do any thing upon general Grounds — My private Creed is that we are beaten; at least that I am. . . — Unless a new Hare starts I am not to my Feelings at Liberty, even if I had the Disposition to enter into the carping & quibbling Peevishness of mere opposition vulgarly

so call'd: — I feel that I should sink myself by it: — besides it is sad to work alone: for the Truth is at this Hour & You best know it, that if You & I had not work'd up that Irish Business, Ld North would have slept thro' the Session at Bushy and Mr Fox at St. Anne's Hill.

Eden shortly resolved his dilemma by transferring his allegiance to Pitt, but others more scrupulous of their honour languished in seemingly endless exile. The failure of the whigs in 1788-9 only reinforced their sense of hopelessness, and by heightening the tensions within the party that failure also helped to pave the way for the splits of the mid-1790s[1].

For a few years in the wake of those splits the rump, more determined than ever to demonstrate its righteousness, was vigorous in its opposition to and criticism of a wide range of government policies. Yet their sense of moral rectitude was insufficient to carry these frustrated noblemen over the long miles to London simply to take part in divisions which they were bound to lose. In the last years of the century many whigs became overwhelmed by a sense of futility: without any chance of defeating or even modifying government policies they refused to budge from their estates and cared little whether attacks were made at all. By 1798 most had seceded from parliament. Once again demoralization and splintering became endemic[2].

This demoralization only heightened the need for effective leadership. Whigs did not simply appear by chance on the occasion of debates. Such confrontations required careful preparation if they were to be at all successful. Several peers had to follow the course of business, keeping their colleagues informed of its progress. Proxies had to be distributed among the allies in town, and absentees had to be summoned for important confrontations[3]. The task of recruiting

1 Auckland Papers, Add. MS 45728, fos. 62-3, Eden to Sheffield, 22 Oct. 1785; L. Mitchell, *Fox and the Whigs*, 99-101, 147-50; J. Derry, *The Regency Crisis and the Whigs* (Cambridge, 1963), 192-7.

2 Holland House Papers, Add. MS 51660, fo. 70, Bedford to Holland [no date]; *ibid.*, Add. MS 51571, fo. 48, Thanet to Holland, 18 Nov. 1800; *ibid.*, Add. MS 51682, fo. 55, Lansdowne to Holland, 24 Jan. 1800; R. Willis, 'Fox, Grenville and the Recovery of Opposition, 1801-1804', *Journal of British Studies*, xi (1972), 30-3.

3 The whigs evolved an efficient technique for summoning adherents. From the 1780's lists were kept of potential supporters, and by the opening of the nineteenth century the appeals sent to these peers were on printed forms. After 1804 the earl of Albemarle seems to have become an informal whip; Holland, Grey and Grenville each at various times noted that he was the proper person to send out the applications for attendance. F. O'Gorman, *The Whig Party and the French Revolution* (London, 1967), 21; Holland House Papers, Add. MS 51661, fos. 97-8, Bedford to Holland [no date]; *ibid.*, Add. MS 51530, fos. 85-6, Grenville to Holland, 16 May 1808; *ibid.*, Add. MS 51593, fo. 60, Albemarle to Holland, 18 May 1808.

speakers for these occasions was always a difficult one given the general reticence of the peers, and even the most seasoned participants had to be coached on the proper line of attack. Planning was essential, and from the time parliament met leading members of the party were periodically summoned to consider strategies and to define positions.

The whigs did, in fact, make tentative steps towards developing the post of leader of the opposition in the house of lords. From 1783 until he joined Pitt in 1794 the duke of Portland strove to organize the whig forces in the upper house, but he had no apparent successor until the end of the decade when the young Lord Holland attempted to weld the beleaguered party into some shape.[1] Holland's tenure was informal and brief: in the early years of the nineteenth century he was on the continent, and once again the whigs lacked a leader.[2] Only when the party coalesced with the Grenvillites in 1804 did it gain an effective, active and officially recognized commander, Lord Grenville.[3]

How the whigs fared in the intervals between Portland and Holland and Grenville is unclear. Though he had little faith in the critical capacities of the peerage, Charles Fox did give some advice to his allies in the upper house on how to proceed; he called meetings to plan strategy and even helped to secure attendances.[4] After 1798, however, Fox withdrew from politics and did not return until 1803. In the meantime the party probably required very little direction. During its leaderless periods it only had a handful of followers in the lords. No elaborate organization was required to mobilize a group whose active strength varied from ten to fifteen; private initiative and word of mouth sufficed.

1 *HMC, 15th R.,* vi, *Carlisle MSS,* 645; Portland Papers, Pwf. 7027, Mansfield to Portland, 9 June 1791; Percy Family Papers, 1vii, fo. 62, Portland to Northumberland, 3 Dec. 1790.

2 If Holland was not the official leader of the opposition in the house of lords during the late 1790s, his correspondence with various whig peers indicates that he was the focal point of its organization, arranging attendances, recruiting speakers and distributing proxies. Holland House Papers, Add. MS 51821, fos. 193-4, 236, 293, Oxford to Holland, 21 Mar. 1799, 27 Jan., 17 Nov. 1800; *ibid.,* Add MS 51572, fos. 55, 63-4, King to Holland, 20 Apr., 17 Nov. 1800; *ibid.,* Add. MS 51571, fos. 48, 62, Thanet to Holland, 18 Nov. 1800, 25 Oct. 1801.

3 Fox conceded Grenville the leadership of the upper house without hesitation, believing the commons, where he had the lead, to be of far greater importance. Fox Papers, Add. MS 47564, fos. 197-8, Fox to Lauderdale [1804].

4 *Memorials and Correspondence,* iii, 139-40; Percy Family Papers, 1viii, fos. 109-10, Fox to Northumberland, 4 Sept. 1796; Fox Papers, Add. MS 47564, fos. 94-5, Fox to Lauderdale, Wednesday; *ibid.,* Add. MS 47561, fo. 100, Fox to Portland, 29 Jan. 1789; Grafton Papers, 423/159, Fox to Grafton, 17 Jan. [1794?].

More ' serious than the gaps in the leadership were the personal limitations of the leaders themselves. Under Portland's aegis the party established an organizational structure, but the duke himself lacked confidence in his own judgment and was unwilling to impose his views on others. Holland was an intelligent man with a warm personality. But his claim to authority rested primarily on his close relationship to Charles Fox and his convenient, entertaining household in Kensington; certainly he was too young and inexperienced to rally his disheartened colleagues. Grenville, on the other hand, had the stature and ability to do so and amply proved his worth in 1804. However, after his failure to gain office in that year, his enthusiasm for political combat apparently diminished.[1]

One consequence of the hesitant leadership of these men was that their allies attacked the government from weak, even ridiculous positions. Sir Gilbert Elliot described to his wife in 1789 how he and others were summoned to Burlington House, Portland's London residence, to prepare a protest during the regency crisis. When, after considerable labour, Elliot and his colleagues delivered the results to the house of lords, they found that 'the protesting Lords had signed Lord Loughborough's vile bald stuff, and entered it on the journals'.[2] Portland had failed to inform his associates in the lords of Elliot's activities.

Unfortunately, for the whigs, the incidence of such mishaps was high. Lacking firm direction the party all too often followed well-meaning individuals whose unsupervised campaigns caused more damage to itself than to the enemy. *The Times* noted pointedly in 1791 that Lord Porchester's whig colleagues refused to vote on his motion for Indian papers so as not to reveal their small numbers. During the early nineteenth century the earl of Darnley developed an unhappy propensity for putting his allies in unfavourable positions. On one occasion Lord Spencer complained that a motion of Darnley's would only 'produce an embarrassed debate in which they [the ministers] will have so much the advantage on the plea of Candour that it can produce no good'. On another, Darnley moved for papers which he hoped would indict Lord Melville without consulting Lord Grenville. Grenville disliked the whole attempt to defame Melville; he believed, moreover, that the only consequence of Darnley's ill-conceived

---

1 O'Gorman, *The Whigs and the French Revolution,* 6-7. Grenville told Holland in 1808 that he would not attend a particular debate because he believed such attendance was futile. Holland House Papers, Add. MS 51530, fos. 85-6, Grenville to Holland, 16 May 1808.

2 *Minto Papers,* i, 250-2.

manoeuvre would be to fix censure on his ally, Lord Spencer. Yet he was unable to stop the enthusiastic earl.[1]

Another more serious consequence of the whigs' poor organization was that they frequently approached great questions with so little preparation that their arguments were facile or worse. Shortly prior to the opening of the 1787 session Fox wrote to Portland expressing the hope that his presence would not be required at the whigs' preliminary consultations on the French Commercial Treaty. When the measure came before the house, it was evident that his noble colleagues had been as lax as Fox: whig comments on the fabulous wealth of the Portuguese trade which was supposedly going to be sacrificed by the treaty and also their allusions to the perfidiousness of France were both ignorant and inflammatory.[2] Far more costly, however, were their blunders during the early phases of the Regency Crisis of 1788-9. Without taking the trouble to analyse the complicated technicalities of the question, Fox seized upon Loughborough's contention that the regency belonged by right to the Prince of Wales. This argument outraged innumerable members in both houses who consequently provided Pitt with the support which enabled him to implement a policy of delay and remain in power throughout the king's illness.[3]

The organizational shortcomings of the whigs were compounded by their leaders' lack of practical administrative experience. Exiled from the inner circles of power, leading whigs lacked the opportunity to familiarize themselves with the business of government. Of the party's ten leading spokesmen prior to the French war, Fitzwilliam, Porchester and Moira had never held an important post in the central government. Carlisle, Derby and Manchester had occupied some of the more ceremonial offices, and even Portland had only served for twelve months in important posts.[4] Alone among these men, the Northite peers, Lough-

1 Grenville Papers, Add. MS 41854, fos. 204-5, Spencer to Grenville, 7 May 1803; Spencer Papers, Box 59, Grenville to Spencer, 19 May 1805; *Courts and Cabinets*, iii, 418-9.

2 Fox Papers, Add. MS 47561, fos. 90-1, Fox to Portland, 12 Dec. 1786; *PH*, xxvi, 514-96, 23 Feb., 1, 5, 6 Mar. 1787.

3 Derry, *The Regency Crisis*, 87-119.

4 *Frederick*, fifth earl of Carlisle (1748-1825), treasurer of the household, 1777-9; commissioner to treat with America, 1778; first lord of trade, 1779-80; lord lieutenant of Ireland, 1780-2. *Edward*, twelfth earl of Derby (1752-1834), chancellor of the duchy of Lancaster, Aug.-Dec. 1783. *George*, fourth duke of Manchester (1737-88), lord of the bedchamber, 1762-70; lord chamberlain, 1782-3; ambassador to Paris, Apr.-Dec. 1783. *William*, third duke of Portland (1738-1809), lord chamberlain, 1765-6; lord lieutenant of Ireland, Apr.-Aug. 1782; first lord of the treasury, Apr.-Dec. 1783.

borough, Sandwich and Stormont, had extensive experience in conducting the judicial, foreign or naval business of the country.[1]

Death and the breach within the party deprived the whigs of its most experienced leaders: of the original group of former office-holders Derby alone remained in 1794. He was joined by North's son, the third earl of Guildford and the brilliant marquess of Lansdowne, whom the whigs in their adversity admitted to the party. Among the other peers who led the opposition against Pitt's government only Earl Stanhope, whom members on both sides believed to be unbalanced, and the young Lord King manifested a detailed understanding of complex national questions.[2] Holland, Moira and the dukes of Bedford and Norfolk made effective contributions, but they lacked the knowledge and experience to challenge such experts in the business of government as Auckland, Grenville or Liverpool.

Whig leaders never, in fact, accorded to efficient administrators the same degree of respect that the latter received from Pitt. The whig party was an avowedly aristocratic one. Rank and fortune, Burke asserted, were sufficient to entitle such magnates as the duke of Portland or Earl Fitzwilliam to claim the highest posts in government. Portland himself acknowledged that men of his station were obliged to take a leading part in the direction of national affairs, and Fox yearned for a party composed of Cavendishes and Russells, a party whose independence was of such purity that it would effectively stand forth as the preserver of liberty.[3] Unable to gain administrative experience or to recruit talented but ambitious politicians, the whigs instead exalted the titled amateur, their only available resource.

Unfortunately, the arguments presented by these noblemen in the house of lords were often superficial or misleading. In chapter 4 we

1 *Alexander Wedderburn* (1733-1805), solicitor general, 1771-8; attorney general, 1778-80; chief justice of the common pleas, 1780-93; cr. Baron Loughborough, 1780. *David*, seventh Viscount Stormont (1727-96), envoy to Dresden; envoy to Warsaw, 1756-61; ambassador to Vienna, 1763-72; ambassador to Paris, 1772-8; secretary of state, northern department, 1779-82; lord president of the council, Apr.-Dec. 1783; representative peer of Scotland, 1754-96. *John*, fourth earl of Sandwich (1718-92), general, 1772; lord of the admiralty, 1744-6; first lord of the admiralty, 1749-51; joint vice-treasurer (Ireland), 1755-63; secretary of state, northern department, 1763-5; joint postmaster general, 1768-70; first lord of the admiralty, 1771-82; ranger of St. James and Hyde Parks, 1783-4.

2 Fox told Holland in 1795 that *'existing circumstances. . .have made Lansdowne more cordial to us all. . .' Memorials and Correspondence*, iii, 126-9; Holland, *Memoirs*, i, 38-45.

3 *The Correspondence of Edmund Burke*, ed. T. W. Copeland (Cambridge, 1968), vii, 307-8; Earl of Rosebery, *The Windham Papers: The Life and Correspondence of the Rt. Hon. William Windham, 1750-1810* (London, 1913), i, 199-209; *Memorials and Correspondence*, iii, 397-400.

examined the shallowness of the opposition's challenges to certain of Pitt's financial or commercial policies.[1] In fact, the whigs made only two efforts of their own to question the success of Pitt's financial administration before 1792. Both reflect an amateurishness which was characteristic of so many of their endeavours. Contending that the country had suffered a deficit of £2.4 million each year since Pitt had taken power, Lord Rawdon moved in 1789 for papers on the financial state of the country. Though warmly supported by those perennial stalwarts of opposition — Stormont and Loughborough — Rawdon could not produce any evidence to prove that the figures he cited were accurate. Consequently, the government speakers were in a strong position when they replied that Rawdon's figures reflected the disappointed hopes of the opposition, not fiscal realities. Two years later Rawdon moved for a committee on the state of the nation by which time his figures had been radically revised and his argument reversed. Instead of exposing vast deficits, he this time complained that the public was being gouged and the nation's credit ruined to support the burden of heavy government expenditure. Though he was able to demonstrate the foolishness of paying money into the sinking fund at a time when there were deficits, his allusions to overburdened taxpayers and impending financial ruin were absurd.[2]

The accession of William, Lord Grenville to the whigs in 1804 is significant precisely because he brought to the party qualities which had hitherto been in meagre supply. Henry Brougham justifiably acknowledged this fact:

> all the qualities in which their [the whigs'] long opposition and personal habits had made them deficient, Lord Grenville possessed in an eminent degree. Long habits of business had matured his experience and disciplined his naturally vigorous understanding. . . . His tried prudence and discretion were a balance much wanted against the opposite defects of the Whig party, and especially their most celebrated leader.[3]

Grenville's career will be discussed later in this chapter. The extent to which effective opposition depended upon the whigs' ability to

1 Throughout these years the most intelligent critical discussion of Pitt's commercial or financial projects came from individuals outside the whig party: Lansdowne and Sackville on the Irish commercial resolutions, Stanhope on the sinking fund and Lansdowne and Watson, bishop of Landaff, on the French Commercial Treaty.

2 *The Times*, 14, 15 July 1789; *ibid.*, 31 Mar. 1791. In contrast to the whigs, Pitt earned the admiration of several noblemen for his handling of financial or commercial matters. See *Lord Granville Leveson Gower, Private Correspondence, 1780-1821*, ed. Countess Granville (London, 1916), i, 5-6; *PH*, xxv, 835, 8 July 1785.

3 Brougham, *Statesmen*, i, 330.

recruit such able men can be seen, however, by comparing two series of debates on monetary policy. In 1797 the duke of Bedford blamed the suspension of cash payments on the subsidies which England had payed to its continental allies. Though this analysis may have suited Bedford's view of the evil consequences of the war, it was also superficial and easily demolished by a true expert like Liverpool. Five years later, even before their alliance was officially confirmed, Grenville and the young whig, Lord King, initiated a series of interesting, intelligent discussions on the consequences of the 1797 suspension. In essence those peers contended that an overly large issue of paper had led to a sharp rise in prices. While they did not carry a majority of the house with them, they were successful in two other respects: they forced ministers to acknowledge and explain in their own way the phenomenon of inflation, and they presented arguments which, though disputed, were never successfully rebutted.[1]

The third and last of those factors which weakened the whig's ability to function as an effective, critical opposition was the constricting sense of rectitude which held Fox and others in its grasp. Lady Holland justifiably complained that there was 'a bigotry in their adherence to their ineffectual principles that borders upon infatuation'.[2] However, neither her husband nor Fox ever seriously questioned the righteousness of their interpretation of past events or their own conduct in them. The whigs' belief that they possessed a monopoly of truth and virtue sometimes made it difficult for them to work effectively with those who did not share their vision.[3] More seriously, their continuing adherence to the myth of royal despotism, by severely restricting their perception of reality, blunted their capacity to function as plausible critics, particularly during the 1790s.

So limited were they by their static concept of politics that Fox and his coterie could not appreciate the cataclysmic impact which the French Revolution had on the political nation. While whig alarmists asserted that the revolution had made earlier controversies irrelevant, the major theme of the Foxites remained the same: Pitt had acted criminally in 1784, and he compounded his crimes a decade later. An overblown executive still posed the most serious threat to liberty and the constitution, and the war seemed to the whigs to offer ministers additional opportunities to expand their powers. Unlike the rest of the

---

[1] *PH*, xxxiii, 517-41, 15 May 1797; *ibid.*, xxxvi, 1156-7, 1247-58, 22 Feb., 3, 13 May 1803; *Hansard*, i, 697-713, 5 Mar. 1804.

[2] *Lady Holland's Journal*, i, 148-9.

[3] Fox Papers, Add. MS 47574, fos. 128-30, Holland to Fox [Jan. 1801]; *Memorials and Correspondence*, iii, 423-6.

political nation they discounted the French menace, arguing that France would welcome negotiations: when those proved abortive, the whigs complained that ministers had made no significant concessions.[1] Such views reveal at once the strength of the whig 'myth' and the extent to which the party's leading spokesmen could disregard or misinterpret events.

Not surprisingly, its members' rigidity weakened the party's political position in the house of lords. The whigs' adherence to one line blunted the effect of their valid criticisms of the ministerial reign of terror or of the government's mismanagement of the war. More seriously, their idle charges gave rise to suspicions about the whigs' loyalty. The duke of Atholl and the earl of Warwick, for example, were only two among many peers to charge in the house of lords that whig criticisms and complaints strengthened the hand of the French party in England, a group with which some peers suspected Fox was working. Such suspicions in turn raised doubts about the party's capacity to govern. In fact, the peerage had by the 1790s no choice but to accept Pitt's leadership: 'Mr. Fox's party is dreaded and disliked', wrote Lord Auckland, 'and there is no other at present'.[2]

For all their failings, however, the whigs brought to the house of lords a sense of decency which otherwise would have been lacking. Though their campaign against Hastings degenerated into a cruel farce, it represented at its best a sincere effort to improve the government of India. More than any other group of politicians whig leaders helped to create the environment in which all eventually admitted the need for some reform of the Indian administration. At the outbreak of the French war when basic constitutional liberties were being attacked out of irrational fear and Pitt's associates arrogantly asserted that they alone had the capacity to preserve the true principles of the constitution, only the whigs challenged the exaggerated reports used to justify the government's draconian measures, only they asked for evidence to support the notion of conspiracies, only they pointed out the constitutional consequences of such acts. Similarly, in the years just before and after the Irish rising of 1798 they urged a policy of conciliation,

1 L. G. Mitchell, *Fox and the Whigs,* 194-238; Fox Papers, Add. MS 47573, fos. 228-36, Memorandum in Lord Holland's hand; *PH,* xxxi, 962-94, 30 Dec. 1794; *ibid.,* xxxii, 1494-1508, 30 Dec. 1796; *ibid.,* xxxiv, 1204-41, 28 Jan. 1800.

2 *Ibid.,* xxxiii, 189-90, 744, 27 Mar., 30 May 1797; *Auckland Correspondence,* iii, 280-2; Morley Papers, Add. MS 48244, fos. 265-7, 'Memoirs of the earl of Morley'. The dilemma pointed out by Auckland created particular difficulties for whigs. See, for example, Portland Papers, Pwf. 1442, Darnley to Portland, 16 Jan. 1794.

they decried the army's brutal repression and predicted that it would drive the Irish to rebellion.[1] No doubt these arguments were adopted at least partially to contradict the government's policies, but the same confidence in their rectitude which limited the whigs' perception of realities also made them impervious to the opinions of others. Within the traditional political nation they composed the one group willing to risk unpopularity, even anathematization for their views, and in espousing unpopular causes they challenged, if only slightly, the constricting conformity of the majority.

Despite the large number of peers who held office in the governments of this period no more than three or four took a prominent part in the business of the house of lords at any one time. All cabinets contained great peers whose rank and territorial connections compensated for any lack of talents. Some less exalted ministers were also undistinguished, even incompetent, and the soldiers and professional heads of the admiralty rarely took part in parliamentary discussions. Still other ministers, while competent administrators of their departments, confined their speeches in the lords to topics pertaining to their official responsibilities. Only the chancellor, one or perhaps two men of business and the same number of politicians spoke intelligently on a broad spectrum of public issues.

What distinguished these last men from their colleagues was their wide-ranging competence and authority. Though never part of Pitt's inner circle, Thurlow, Loughborough and Eldon exercised extensive influence in the house of lords: their intelligence, strong personalities and close connections with the king enabled them to secure a relatively independent and respected position in that body. On the other hand, all the politicians and men of business who functioned as effective leaders in the upper house worked closely with that minister in formulating policy. Their intimate involvement in the business of government was, in fact, an essential prerequisite for their leading role in the house; from it they derived the authority and knowledge which enabled them to assume a commanding position.

With the exception of Hawkesbury, who first sat by right of his father's barony, none of the small band of prominent peers were drawn from the ranks of the existing nobility. Few noblemen manifested any

---

1 For the whig opposition to the Aliens Bill see *PH*, xxx, 161-70, 26 Dec. 1792; the Seditious Assemblies Bill *ibid.*, xxxii, 527-54, 9, 14 Dec. 1795. Their basic disagreements with the government's Irish policy are outlined in *ibid.*, xxxiii, 127-39, 21 Mar. 1797.

inclination to follow the example of the leading Pittite administrator-politicians: even among politicians of the second rank only Leeds, Richmond and Spencer inherited their titles, and the first proved himself to be quite incompetent. Each of the leading lawyers in this period was a new peer. Some important house of commons men such as Grenville or Hawkesbury were sent by ministers specifically to restore order in the lords. Others, including Liverpool or Auckland, actively solicited their peerages from a minister who acknowledged on one occasion that it was useful to have able men of business in the upper house.[1] Talent in this period was recruited from the house of commons. The peerage itself did not produce men capable of giving effective direction to ministerial forces.

Finally, ministers assured the loyalty of the house by selecting one from among these leading peers to command their forces there.[2] During the course of our period, the post of leader of the house of lords was substantially transformed; where once its occupant had merely organized the government majority, after 1790 he also served as the administration's leading spokesman. Through the agency of loyal, powerful leaders Pitt and Addington not only were able to prevent disgruntled cabinet ministers from challenging them in that body; the leaders also provided an effective counterpoise in the nineteenth century to an increasingly powerful opposition.

Government business in most instances flowed smoothly through the house of lords as long as the administration's majority remained intact. Consequently, the initial responsibility of the leader was to hold ministerial forces together. Periodic appeals for attendance were dispatched in his name, though other ministers sometimes followed up these applications with their own communications.[3] Important supporters were kept up to date with parliamentary affairs, at least partially so they would not waste their time on needless attendance, and leaders also had to keep the king informed of the state of

---

1 *Later Correspondence,* ii, no. 1626.

2 The evolution of the leadership of the house of lords is described by J. C. Sainty, 'The Origin of the Leadership of the House of Lords', *BIHR,* xlvii (1974), 53-73.

3 Hardwicke Papers, Add. MS 35622, fos. 200-1, Sydney to Hardwicke, 13 May 1784; Verulam Papers, D/EV F29, Grenville to Grimston, 8 June 1800; Hardwicke Papers, Add. MS 35393, fo. 119, Chatham to Hardwicke, 16 May 1797; Grafton Papers, 423/743, Pitt to Grafton, 29 Jan. [1789]. The leader's letter was often followed by another appeal, since many peers regarded his summons, especially at the opening of parliament, as a mere form. Portland Papers, Pwf. 6114, Roxburghe to Portland, 28 Sept. 1801.

130

business.[1] To rally supporters and familiarize them with the details of important policy, meetings were held at which the leader, sometimes aided by Pitt, discussed upcoming business: most notably, all adherents were invited to an assembly at the leader's house where the king's speech was read, and after this practice was discontinued in 1801, the leader instead presided over small dinners for leading followers.[2] Finally, the leader, again with the assistance of Pitt and other ministers, recruited and coached speakers for upcoming debates. This was no easy task, and all leaders shared the frustrations of Grenville, who complained on one occasion of 'the general indisposition which prevails in the House of Lords to come forward and take any active part. . . .'[3]

Beyond his performance of these chores, the degree to which a leader shaped events in the house of lords depended on his personality, talents and authority. Lord Sydney, the home secretary from 1783-9, was in a narrow sense very competent. He attended diligently, kept a close watch on the progress of government measures and was able to anticipate many problems before they arose. Though no expert on parliamentary procedure, he was willing to seek out expert advice, and he maintained close contacts with his cabinet colleagues, who in turn consulted with him before acting in the house. Above all, Sydney assiduously cultivated the good will of the government's supporters.[4]

Unfortunately, the effect of Sydney's diligence was undercut by his lack of authority. Even his cousin, Lord Cornwallis, admitted that he was a 'very weak quarter'. He had entered office reluctantly, declaring that he disliked the responsibility and expense of his important post, and there were throughout his tenure persistent rumours of his impending resignation. Pitt's most recent biographer has shown that the minister conducted much of the business of the home office, an arrangement to which Sydney originally acquiesced. As he later learned, however, this intrusion detracted from his authority within the

1 Egerton MS (Hertford Papers), Eg. 3262, fo. 60, Portland to Hertford, 12 July 1783; Newcastle Papers, NeC. 2387, Sydney to Newcastle, 22 Dec. 1788; Liverpool Papers, Add. MS 38232, fo. 121, Grenville to Liverpool, Monday; Auckland Papers, Add. MS 34452, fos. 510-11, Grenville to Auckland [no date]; *Later Correspondence,* i, nos. 29, 81, 83, 737.

2 *Leeds Political Memoranda,* 128; *Lord Fife and His Factor; Being the Correspondence of James Second Lord Fife, 1729-1809,* ed. A. and H. Tayler (London, 1925), 221; *Later Correspondence,* iii, 476, n.1; Chichester Papers, Add. MS 33128, fos. 255-6, Pelham to Chichester, 20 Oct. 1801.

3 *Auckland Correspondence,* iii, 168-70; *Harcourt Papers,* iii, 174-5; *HMC, 13th R.,* iii, *Fortescue MSS,* vi, 424.

4 Sydney Papers, Box 1, Bathurst to Sydney [no date]; *ibid.,* Box 1, Hatsell to Sydney [no date]; *ibid.,* Box 2, Sydney to Northumberland, 27 Feb. 1787 (copy); Hardwicke Papers, Add. MS 35622, fos. 204, 210, Sydney to Hardwicke, 14, 19 Feb. 1785.

government, and he further diminished his stature in the house of lords by repeatedly offering excuses as to why he should not answer opposition questions and challenges.[1] In fact, after his dismal performance during the debates on the Anglo-Irish commercial propositions Sydney never took a lead on any important measure: during the last four years of his tenure others more competent to fill this role served as the government's spokesmen, and Sydney performed the more mechanical chores of the leadership.

Sydney's successor, the duke of Leeds, was even less qualified to present important government business. Lazy and subject to fits of depression, this charming noble poet was better suited for the fashionable drawing room than the foreign office where Pitt in any case conducted much of the business. Before becoming leader the duke had taken no significant part in parliamentary affairs, nor did he make any mark during the one session that he held that post.[2] Under his aegis the government forces, as we shall see, began to show signs of splintering.

The weakness of Sydney and Carmarthen meant that the burden of defending ministerial policy fell more heavily upon their cabinet colleagues. Regrettably, this was a task that most were ill-equipped to perform. Though Wraxall's remark that Pitt's was the weakest front bench in memory is an exaggeration, the noble ministers' talents were not, with the exception of Thurlow's, overly impressive.[3] Gower, the lord privy seal, Lord Howe and his successor at the admiralty, Chatham, almost never spoke. The duke of Richmond was more able and better informed. Sympathetic to many of Pitt's projects, he took some part in the formulation of government policy and could speak with authority. However, he worked in spurts, lacked tact and was disliked by the king and many peers on account of his former radicalism.[4] Throughout the 1780s the respected and venerable Earl Camden was, aside from Thurlow, Pitt's most reliable and able colleague in the lords. In 1785, for example, he tried valiantly to retrieve the government's position on the Anglo-Irish commercial resolutions, and during the Regency Crisis he was appointed to present the ministerial case to the house of lords.

1 Mann (Cornwallis) Papers, U24/C1, Cornwallis to J. Cornwallis, 7 Nov. 1788; Wraxall, *Memoirs*, iv, 5; Pitt Papers, PRO 30/8/181, fo. 257, Sydney to Pitt, 24 Sept. 1784; Ehrman, *Pitt*, 310; *Courts and Cabinets*, ii, 155. For examples of his unwillingness to speak in the lords see *PH*, xxv, 821, 7 June 1785; *The Times*, 30 July 1785; *ibid.*, 22 May 1787.

2 Ehrman, *Pitt*, 185, 570-1; Wraxall, *Memoirs*, iv, 5; Leeds Papers, Add. MS 28064, fo. 330, Leeds to Thurlow, 2 May 1790; *PH*, xxviii, 766-9, 6 May 1790; *The Times*, 7 May 1790.

3 Wraxall, *Memoirs*, iv, 4-6.

4 A. Olson, *The Radical Duke*, 9-10, 79-90; Pitt Papers, PRO 30/8/171, fos. 89-91, 163, Richmond to Pitt, 30 May 1786, 7 Dec. 1790.

However, he was an old man at the end of his career and without any real enthusiasm for office.[1]

Fortunately for Pitt there were several able men of business in the house of lords. During his career the second Lord Walsingham served in many minor offices where he seems invariably to have been efficient. As an expert in parliamentary procedure he often took the chair in committees, and as one of the few peers who sat on the board of control he was of some use during the many Indian debates.[2] Far more formidable was Charles Jenkinson, Baron Hawkesbury and in 1796 first earl of Liverpool. Wraxall implies that Jenkinson was sent to the house of lords because no one else could lead the debates there on the French Commercial Treaty. Though there is no evidence to support this assertion, it is plausible; Liverpool was above all a man of business for whom politics were secondary to administration. Awkward and rather pompous, he never became an intimate of Pitt, whom he openly criticized on some occasions. In fact, Liverpool was so confident of his own expertise and the righteousness of his conservative principles that he had little patience with those who tried to challenge him. Nevertheless, he was an indispensable colleague: no man did more to shape Britain's commercial policies in this period, and few had wider contacts in the mercantile and manufacturing communities. In the house of lords Liverpool was never a brilliant speaker, but his vast knowledge and good sense gave his efforts an authority and soundness quite in contrast to the vague or unfounded arguments he most effectively attacked. When in 1786 he requested a peerage, Pitt wrote to him 'that the Sense of the Advantage which Government receives on many occasions from your abilities and knowledge and particularly in the very important Department you are so good as to execute, makes it impossible for me not to take a warm Interest in any object which you have at Heart'.[3]

Outwardly the weaknesses of Sydney and Leeds made no difference to the successful execution of government business. Though Pitt's measures were lamentably presented on many occasions, neither the fumbling nor the silences of these men jeopardized their passage. The problem posed by their incapacity was not that the whigs might destroy some bill, but rather the consequent prominence in which Thurlow and

---

1 *Grafton Autobiography*, 396; *PH*, xxv, 838-46, 8 July 1785; *ibid.*, xxvii, 1040-4, 22 Jan. 1789; *ibid.*, xxviii, 124-9, 31 Jan. 1789. According to Lord Campbell Camden refused on account of his age to take part in debates after the Regency Crisis. Campbell, *Lord Chancellors*, vi, 395.

2 For more information on Walsingham see above, chapter 5, pp. 108-10.

3 Wraxall, *Memoirs*, iv, 419-20; Ehrman, *Pitt*, 330-41; *PH*, xxvi, 553-66, 1 Mar. 1787; *The Times*, 20 Apr. 1787; Liverpool Papers, Add. MS 38192, fo. 51, Pitt to Jenkinson, 8 Jan. 1786.

Liverpool were placed. In 1790 George III correctly asserted that these two were the only effective government spokesmen in the house.[1] Thus, Pitt had to rely in the lords on men who disliked him and some of his policies with increasing vehemence in those years.

Chancellor Thurlow's waywardness is familiar to all students of the period. The growing emnity between Pitt and his chancellor developed gradually as a result of personality conflicts, differences over official appointments and the questions of Hastings and the slave trade. Above all, Thurlow resented Pitt's growing influence at court and in parliament.[2] Evidence of their falling out began to accumulate publicly in 1788. That year the chancellor attacked Dolben's Slave Bill even though he knew that the minister favoured it. During the early phases of the Regency Crisis in the fall of the same year he scarcely bothered to veil his overtures to the whigs. In both 1789 and 1790 he assailed the government's tobacco bills in the house, and his diatribe against the second bill, quoted earlier in this chapter, was aimed directly at Pitt. Two years later he complained to Lord Kenyon that Lord Grenville, the new leader, gave 'the silliest reasons for going on with the silliest of Bills', among these being the Catholic Relief Bill which he did his best to obstruct. These incidents represent only the more open, parliamentary manifestations of his fractious behaviour. In private he was rude and sarcastic with his colleagues, raising innumerable petty objections to their various requests or proposals. His conduct in the cabinet was equally provoking, for he either opposed what was put before him or refused to participate, often feigning sleep.[3]

The importance of Thurlow's unruly conduct cannot be overstressed. He was an able speaker, a watchful observer and a deft parliamentary tactician. George III warmly admired him, and his prestige in the house of lords was immense. The archbishop of Canterbury, for example, believed that unbearable as he was personally the house 'would be a wretched, unsupportable place' without him, and Liverpool wrote during the Regency Crisis that Thurlow's recent performances had raised his reputation with all parties and gave him 'an ascendancy in this Country, which few have ever attain[d]'.[4] Still, to focus entirely on the

1   Stanhope, *Pitt*, i, 491.

2   R. Gore Browne, *Chancellor Thurlow*, 234-5, 245-50, 283.

3   *PH*, xxvii, 641-2, 25 June 1788; *The Times*, 30 July 1789; *ibid.*, 4 June 1790; G. Kenyon, *Kenyon*, 245-6; *The Times*, 7, 8 June 1791; Gore Browne, *Chancellor Thurlow*, 281-2; Camden Papers, U840 C3/24, Camden to Lady Londonderry, 21 May 1792.

4   Stanhope, *Pitt*, i, 488-9; *Auckland Correspondence*, ii, 217-8; Sackville Family Papers, U269 C182, Hawkesbury to Dorset, 26 Jan. 1789.

problems he created simplifies the dilemma which Pitt faced in the house of lords during the late 1780s.

Thurlow's opposition was open, even belligerent, but at least four other important government peers were also unhappy with their situations. Sydney had come to resent the intrusions that Pitt made on his department and was also shocked by the minister's brusque treatment of his colleagues during the disputes over Dolben's Slave Regulation Bill. In June 1789, he resigned his post. Liverpool, as we have seen, was equally disturbed by Pitt's conduct on the slave bill: along with Thurlow he considered the Tobacco Bill of 1789 'ill-constructed', and both he and Richmond voted for the chancellor's amendments. Indeed, Liverpool's frank admiration for the unruly Thurlow raised doubts about his own loyalty[1]. The duke of Richmond was also unhappy with his position. He too publicly proclaimed his objections to the Tobacco Bill of 1789, and he strongly protested when Pitt sent Grenville to take the lead in the house of lords, implying that he himself should have had the post. Perhaps the clearest symptoms of his discontent, however, were his prolonged absences from London and his increasing unwillingness to attend the house of lords. Finally, the duke of Leeds complained about a want of communication even on matters relating to his own department: he confessed, for example, that he did not know what the government's policy was during certain phases of the diplomatic crisis with Spain arising from the Nootka Sound incident[2].

Pitt always tended to formulate policy with a few favourites and inform the rest of his colleagues of his decisions. By the late 1780s the dissident peers deeply resented this practice and complained openly of their exclusion from the inner circle. 'Mr Pitt', Liverpool told the duke of Dorset, 'goes on triumphantly & communicates with neither the Chancellor the Duke of Leeds nor myself nor any one with whom I have any connection with'. In 1791 Thurlow complained to Liverpool that cabinet meetings were deliberately scheduled while the court of chancery was sitting and that he never received any cabinet papers, a 'mortification' which Liverpool also had to endure. More seriously, Thurlow and Leeds agreed that the want of communication was 'not only unpleasant to individuals but injurious to the general interests of the Govt'[3].

1 Liverpool Papers, Add. MS 38223, fo. 96, Sydney to Hawkesbury, 29 June 1788; Sackville Family Papers, U269 C182, Hawkesbury to Dorset, 4 July 1788, 10 July 1789; Camden Papers, U840 C3/24, Camden to Lady Londonderry, 2 May 1792.

2 A. Olson, *The Radical Duke*, 89-101; Leeds Papers, Add. MS 28064, fo. 330, Leeds to Thurlow, 2 May 1790.

3 Sackville Family Papers, U269 C182, Hawkesbury to Dorset, 2 July, 1789;

In this last respect these two peers were correct. Pitt's aloofness made it difficult to deal with problems when they arose in the lords. The poorly drafted Cocoa Nut Duty Bill, for example, provoked much criticism there, and when Thurlow tried to raise the matter with Pitt, the latter responded 'in a manner which made it impossible to proceed'. Consequently the bill was rejected on a motion of the duke of Leeds.

Similar but more serious episodes were inevitable. Thurlow was claiming by this time that he could not be bound to carry measures through the house which he did 'not know from their beginning'. His colleagues' opposition to Dolben's Slave Bill and the Tobacco Bills of 1789 and 1790 demonstrates that they shared his indisposition. No minister could long tolerate this sullen group in the lords, particularly so long as it was presided over by so powerful a man as Thurlow. As Pitt told George III in 1790, 'in the present state of the House of Lords, and while the Chancellor's disposition is such as is represented, it can hardly be expected that the public business can long proceed without leading to some disagreeable incident'.[1]

It was to subordinate Thurlow and his obstreperous partners that Pitt dispatched his cousin, William Grenville, to the house of lords. Like so many figures of this period, Grenville has had no modern biographer. Instead, most sources cite briefly his experience, his obvious professional competence but also the pride which made it difficult for him to associate easily with other men.[2] The pride of the Grenville's was justifiably legendary: Fox admired a certain 'Stoutness in the way in which they declare that a Gov^t without a Grenville or (as the old phrase used to be concerning them) at least one of the *Cousinhood* is scarcely a legitimate Government'. This steadfastness, many called it arrogance or greed, naturally made the family unpopular, and because he was awkward and shy, Grenville appeared particularly aloof and haughty. Like Pitt he was unable to establish casual friendships, and his closest allies were either relatives or men who had worked with him for some time.[3]

Liverpool Papers, Add. MS 38192, fos. 151-2, Thurlow to Hawkesbury, 10 Aug. 1791; *Leeds Political Memoranda*, 149.

1 Leeds Papers, Add. MS 28064, fo. 198, Thurlow to Leeds [no date]; Granville Papers, PRO 30/29/4/6, fos. 843-6, Sir A. Macdonald to Lady Stafford, 11 Aug. 1789; *Later Correspondence*, i, no. 635. The threat which Thurlow posed to Pitt's government is illustrated by the former's last attack on an administration bill. In May 1792, Thurlow, who had maintained his high standing at court, carried most of the courtiers with him and nearly defeated Pitt's pet Sinking Fund Bill. Spencer Papers, Box 11, Spencer to Dowager Countess Spencer, 22 May 1792.

2 Turberville, *The House of Lords in the Age of Reform*, 67-8; J. W. Fortescue, *British Statesmen of the Great War, 1793-1814* (Oxford, 1911), 42-3, 75-8.

3 Chatsworth Papers, Fifth Duke's Group, 1683, Fox to Duchess of Devon-

On the other hand, Grenville's unwillingness to practice the more obvious political arts may have arisen from his ambivalent attitudes towards public life. Grenville was not a compulsive politician: in 1794 he offered during a difficult moment to resign, telling Pitt that 'the notion of indefinite & unlimited Service in such a situation as mine, is not fitted to the frame of my mind'. The fact that his wife inherited a large fortune in the early nineteenth century further diminished his appetite for politics. No longer did he have to rely on his salary to support his household, and his letters written to Lord Holland after the fall of the Talents reveal that he was a very reluctant parliamentary participant.[1]

Whatever the reasons for his aloofness Grenville was among the most able of the Pittite administrator-politicians. He was receptive to new ideas, being, for example, an ardent student of Adam Smith.[2] He served in a whole range of official situations and accumulated extensive knowledge of public business and administration[3] Indeed, one of the notable features of his political career is that he preserved widely diverse interests; even in the late 1790s as he presided over the foreign office and helped to arrange military strategy, the published volumes of his correspondence indicate that he was busily dealing with such unrelated questions as the Irish union or the commutation of tithes. Yet, for all his interests there was nothing dilettantish in his approach to public affairs. During the French war he was the foremost architect of British foreign policy: it was he who defined the goals of that conflict which Pitt after 1797 made his own.[4]

Both George III and Lord Liverpool claimed that Grenville was narrow and rigid in his opinions, and several historians have accepted their judgment.[5] It is interesting, however, that these two men expressed their views at times when the Catholic question divided them sharply from Grenville. Certainly there was nothing narrow about Grenville's advocacy of emancipation; he believed in its justice and necessity and was hailed by Brougham as one of its foremost advocates Similarly, it

shire, 16 Dec. 1802; Wraxall, *Memoirs,* iv, 101-2; Stanhope, *Pitt,* i, 415.

1 Dacres Adam Papers, PRO 30/58/1, Grenville to Pitt, 26 Feb. 1794.

2 *Ibid.,* PRO 30/58/3, Grenville to Pitt, 24 Oct. 1800.

3 Chief secretary for Ireland, 1782-3; paymaster-general, 1784-9; vice-president of the board of trade, 1789; Pitt's private emissary to Holland, 1787; speaker of the house of commons, 1789; home secretary, 1789-91; foreign secretary, 1791-1801.

4 E. D. Adams, *The Influence of Grenville on Pitt's Foreign Policy, 1787-1798* (Washington, 1904), 74.

5 *Glenbervie Diaries,* i, 149-50; *Auckland Correspondence,* iv, 307-9; J. W. Fortescue, *British Statesmen,* 77; A. S. Turberville, *The House of Lords in the Age of Reform,* 68.

has been shown that his unpopular opposition to Addington's peace with France arose from his conviction that it was detrimental to the national interest. This same dedication to what he felt was just and right is also evident in his opposition to the slave trade. Indeed, the immediate cause for the passage of the bill abolishing trade in 1807 was Grenville's willingness to exert all the political influence at his disposal in its favour.[1]

Thus, it may reasonably be asked whether it was not his critics rather than Grenville who were the obstinate ones. His public decisions reflected the intelligence, honesty and extensive experience of a man better qualified than most to make such judgments. Grenville frightened some and offended others, but Charles Fox admired him because he was direct. This honesty and clear perception together with his willingness to pursue that which he believed to be right made him one of the leading politicians of his age. For all his reputed coldness he displayed a greater and more generous enthusiasm for such causes as abolition or Catholic emancipation than almost any other statesman of his day. Lord Holland, whose good opinion any man would have valued, wrote of Grenville: 'I, for one, feel that among the rare gratifications of a public life the reflection of having known and acted with such a man as Lord Grenville is not the least'.[2]

Though Grenville was to dominate the house of lords for ten years, he failed in his first task, that of taming Thurlow. Initially it was hoped that he might serve as an intermediary between Pitt and the chancellor: on his elevation he expressed the hope that he and Thurlow would be able to work 'in the fullest concert', and he did try to modify measures which the latter found objectionable. However, Thurlow was not prepared to accommodate any emissary of Pitt. On several occasions he was inexcusably rude, and by the fall of 1791 Dundas told the marquess of Stafford, an old ally of Thurlow's, that Grenville despaired of establishing any workable harmony with the chancellor. Thus, when in the following spring he opposed and nearly defeated a bill to continue the sinking fund, Grenville supported Pitt in calling for his resignation.[3]

Even before Thurlow's dismissal, however, Grenville had begun to

1 Brougham, *Statesmen*, i, 331-2; Willis, 'Fox, Grenville and the Recovery of Opposition', *Journal of British Studies*, xi, 33-43; R. Anstey, 'A Re-interpretation of the Abolition of the British Slave Trade, 1806-7', *EHR* (1972), lxxvii, 328-9.

2 Lord Holland, *Further Memoirs of the Whig Party, 1807-21*, ed. Lord Stavordale (New York, 1905), 271.

3 *HMC, 13th R.*, iii, *Fortescue MSS*, i, 524, 611, ii, 89-91; Gore-Booth, *Chancellor Thurlow*, 281-2; Granville Papers, PRO 30/29/1/15, Dundas to Stafford, 22 Oct. 1791.

establish himself as the preeminent figure in the house of lords. His brief term as speaker gave him some knowledge of parliamentary procedure which he used to advantage as the following letter from Lord Fitzwilliam attests.

> Ld Grenville has manoeuvered with considerable dexterity: by announcing to the House that Monday next he shall propose to appoint for consideration of the Resolutions, He puts the House off its guard, & gains the point of *fixing a day for the consideration without debate.* He does not summon the House for the question, which he is aware will be the principal question, but surreptitiously carries an apparent unanimity, as to the important point of taking them at all into consideration. We are not so much as apprized of the day, when he will name for the consideration, so that if those who are adverse to any discussion, do not stand sentry at the House without relief, that important point is gain'd as a matter of course, & it goes forth as if the House had unanimously adopted the measure as fit for discussion.

Grenville also enjoyed direct access to Pitt; when problems arose, he could therefore secure the minister's advice. Moreover, despite his reputation for aloofness he worked closely with his subordinates, advising them on the proper line to take during debates.[1]

Above all, Grenville was a superbly able spokesman for the government. Others besides Auckland noted his tendency to lecture his listeners, a consequence perhaps of his unquestioned authority and his personal awkwardness. At times he was shrill and high-handed in his treatment of opposition speakers, but he was also adept at ridiculing their more sententious pronouncements. Lord Holland believed that Grenville became a better debater in opposition,[2] and his performance during the spring of 1804 substantiates this argument. Nevertheless, as leader his experience and understanding of the whole scope of government business made him well-versed in most subjects which came before the house. Endowed with seemingly limitless energy, he led virtually every important debate in the house of lords over a ten year period. Because of his stature and political importance, his speeches had a very compelling authority.[3] He was, in fact, the first leader to assume the responsibility for presenting and defending all important government policies.

1 Holland House Papers, Add. MS 51593, fo. 5, Fitzwilliam to Holland, Tuesday; Auckland Papers, Add. MS 33453, fos. 510-11, Auckland to Grenville [no date]; *ibid.*, Add. MS 34454, fos. 183-4, Grenville to Auckland, 20 Mar. 1798.

2 Holland, *Memoirs*, i, 202.

3 In March 1797, Grenville told his brother that because the chancellor would be absent, he would have to undertake the whole defence against Lord Moira's attack on the government's Irish policy, but he noted that it is not the first time. . .and most probably it will not be the last' such a circumstance had occurred. *Courts and Cabinets*, ii, 866.

Grenville was also fortunate in having a small group of able colleagues. Liverpool's discontents mellowed somewhat after he was elevated
to the cabinet in 1791, and Thurlow's exit in 1792 left him isolated
politically with no one to whom he could complain in the cabinet.
Among the new ministers George John, second Earl Spencer proved to
be an effective first lord of the admiralty; though his speeches dealt
primarily with naval affairs, he did also endeavour to defend the government's foreign policy. Loughborough, of course, was a brilliant speaker
who enthusiastically upheld the government's controversial legislation
to control domestic sedition and warmly advocated the war in its early
phases. The most skillful recruit, however, was William, Lord Auckland.

Though Auckland never attained cabinet rank, he had extensive
knowledge of public topics ranging from Ireland to French commerce.
In fact, he revelled in the details of business and was bitterly
disappointed when out of office: 'the zeal & habitual activity of mind',
he told Pitt, 'which so long led me forward in His Majesty's service,
make it somewhat painful to me to find myself in times like these, an
idle man'. Idle he rarely was. Even before he was given the post office
in 1798, Auckland bombarded Pitt with advice on important questions
and participated in the planning of public policy. In the house of
lords he sat on various special committees and even participated in
judicial appeals. Few men save Grenville spoke more frequently, and
his able speeches covered the entire range of public questions. Unfortunately Auckland was never able to allay contemporary suspicions that
there was something in his character 'which did not convey the impression of plain dealing or inspire confidence'. Nevertheless, as a man of
business he ranked just behind Liverpool and as a speaker he was his
superior.[1]

Other noble cabinet ministers played a negligible role in the house
of lords during these years. While speaking fairly frequently, the earl
of Westmorland rarely made any impact; his speeches were more
distinguished for their rabid conservatism than their perception or
authority. Among Pitt's various relatives and friends, Chatham, the
incompetent first lord of the admiralty, moved through a succession of
dignified offices but never spoke, nor did the second Earl Camden after
his inglorious return from Ireland in 1798. The soldiers, Amherst and
Cornwallis, took no part in parliamentary business, and though active
at the home office, Portland rarely spoke in the lords.

Pitt's wartime cabinet was not without its internal divisions. Gren-

1 Pitt Papers, PRO 30/8/110, fo. 255, Auckland to Pitt, 9 Feb. 1795; *Public
Characters, 1802-3*, 10-14; Wraxall, *Memoirs*, iv, 226-9.

ville himself nearly resigned over the question of peace negotiations in 1797. By 1801 Liverpool was again complaining that he and Lord Westmorland were excluded from the inner circle of the cabinet. So too was Lord Loughborough, who in the late 1790s developed reservations about the manner in which the war was being conducted. But except for the dispute over Thornton's bill to limit the slave trade, these divisions were never publicly displayed in the house of lords. Liverpool was by then at the end of his career: his primary goal was the advancement of his son, and he had no allies, save perhaps the ineffectual Westmorland. Loughborough, as Lord Campbell says, was too mindful of public decorum to speak out against the minister as Thurlow had. Instead, he simply participated less frequently in the business of the house. Above all, none of these men were in a position to challenge Grenville. His hegemony in the house of lords was absolute, even when Pitt's own colleagues were plotting his demise in the closet[1]

For several years after Pitt's resignation the leadership of the house of lords was weak and unsettled. Lacking a suitable ally there to assume the lead, Addington resolved to send up Thomas Pelham, a sickly man of reputed talent. Unfortunately, the implementation of this design was hindered first by Pelham's reluctance to take office and then by the duke of Portland's embarrassing refusal to resign the home office. In the interim Lord Hobart, secretary of state for war, served as leader, and though he admitted it was an expensive and troublesome post, he too stalled before finally surrendering it to Pelham[2]

With so inauspicious a beginning, it is not, perhaps, surprising to discover that Pelham was an unsatisfactory leader. Almost from the moment he took office, he was uncomfortable in his surroundings and incapable of meeting his responsibilities. For example, Lord Hardwicke told his brother that,

> I can say with perfect truth that in the whole of his [Pelham's] correspondence, whether private or official, on the subject of Ireland, not a single sentence is to be found that conveys the least information, not a single answer to any question or point sub-

1 *Glenbervie Diaries*, i, 158; Campbell, *Lord Chancellors*, vii, 464, 476-7, 491.

2 Chichester Papers, Add. MS 33128, fos. 203, 205-7, 210-11, T. Pelham to Lord Pelham, 9 Feb., Wednesday, 18 Feb. 1801. Portland refused to resign until he could find £30,000 which he had borrowed from home office funds and was incapable of repaying. *Later Correspondence*, III, xxi. Hobart told Addington that the latter's announcement that Pelham would take over the lead in the upper house had caused him 'no inconsiderable surprise'. He was chiefly annoyed by Pelham's apparent presumption in claiming to be superior to himself. Once his pride had been restored, he admitted that he was glad to be rid of a dull, troublesome and expensive post. Chichester Papers, Add. MS 33108, fos. 116-7, Hobart to Addington, 7 Oct. 1801; Auckland Papers, Add. MS 34455, fos. 434-7, Hobart to Auckland, 8 Oct. [1801] ; *Auckland Correspondence*, iv, 139-41.

mitted to him. . .that is in any degree satisfactory. . .I consider it therefore as a public evil and a very great drawback on the efficiency of the Ministry that he has been so long suffered to hold the office to the exclusion of abler men.

To make matters worse, Pelham had serious reservations about the government's foreign policy. In March 1802 he formally protested in a minute to the cabinet about what he considered to be the insufficient securities in the Treaty of Amiens. The following month Addington found himself in the unenviable position of being informed by his leader in the house of lords that the Grenvillite arguments against the treaty had made a strong impression upon him 'such a one as I should have found it difficult to resist, informed as I am upon those subjects'. In spite of his criticisms of the peace, Pelham endeavoured with limited success to take a lead in presenting it to the house. Thereafter he made little attempt to explain new policies. Like Sydney he merely organized the government's majority.[1]

Once again the burden of defending ministerial policies fell upon the shoulders of other politicians. Hobart, whose past experience was confined to Ireland and India, demonstrated in his various plans for encouraging military recruitment that he was unequal to the demands of his post.[2] Auckland and Eldon were more formidable figures, but they unfortunately could not manage Lord Grenville.

Even out of office Grenville remained the leading figure in the house of lords. Hobart, for example, pleaded for the former minister's aid and advice during the first months of the new government's existence. Two years later, however, after Grenville had gone into opposition, Hardwicke wrote that only Eldon could cope with him, and Tierney informed Lady Holland that Lord Grenville ruled the roost in the lords: 'the Lords Pelham & Hobart seem to feel themselves out of the question, and the Chancellor is not a match for his noble opponent'.[3]

1 *Later Correspondence,* IV, x; Chichester Papers, Add. MS 33109, fos. 154-7, Pelham's Protest to a Minute of the Cabinet, 14 Mar. 1802; *ibid.,* Add. MS 33109, fos. 202-3, Pelham to Addington, 13 Apr. 1802.

2 Lord Sheffield complained that Hobart's proposals for the militia in 1803 proved that he and his aides did not have 'a competent knowledge of the Country & the details of management'. Richmond, in the same year, found that minister's most recent effort to be 'absurd'. 'If Lord Hobart. . .would at least take the trouble', Richmond wrote, 'to read them [his bills] which He owned to me he had not done in Respect to this Defence Bill, He would save himself & the Counties much trouble'. Chichester Papers, Add. MS 33111, fos. 216-7, Sheffield to Pelham, 12 June 1803; *ibid.,* Add. MS 33111, fos. 277-8, Richmond to Pelham, 17 July 1803.

3 *HMC, 13th R.,* iii, *Fortescue MSS,* vii, 20-1; *Later Correspondence,* IV, x; Holland House Papers, Add. MS 51585, fos. 31-3, Tierney to Lady Holland, 26 Dec. 1802.

Grenville was never able to defeat important government measures, but in 1804 he did prolong the consideration of several important bills and successfully carry many of his amendments to them.

To deal with this unsatisfactory situation in the house of lords Addington adopted the time-honoured policy of sending one of his most able colleagues from the commons to assume the command in the lords. In this instance he chose Lord Hawkesbury, son and heir of the first earl of Liverpool. Hawkesbury's redoubtable father had destined him for high office, taking care for example, to weigh the educational and political value of any post his son was offered before permitting the latter to accept. Fortunately, Hawkesbury was also blessed with a moderation and ease of character which made him an invaluable mediator in this tempestuous political period.[1]

From the beginning Hawkesbury's colleagues in the lords regarded him with some awe. Soon after his appointment Lord Hobart reported to Auckland that 'Lord Hawkesbury has a readiness & confidence about him that will be usefull in the House of Lords — and will put the business there upon a footing, that will be extremely advantageous to the present administration'. A year and a half later his noble colleagues opposed his appointment to the admiralty if it meant that he would have to give up the leadership in their house.[2]

To a certain degree Hawkesbury's reputation was deserved. From the moment he entered the house he, like Grenville, spoke on every major political topic, leading most of the debates for the government. Though his speeches have only a limited rhetorical distinction, they were usually based on sound argument. Hawkesbury was also an adept political organizer who took inordinate pains to assemble his allies at the most crucial occasions.[3]

Nevertheless, he never succeeded in dominating the house of lords to the extent that Grenville had. A month after he arrived in the lords Grenville forced the government to adopt many amendments to the Volunteer Exemption Bill, and in the following April administration forces lost control of the house. Though the aura of doom hung over

1 W. R. Brock, *Lord Liverpool and Liberal Toryism; 1820 to 1827* (London, 1967), **4**, 26-30; *Later Correspondence,* iii, No.1932. Liverpool, who confidently expected that his son would be the next prime minister, opposed his going to the house of lords to take the leadership. Liverpool Papers, Add. MS 38236, fos. 258-62, Liverpool to Hawkesbury, 6 Jan. 1803.

2 Auckland Papers, Add. MS 34456, fos. 40-1, Hobart to Auckland, 19 Dec. [1803]; *HMC, Bathurst MSS,* 45-6.

3 Pitt Papers, PRO 30/8/143, fo. 96, Hawkesbury to Pitt, 14 Jan. 1806; *Later Correspondence,* iv, 595, n. 2.

Addington's government, his ministers' performances may have hastened that collapse in the upper house: their defense of Hobart's Volunteers Bill was weak, and Hawkesbury's presentation was especially flaccid. The government's situation naturally improved after Pitt's return to office: though no new able men were sent up to the house, the opposition's strength abated, and fewer controversial issues were raised there. Even so, Hawkesbury was not always able to answer effectively, far less stifle persistent opposition criticism.[1]

Of course, Hawkesbury's position was more difficult than that which his formidable predecessor had faced. Grenville's majority in the lords had been invulnerable; Hawkesbury lost his in April, 1804, and thereafter had to contend with an opposition of at least sixty peers led by the most able man in the house. In Auckland, Liverpool and Loughborough Grenville had three competent lieutenants. Before April 1804, Hawkesbury had only Auckland and Eldon, and the latter's zeal turned out to be questionable at the end. Thereafter, Hawkesbury's position grew even worse; aside from Eldon his two most able colleagues were soon crippled — Melville by his impeachment, Harrowby by illness. Finally, there was a substantial difference in the stature of these two men. Grenville was one of the nation's leading statesmen, a man of proven ability, a forceful personality. Hawkesbury had had extensive experience, but he was young and awkward: though able, his tenure at the foreign office had been disappointing, and he had yet to establish his reputation.

By providing a counterpoise to dissident ministers and to the opposition, Grenville strengthened the ministerial hold over the house of lords. Pitt had told his mother in 1790 that his cousin's appointment would give ministers 'more strength than has belonged to us since the beginning of the Government'.[2] This was a remarkably accurate prediction: by overwhelming opposing ministerial voices, Grenville soon halted the disintegration which might otherwise have jeopardized the government's hold on the house of lords, and no opposition politician successfully challenged him during his tenure.

The lesson of his achievement was soon appreciated by other politicians. When Grenville contemplated resigning in 1797, Henry Dundas informed the duke of Buccleuch that he had considered going to the lords in order to prevent the administration from being broken up 'from the want of a Person there to do the business of Government and

---

1 *Hansard*, i, 1022-6, 27 Mar. 1804; Spencer Papers, Box 55, T. Grenville to Spencer, 20 Mar. 1804; *Hansard*, iv, 581-2, 719-22, 21 Feb., 6 Mar. 1805.

2 Stanhope, *Pitt*, i, 377-8.

maintain the Credit of Administration'. Hawkesbury never enjoyed Grenville's unchallenged authority; he did, however, help to restore ministerial preponderance in the house of lords. Consequently, when Pitt sought a replacement for Melville at the admiralty in 1805, he was forced to pass over that peer because it was impossible to replace him as the leader.[1]

Yet, to isolate these men as the cause for the government's strength in the upper house is to distort the nature of ministerial leadership in the lords. Leadership was invariably collective: it consisted of three or four able men of whom the leader was, after 1790, generally the most visible and important. Superior to their ministerial colleagues in point of knowledge and ability, these men also presented a sharp contrast to their whig opponents. To be sure, government leadership in the house of lords was very weak during the early years of Pitt's first administration and throughout his second. But in between administration spokesmen usually demonstrated a far better command of policy and detail than their inexperienced adversaries. Indeed, Liverpool, Grenville, Hawkesbury, Eldon or Auckland not only strengthened the government's position in the upper house; each also increased by his presence the significance of the lords' proceedings.

1   Buccleuch Papers, SRO GD 224/30/4, Dundas to Buccleuch, 16 July 1797; *HMC, Bathurst MSS*, 45-6.

7

THE KING'S FRIENDS

The core of any government's majority in the house of lords was composed of those members who supported every minister in whom the king had confidence. In 1785 and 1805 the combined total of the independent and political peers barely exceeded the number in this group, and in 1795 they formed an absolute majority.[1] When joined by cabinet ministers, office holders and the minister's personal followers, the crown's adherents were able to render any administration's position unassailable in the upper house.

The peers who formed this important group were the king's friends not his minions. Most, though not all, tended to be uninterested in the complex, detailed questions with which late eighteenth-century governments were forced to deal, and only a very few had any particular aptitude for business. This lack of involvement or general interest in politics left the majority particularly susceptible to the influences of patronage, friendship or family tradition. Yet, the king's friends did have definable political objectives: they were deeply conservative men who assumed that a strong monarchy was an essential prerequisite for stable government and that systematic opposition or political innovation inevitably led to disruption and dislocation. Even more than patronage or friendship, factors whose impact varied from peer to peer, their conservative principles bound members of this group to the crown.

An analysis of their parliamentary participation indicates that the king's friends were primarily concerned to uphold his government. Serious, potentially dangerous party confrontations monopolized their attention. In 1795 major divisions occurred at one out of every two sessions which 35 per cent of the group attended; an additional 24 per cent witnessed such events at one-third or more of the meetings in which they participated. Even when they could not attend in person, the king's friends were concerned to uphold his government: invariably a large portion of them who were not in London left their proxies with allies who remained in town.[2]

---

1 The following figures are based on my own calculations; without division lists it is impossible to guarantee that they are even reasonably accurate.

	1785	1795	1805
King's Friends	76	100	125
Political Parties	c. 50	c. 60	c. 110
Independents	c. 35	c. 30	c. 20

2 Large demonstrates that members of his 'party of the crown' were particularly

Men who limited their attendance primarily to party confrontations were unlikely to take a direct or active part in the formulation of public policy. Much of the business which came before the house of lords was entirely uncontroversial and understandably failed to stimulate any general interest. Yet the reasons for the lassitude of the king's friends are more profound. For some the weight of personal inertia precluded any constructive activity. Many recognized that they lacked the talent to be of service, and a few of the frankest admitted that their indifference arose from the conviction that they would derive no personal benefit from politics.[1]

Slightly different considerations induced most of the bishops to refrain from overt political activity. Unlike their lay colleagues the prelates had very specific parliamentary duties: they were obliged to protect the interests of the church, promote general moral improvement and a few even claimed some responsibility for relieving the unfortunate. According to Hinchcliffe of Peterborough these obligations were so compelling that if the bishops were 'not fit to be consulted on such a business as immediately concerns our religious establishment, I cannot see what business we have in the house at all'.[2]

Though there is no direct evidence to show that his colleagues shared Hinchcliffe's sense of priorities, their parliamentary behaviour indicates their implicit agreement. Being naturally anxious to uphold established authority, the bishops supported the king's government. With few exceptions, however, they refrained from any direct participation in the secular business of the nation: civil affairs were the province of laymen, and the prelates normally took an active part in

---

assiduous in their attendance at divisions. Large, 'The Party of the Crown', *EHR*, lxviii, 672-4. They were also careful to leave their proxies in the hands of adherents of the government: of the twenty-five men who held court offices in 1785, seventeen left their proxies, and in 1795 twenty of twenty-nine did so.

1 *Edward Jeringham and His Circle*, ed. L. Bettany (London, 1919), 91-2. Protestations of inadequacy greeted ministerial applications for aid in moving or seconding the address to the king at the opening of the session. Sydney Papers, Box 2, Harrington to Sydney, 9 Nov. 1787. Among the few who ventured to speak, Lord Winchelsea emerged unscathed. His sister reported that 'he seems vastly happy in his having opened his mouth in ye House, having express'd it several times, and has no fancies about having done anything awkward. . . .' P. Finch, *History of Burley on-the-Hill* (London, 1901), i, 332. On the other hand, Lord Glasgow muddled his first speech so badly because of his nervousness that he asked, through an intermediary, for another opportunity to prove himself. Melville Castle MSS, SRO GD 51/1/44, W. Garthshore to Dundas, 26 Aug. 1797. Among those king's friends who proclaimed their indifference to or ignorance of politics were Wentworth, Southampton and Hurd, bishop of Worcester. *The Noels and the Milbankes*, 208-9; Cornwallis Papers, PRO 30/11/270, fos. 74-7, Southampton to Cornwallis, 19 Feb. 1792; *Later Correspondence*, iii, no. 2098.

2 Grafton Papers, 435/755, Hinchcliffe to Grafton, 2 July 1780.

the house only when matters pertaining to the church were under consideration.

Their unwillingness or inability to partake in public affairs left many of the king's friends particularly susceptible to the influence of patronage. In a system where power was inherited from generation to generation patronage was an essential feature of the political structure. The patronage system provided a livelihood for a few, rank and status for many more. Most magnates counted upon the government's largesse to help them maintain or extend their electoral interests, and some peers found they could not even enter parliament without its support.

'Whether one lives in the town or the country', wrote Charles Fox, 'it is a great thing in this country to have some influence, and no influence is to be had but from consequence in Parliament'. For Scottish peers in particular the truth of Fox's statement was cruelly apparent. Having failed to secure his election to the representative peerage in 1790, the seventh earl of Galloway applied for a British peerage. That lord had been shocked to find that soon after his defeat his neighbours had concluded he had fallen out of favour in London. Only so substantial a reward as a British peerage, he argued, could correct this misapprehension and convince his countrymen that the earl would continue to provide them with the small posts and favours they required.[1]

Innumerable peers asked nothing more of ministers than the right to dispose of local patronage. For Galloway as for others the ability to insure that a steady supply of posts and favours reached their followers was a key test of their local standing. Consequently, they were annoyed when their applications were ignored. The duke of Hamilton, for example, complained to Pitt that his dilatory handling of the duke's 'trifling' requests made his grace 'appear in an odd point of view to those who press me to ask favours, & who look up to me as the channel through which those favours are to come'.[2] Some peers even threatened to reassess their political allegiances if they found after years of steady support that ministers disregarded their petitions.[3]

Other noblemen sought ministerial patronage as a means of enhanc-

1 Holland House Papers, Add. MS 51467, fo. 24, Fox to Ilchester, 5 Sept. 1783; Melville Castle MSS, SRO GD 51/1a/22, Galloway to Dundas, 16 Aug. 1793.

2 Pitt Papers, PRO 30/8/141, fo. 121, Hamilton to Pitt, 26 May 1791.

3 See *Diaries and Correspondence of Rose*, i, 58-9; Percy Family Papers, 1v, fos. 263-4, Northumberland to Blackett, 6 Aug. 1786 (draft); Pitt Papers, PRO 30/8/119, fo. 9, Cadogan to [?], 19 Nov. 1798; Melville Papers, Box 1041, fo.77, Grosvenor to Dundas, 24 July 1799.

ing their personal or familial prestige. The second marquis of Hertford and the second earl of Hardwicke maintained extensive electoral interests to enrich their families. Both were steady adherents of government; both demanded that their dependents in the commons follow the same course regardless of their political principles.[1] In return for the support they and their allies provided successive ministers, these potentates expected and received handsome dividends — dividends which supplemented the income, if not always the dignity of the houses of Seymour and Yorke.[2]

However, the classic eighteenth-century political character was one such as the first earl of Clarendon who trimmed his sails to the political winds because he delighted in the status which office conferred. Having started life as a diplomat, Clarendon returned home to collect a peerage and occupy minor but lucrative offices including a joint mastership of the post office and the chancellorship of the duchy of Lancaster. Nor did his appetite abate with age: after being dismissed by Shelburne, he pressed Portland, North and then Pitt for some new post. Only by holding office, he believed, could he demonstrate to the world that the king appreciated his earlier services.[3]

This anxiety for recognition is but one example of a more general phenomenon: by the late eighteenth century the British aristocracy had become acutely sensitive to questions of rank. The clearest manifestation of this obsession was what can only be described as a peerage mania. For innumerable reasons countless individuals suddenly decided in

1 Hardwicke papers, Add. MS 35381, fo. 240, Hardwicke to P. Yorke, 3 Feb. 1784; Hertford Papers, Eg. 3260, fos. 104-6, Hertford to Lord R. Seymour-Conway [1804?].

2 *YORKES: James Yorke* (d. 1808), bishop of St. David's, 1774; translated to Gloucester, 1779; to Ely, 1781. *John Yorke* (1728-1801), clerk of the crown in chancery, 1746-1801; patentee for commissioners of bankruptcy, 1755-1801; lord of trade, 1761-3; lord of the admiralty, 1765-6; *Joseph Yorke* (1724-92), col. 5th dragoons, 1760-87; lt. gen., 1760; gen., 1771; col. 22 lt. dragoons, 1787-9; 1st life guards, 1789-92; minister at the Hague, 1751-61; ambassador, 1765-80; cr. Baron Dover, 1788. *Philip Yorke,* second earl of Hardwicke (1720-90), teller of the exchequer, 1738-90.
SEYMOURS: Francis Seymour, second marquis of Hertford (1743-1822), sec. to lord lieutenant of Ireland, 1765-6; constable of Dublin Castle, 1766-1822; lord of the treasury, 1774-80; cofferer of the household, 1780-2; master of the horse, 1804-6; lord chamberlain, 1812-21. *George Seymour-Conway* (1763-1848), commissioner of the excise, 1801-22; chairman of the board of excise, 1822-33; deputy graver and wharfinger (Ire.). *Henry Seymour-Conway* (1746-1830), joint clerk of the crown, king's bench (Ire.), 1790-1830. *Hugh Seymour-Conway* (1759-1801), captain in the navy at the time of his death. *Robert Seymour-Conway* (1748-1831), joint clerk of the crown, king's bench (Ire.), 1790-1830; sole clerk, 1830-1.

3 Clarendon Papers, C347, fos. 563-4, 572-5, 589, Clarendon to Portland, 24 Feb., 16 Apr. 1783, Clarendon to North, 23 Aug. 1783.

the last decades of the eighteenth century that they deserved a peerage. By exploiting this seemingly insatiable appetite to their own advantage, the governments only reinforced the demand for honours. As early as 1786 the solicitor general, Sir Archibald MacDonald, perceived the inflationary effect of creations: 'by making one peer', he wrote, 'ten enemies are made, & twenty claimants'. Early awards only awakened the ambitions of men who considered themselves no less rich, loyal or important than those previously rewarded. Because their self-estimations were often correct, ministers could not logically refuse the applications but only hope to stem the flood by making vague promises for the future.[1]

The sudden burst of new creations naturally alarmed the old nobility and inflated their own demands for elevation. When the earl of Salisbury discovered that the creation of several marquises had removed him from the pinnacle of the noble hierarchy, he at once demanded a marquisate for himself. Similarly, Lord Courtenay was distressed to find that 'every person in the County, even those below me before, have been put over my head, & many others also, whose family is, as it were, but of yesterday'. While his lordship had no doubts that such men amply deserved their rewards, he also believed that his extensive properties and ancient lineage entitled him to be raised above them all.[2]

Unfortunately not all of the king's friends could afford to worry about increasing their political power or social status. Lords Essex and Onslow were in such financial straits that their pensions from the secret service fund were secretly transmitted in 1782 so as not to attract the attention of creditors. Both men depended heavily upon the £1,000 which they annually received as lords of the bedchamber.[3] Likewise, the income of some bishoprics was so small that their occupants were reduced to virtual penury. Ministers like Pitt, who wrote on one occasion that 'a bishop is always something gained', were quite prepared to test the strength of an impoverished prelate's convictions by dangling the prospect of translation before him. Not only did such men find it

---

1 Granville Papers, PRO 30/29/2/5, fos. 737-8, A. Macdonald to Lady Stafford, 24 July 1786; Pitt Papers, PRO 30/8/157, fos. 351-4, Dundas to Pitt, 28 Jan. [1784]; *ibid.*, PRO 30/8/195, fo. 88, Pitt to E. Lascelles, 21 Sept. 1788; *ibid.*, PRO 30/8/195, fo. 92, Pitt to J. Rous, 14 June 1794.

2 *Ibid.*, PRO 30/8/175, fo. 60, Salisbury to Pitt, 17 June 1789; *ibid.*, PRO 30/8/126, fos. 58-9, Courtenay to Pitt, 29 May 1796.

3 *Ibid.*, PRO 30/8/229, fo. 74; *The Noels and the Milbankes,* 91; C.E. Vulliamy, *The Onslow Family, 1528-1874* (London, 1953), 172; Pitt Papers, PRO 30/8/164, fos. 134-5, Onslow to Pitt, 29 May 1796.

almost impossible to resist the temptation; they themselves became adept at plotting their own promotions.[1]

Yet, however much importance some peers may have attached to the rewards which they received in return for their loyal adherence to the crown, not all of them entered the king's service solely to attain those prizes. On receiving the yeomen of the guard in 1804, the fourth earl of Macclesfield told the king:

> My family have indeed ever been the faithful adherents and servants to yours, and are and have been ready to endure any sacrifice to evince their attachment: an attachment which has encreased with succeeding generations and which your Majesty's singular and I may add paternal goodness to myself has infinitely strengthened and confirmed.

Macclesfield was but the first of his family to hold court office. For many others, however, service at court had become an established family tradition. Innumerable Finches, Thynnes and Waldegraves received court appointments in the late eighteenth century, intermarried and produced heirs who in turn spent most of their lives in royal service. In fact, twenty-two of the fifty-five men who held court offices between 1783 and 1806 had some near relation who had held similar positions before them.[2]

Especially prominent among these court families were the Brudenells. The head of the family, the first duke of Montagu, served not only as the master of the horse and governor of Windsor Castle but also as governor of the two eldest princes. His brother, Cardigan, succeeded him at Windsor Castle after having served as master of the robes for thirty years, and the second brother, Ailesbury, after eleven years in the bedchamber resigned to become the queen's chamberlain and subsequently her treasurer. Unable because of their limited talents to make a mark in the political world, these men achieved the standing they so craved by filling dignified, ceremonial court offices, by cultivating the royal family and by accepting the ribbons and other honours which their grateful sovereign showered upon them. In the course

---

1 Pretyman Tomline Papers, HA 119/TA108/42, fo. 262, Pitt to Tomline, 25 Sept.; Pitt Papers, PRO 30/8/125, fos. 274-6, J. Cornwallis to Pitt, 8 Jan., 9 May 1787; *ibid.*, PRO 30/8/155, fo. 5, S. Madan to Pitt, 5 Sept. 1793; Dacres Adam Papers, PRO 30/58/6, E. Vernon to Pitt, 29 Jan. 1805.

2 *Later Correspondence,* iv, no. 2896. Aylesford, second Lord Amherst, Boston, Chesterfield, second and third earls of Dartmouth, Delawarr, Dorset, fourth earl of Effingham, fifth earl of Essex, Falmouth, Fauconberg, Harcourt, Jersey, Poulett, second Lord Rivers, fourth Earl Waldegrave, Willoughby de Broke, Winchelsea, Montagu, Ailesbury and the fifth earl of Cardigan.

of their long service they also became the king's personal friends and loyal servants.[1]

Of greater political significance was the connection established by the North family. The head of the clan, Francis, first earl of Guildford, was a lord of the bedchamber to Frederick, Prince of Wales and later governor to his son, the future George III. From 1773 until his death in 1790 he was treasurer of the queen's household. Guildford's stepson, the second earl of Dartmouth, served as the Coalition's lord chamberlain, and his grandson, the third earl, was successively lord steward and lord chamberlain in the early nineteenth century. Finally, Guildford's son-in-law, Lord Willoughby de Broke, was a lord of the bedchamber from 1761 to 1816.[2]

Beyond the ties established in the course of court service were those of friendship. Guildford, who laid the basis for his family's intimate connection with George III, told Mrs Delaney at the end of his life that 'it is not as King and Queen *only* that I love and respect them, but as *two of the best persons I know in the world!*' In the course of serving their sovereign and his family the duke of Roxburghe and Lord Aylesford, Bishops Hurd of Worcester and Manners-Sutton of Norwich became the King's close companions.[3] On the other hand, Lords Chesterfield, Harcourt and St Helens were only drafted into court service after they became friendly with members of the royal family, and several of the king's closest associates never held court office.[4]

---

1 *George*, fourth earl of Cardigan, constable of Windsor Castle, 1752-90, knight of the garter, 1752; cr. duke of Montagu, 1766; governor of the Prince of Wales, 1776-80; master of the horse, 1780-90. *James*, fifth earl of Cardigan (succeeded his brother in 1790), keeper of the privy purse, 1760-1811; master of the robes, 1760-91; cr. Baron Brudenell, 1780; constable of Windsor Castle, 1791. *Thomas*, succeeded his uncle as Baron Bruce, 1747; lord of the bedchamber, 1760-76; cr. earl of Ailesbury, 1776; chamberlain to the queen, 1780-92; treasurer of the queen's household, 1792-8. For a discussion of the lives of these brothers see J. Wake, *The Brudenells of Deene* (London, 1953), 247-344.

2 *Francis*, third Baron North, lord of the bedchamber to the Prince of Wales, 1730-51; governor of George, Prince of Wales, 1750-1; treasurer of the queen's household, 1773-90; cr. earl of Guildford, 1752. *William*, second earl of Dartmouth, first lord of trade, 1765-6, 1772-5; secretary of state for colonies, 1772-5; lord privy seal, 1775-82; lord steward, 1783. *George*, third earl of Dartmouth, lord warden of the stannaries, 1783-98; president of the board of control, 1801-2; lord steward, 1802-4; lord chamberlain, 1804-10; knight of the garter, 1805. *John*, fourteenth Lord Willoughby de Broke, lord of the bedchamber, 1761-1816.

3 *The Autobiography and Correspondence of Mary Granville, Mrs. Delaney*, ed. Lady Llanover (London, 1862), iii, 291-3; Paget Papers, Add. MS 48403 (Provisional Classification), Uxbridge to Lord A. Paget, 20 Mar. 1804; *Later Correspondence*, iv, no. 2880; *Harcourt Papers*, iv, pt. 1, 51.

4 *Ibid.*, vi, 32-3, 43-4, 47-8; *The Farington Diary*, i, 41; *Later Correspondence*, iii, *no. 2355; ibid.*, iv, 181, n. 3.

The ties which arose from a long family tradition of court service or from close friendship with the king were not those of servile dependency. Few courtiers relied financially on salaries which were often insufficient even to meet the expenses they incurred in performing their duties.[1] The main benefit they received from their association with the monarch and from the rewards he granted them was psychological — a reinforced sense of their own dignity and stature. Proximity to majesty, new peerages or ribbands, these made the courtier seem important.

Certainly, friendship and family tradition, independent of any desire to reap rewards or achieve recognition, focused and enkindled the allegiance of some of these men. The first earl of Uxbridge, one of George's closest friends, abhorred factious politics because it tended to 'distress our best of Kings'; in 1804 he thus threatened to remove an unruly son from the house of commons lest the latter vote in opposition to the king's government. In consistently committing their resources to ministers men like Uxbridge believed that they facilitated the process of government and thereby eased the enormous burden which fell upon the shoulders of their sovereign and friend.[2]

Standing beside these peers who took relatively little part in conducting the nation's business was a much smaller group of noblemen, also the king's friends, who relished the opportunity of holding efficient positions in government. Like William, tenth Lord Cathcart, their ambition was 'to come forward in business, to be useful, and therefore to be employed'. Concerned above all with the orderly administration of government, they were professional men of business, the forerunners of the modern civil servant. That they should regard themselves as the crown's servants was entirely logical: amid the comings and goings of politicians, the men of business provided the continuity and expertise essential to the smooth functioning of the king's government.[3]

The house of lords never contained more than five or six such men at a time. The existing peerage produced few men of business: Corn-

1 J. M. Beattie maintains that officers of the court of George I often spent much of their salaries in meeting the expenses incurred in fulfilling their duties. *The English Court in the Reign of George I* (Cambridge, 1967), 205-8.

2 Paget Papers, Add. MS 48403 (Provisional Classification), Lady Uxbridge to Lord A. Paget, 3 May [1804?], 17 Apr. [1805]; *HMC, 15th R.*, vii, *Ailesbury MSS*, 280.

3 For discussions of the political loyalties of eighteenth-century men of business see I. R. Christie, 'John Robinson, M. P., 1727-1802', *Myth and Realities*, 145-82; F. B. Wickwire, 'Kings Friends, Civil Servants or Politicians', *AHR*, lxxi (1965), 18-42.

wallis and Walsingham were, in fact, the only crown servants of note during our period to inherit their titles. Especially able men of business in the commons such as Jenkinson were ennobled, and towards the end of our period it became the practice to reward distinguished ambassadors or colonial governors with a peerage. But most such men only reached the house of lords at the end of their careers.[1]

In spite of their small numbers these noble men of business were extremely important. Liverpool and Cornwallis continued to play a leading role in framing and executing various national policies. Cathcart, John Warren, bishop of Bangor, and Walsingham restricted their activities during this period more to the house of lords. As successive lord chairmen of the committees each helped to insure the smooth functioning of that body. Walsingham, as was seen in chapter 5, revolutionized the manner in which the house dealt with the mass of private and local bills.

What gave coherence to this diverse collection of peers whom we classify as the king's friends was a commonly shared if vaguely enunciated political ideology. Patronage, family tradition, friendship or a desire to participate in the execution of public policy were important factors in determining the group's allegiance to the crown, but the impact of each of these varied from individual to individual. On the other hand all attached great importance to the preservation of a strong monarchy, all believed that the support of the nation's property was an essential prerequisite for continuing stability, and most had a horror of systematic opposition or substantial political innovation.

Perhaps the most remarkable characteristic of this group was its profound respect for monarchial authority. Some peers exalted the king's position because they were his close friends, but the more conservative clung to the notion that the sovereign possessed a spark of the divine. In the midst of the political turmoil of the early 1780s Lord Rivers lamented that the spirit of the age permitted men to confound the entirely wholesome doctrine of 'divine appointment of Monarchial Government' with the 'divine Right of a particular family'. Twenty years later, after exulting at the king's escape from an assassin's bullet, Bishop Hurd concluded that the angel of the Lord tarried closer around 'good and Godly' princes than ordinary mortals.[2]

1 Among the ambassadors in this group to be elevated to the peerage were Joseph Yorke, Lord Dover and Alleyn Fitzherbert, Lord St. Helens. George Macartney was the only colonial governor during this period to receive a peerage.
2 *Correspondence of George III*, vi, no.4329; *Later Correspondence*, iv, no. 2710.

154

Few peers cared to emulate these flights of fancy, but many believed that orderly government required the existence of a strong monarchy. In a memorandum composed in the autumn of 1783, Lord Clarendon wrote:

> business concerning the nation cant be properly transacted unless the King has a confidence in his ministers & they a due deference for HM^{ty}. I w^d have all measures agreeable to the public appear to spring from the King. The ministers will be sufficiently rewarded & acquire additional security if they in return, gain his good will.

Clarendon decried those 'false plans of economy' which were designed to curtail prerogative. Such measures had already deprived the executive of needed influence, and unfortunately they only betokened a worse state of affairs to come: 'a levelling principle prevails, Democracy is assisted by Aristocracy to render Monarchy insignificant, &, if successful, will break the texture of the finest government ever formed. . . .'[1]

Clarendon's respect for monarchial authority had very practical foundations. The experience of 1783-4 proved clearly that stable government was possible only when relations between the closet and the cabinet were harmonious. Where discord existed he and others of the king's friends expected the politicians to defer to the king not only because he was their sovereign, but also because any other behaviour would lead to chaos. However unpleasant the process, ministers could be replaced without serious disruption; monarchs could not.

Repeated ministerial crises also confirmed the king's friends in their belief that order could not be maintained without the steady support of the nation's property and talent. Steadiness, of course, was the mark of this group, and in spite of whig taunts its members were proud of their conduct. During his fifty years of service, Lord Liverpool told Addington, he had always endeavoured to act 'in a manner that merited his Majesty's approbation'. Few of his colleagues were men of business who aspired like Liverpool to reform the coinage system. Yet they did share his conviction that loyal adherence to the crown contributed to stable government. Ministers continued to summon peers to divisions even when the opposition was numerically insignificant. Nothing but a persuasion that their presence at such occasions materially reinforced the strength of the administration and improved the prospects for continuing effective government could have induced the aged, gouty Earl Poulett or a Scot like the duke of Roxburghe to

1   Clarendon Papers, C347, 'Thoughts on our Situation in 1783. . . .'

consider making the long, uncomfortable journey to participate in divisions their allies were bound to win.[1]

This same desire for stable government, this same belief that such government depended on the adherence of property and talent is revealed in the third duke of Marlborough's admonition to his talented member for Heytesbury, William Eden. Eden, who had been instrumental in bringing Fox and North together in 1783, went into opposition after Pitt took power. The duke deprecated such conduct.

> The more the late Members of Opposition keep together, the more the present Government will be embarassed — But that does not seem to me to be a good reason for their keeping together. I should hope that they would not keep together, but that some of the late opposition who are Men of Business, would think it for the good of the Country to offer their assistance & come over, or be Rats, if you please.[2]

For Marlborough systematic opposition seemed senseless and needlessly disruptive. Other peers viewed Fox and his allies in darker terms. Markham, the fanatical archbishop of York, told his son in the troubled spring of 1780 that 'the same wicked faction which has been so long active in contriving the ruin of this country has brought its designs to a dreadful explosion'. Similarly, when his sister dared to blame the nation's awful situation on the incompetence of North and his colleagues, Lord Wentworth furiously replied

> that we are not in a scrape owing to the measures of those I have supported — But I lay it solely on those Patriots who by thwarting every good design, & by depreciating the wealth, the power, ye legal government (in all its branches) of this country, have given encouragement to our enemies and made them spring up like mushrooms.[3]

The king's friends reveal in their loyal adherence to the crown and

1   Liverpool Papers, Add. MS 38236, fo. 280, Liverpool to Addington, 17 Aug. 1803; Sydney Papers, Box 2, Roxburghe to Sydney, 30 Oct. 1787; *ibid.,* Poulett to Sydney, 9 Jan. 1785. The king's friends often insisted that their adherence to the crown was based on their independent judgment, and they reacted strongly to any implication that those of them who served at court were the crown's tools. *Memorials of the Bagot Family,* ed. Lord Bagot (Blithfield, 1824), 94; *PH,* xxvii, 1044-5, 1282-3, 22 Jan., 17 Feb. 1789.

2   Auckland Papers, Add. MS 34419, fo. 385, Marlborough to Eden, 4 Apr. 1784.

3   D. F. Markham, *A History of the Markham Family* (London, 1854), 60; *The Noels and the Milbankes,* 184. The true king's friend never openly opposed the government even if he disagreed sharply with its policies. According to Lady Holland, the duke of Queensberry was violent against the war by 1797; however, he had also 'made a resolution never to vote against Government'. Likewise, Thurlow told Lord Kenyon that he would not attend the house because, for all his hatred of ministers, he did not think '. . .that either House of Parliament should manifest any signs of disloyalty to his Majestie's Ministers. . . .' *Lady Holland's Journal,* ii, 108; *HMC, 14th R., Kenyon MSS,* 540.

their strong disapproval of systematic opposition the full extent of their conservatism. Stability was their object, and strong, efficient government was the agency by which stability would be preserved. A strong administration was in itself a monument to the continuing vitality of the eighteenth-century constitutional system: it obviated by its very existence the need for substantial political innovation.

Thus, it was logical for the king's friends to villify Fox and his cohorts. At best the whigs complicated the task of ministers. At worst, the king's friends suspected, certain whigs endeavoured to arouse popular passions by proposing sweeping constitutional or political changes in order to return to power. The techniques of these whigs were demagogic and dangerous: their proposals, if implemented, would destroy the harmony and balance which was integral to the functioning of the traditional political order.[1] For the king's friends substantial political change was anathema.

Conservative as they were, the king's friends did not rigidly oppose all change. Pitt's administrative reforms, his innovations in commercial and taxation policies and the union with Ireland were accepted without demur. Some men in this group promoted change themselves by introducing or sponsoring legislation designed to facilitate growth in a developing sector of the economy. Nor were they without humanitarian instincts: despite the king's opposition many supported a bill to limit the slave traffic on the west coast of Africa. A few peers were even prepared to extend or protect further individual political rights.[2] However, they invariably opposed proposals which they felt might disrupt the existing political order.

Amidst the multitude of specific objections that the king's friends raised against such bills, there emerges one preoccupation: that the most modest alteration would overwhelm the entire political structure. Thus, when in 1789 Earl Stanhope introduced a bill to remove certain archaic religious penalties, the Archbishop of Canterbury complained that if

> unrestrained speaking, writing, printing and publishing of religious opinions were permitted, there was scarcely a mischief to the church, or to civil society. . .which might not be effected. . . If the Athiest were to be allowed to defend his Atheism by argument, he

1 *Auckland Correspondence*, iii, 280-2; *PH*, xxxi, 1282, 3 Feb. 1795; *ibid.*, xxxiii, 188-89, 27 Mar. 1797.

2 In the tumultuous months following the Coalition's dismissal, Earl Fauconberg supported the Yorkshire Association's demand for a redistribution of parliamentary seats because such a reform, he believed, would undercut the influence of Fox and North. N. C. Phillips, *Yorkshire and National Politics, 1783-4* (Christchurch, N. Z., 1961), 55-6.

saw no reason why the thief might not be permitted to reason in
behalf of theft, the burglarer of burglary, the seducer of seduc-
tion. . . .

Nine years later the second marquis of Downshire replied with similar
vehemence to a suggestion that various reforms might be necessary in
Ireland.

> The system of parliamentary reform and catholic emancipation is
> the thinnest disguise imaginable to the treason of the Irish rebels,
> whose efforts tend to disunite their country from the crown of
> Great Britain, and reduce it to a province of the French Republic.
> With men of such designs and dispositions no conciliatory measures
> could produce any good effect.[1]

Underlying the hysterical element in such statements is an apprecia-
tion of the precarious nature of the political system and the relentless
dynamic of change. The dukes of Marlborough and Northumberland
and the second earl of Hardwicke viewed Pitt's proposals for parliamentary reform in terms which were from their perspective very
reasonable. All complained that an enlarged electorate would make the
cost of maintaining an electoral interest ruinous. As the influence of
property owners thus declined, the way would be opened for dema-
gogues and agitators who, in order to obtain a following in the enlarged
voting population, would propose increasingly wild political reforms.
Governments that refused to bow to their demands would only reinforce the public cry for change and thus exacerbate an already tumultuous political environment. On the other hand, these radical proposals,
if once accepted, would render all lawful government untenable. Such
views were not, of course, unique to courtiers. Even moderate men
began in the 1790s to hold similar opinions. The important point is
that several years before the outbreak of the French Revolution these
peers had a distinctly Burkean distrust of reformers and political
change.[2]

Like other great landlords the king's friends naturally strove to preserve the existing political system and the social hierarchy from which
it emanated. However, without any direct administrative or political
experience they were less likely than some of their noble colleagues to
appreciate the necessity of such remedial reforms as Catholic emancipation. Many also found their conservatism reinforced by the
institutions to which they were attached. Within the ranks of the

1   *PH*, xxviii, 115-7, 9 June 1789; *ibid.*, xxxiii, 1356, 26 Mar. 1798.

2   Hardwicke Papers, Add. MS 35382, fos. 266-7, 312-3, Hardwicke to P. Yorke,
2 Feb., 27 Mar. 1785; *ibid.*, Add. MS 35623, fo. 265, Northumberland to Hardwicke, 2 Apr. [1785]; Auckland Papers, Add. MS 34419, fo. 459, Marlborough to
Eden, 12 Jan. 1785.

king's friends, for example, were many of the bishops, representatives of an organization whose political aims became, if anything, more conservative during this period.[1] Likewise, the courtiers found that in exalting the authority of the king they not only justified the existence of a large, expensive court, but also implicitly enhanced their own stature and prestige.

No other faction or party of peers equated stability so intimately with the preservation of a strong monarchy during our period. No other group so loyally supported the king's government or so bitterly condemned factious opposition. While only a small number of lords ever advocated substantial political innovations, few members of the peerage opposed all such measures with the same consistency and vehemence as the king's friends. These men composed, in fact, the most conservative group in the house of lords.

The group whose members we classify as king's friends has been described by other historians as a 'party of the crown'. The court party, they claim, was an amalgam of several distinct groups, including the newly honoured peers, the courtiers, the bishops and the representative peers of Scotland. What bound this group together and united it firmly to the government was 'the settled influence of the crown' or, in plain language, patronage. Like the Foxite whigs, these historians apparently assume that men who so consistently supported the crown had to be its captive creatures.[2]

This theory is mechanistic and in certain respects factually insubstantial. Lacking identifiable leadership or organization, the king's friends never constituted a party in the sense that the whigs were a party. Nor was this group a mere composite of those portions of the house which were most susceptible to the crown's influence. Indeed, the extent to which the king or his ministers were able to sway these men through disposal of offices and other favours has been unduly exaggerated.

Unlike the whigs the king's friends had no distinct, continuous leadership.[3] George's interventions against the India Bill or his opposi-

---

[1] For a discussion of the political attitudes of the episcopacy in the last decades of the eighteenth century see R. A. Soloway, *Prelates and People*, 19-84; see also above, chapter 3, 51-3.

[2] The most complete statement of this thesis is contained in D. Large, 'The Decline of the "Party of the Crown" and the Rise of Parties in the House of Lords, 1783-1837', *EHR*, lxviii (1963), 669-95.

[3] The king's friend prided himself on his loyalty to the crown. He supported successive ministers but without acknowledging them as his political mentors.

tion to Pitt's proposals for Catholic emancipation undoubtedly influenced the attitudes and conduct of a number of these peers. Favourites were also called upon to uphold his majesty's views when business relating to the royal family came before the house, and in 1799 the court exerted its influence to defeat Thornton's slave trade bill.[1] But generally the king refrained from expressing his opinions on controversial public questions; instead, he left the conduct of the government and the marshalling of its supporters to his ministers.

It is evident, moreover, that the king's friends arrived at their positions on a number of important questions independently, without any prodding from George III. In 1785 George protested to his irate minister that he had done nothing to incite his allies against parliamentary reform. In 1799, when the court opposed a bill which would have banned the slave trade along certain parts of the west African coast, the bishops who participated in the decisive division nevertheless voted in its favour. Again, two years later many court peers and bishops announced their objections to Catholic emancipation well before the king's sentiments were publicized.[2]

In fact, his close associates on certain occasions shaped the king's mind, not he theirs. A number of these men shared and reinforced George's dislike of reformers, dissenters and abolitionists. Moore, the archbishop of Canterbury, and several other prelates reinforced his misguided notion that the approval of Catholic emancipation would constitute a violation of the coronation oath. Lords Camden and Malmesbury even claimed that Pitt resigned in 1801 because he believed that the courtiers rather than the ministers controlled the king's mind.[3]

Without a recognized leader it was impossible for the king's friends to evolve a distinct, coherent organization. They like other followers of any government were summoned to the lords by the leader of the house or their particular friends within the government.[4] The king might

Pitt, in any case, was an unsuitable leader for this group: he was inattentive to its applications and espoused policies — reform and emancipation — which were highly unpalatable to these men. Addington avoided such excesses and enjoyed a certain popularity with the king's friends, but this did not prevent many of them from deserting him in 1804.

1 *HMC, 15th R.,* vii, *Ailesbury MSS,* 265; Stanhope, *Pitt,* ii, 322-3.

2 Pitt Papers, PRO 30/8/103, fos. 149, George III to Pitt, 20 Mar. 1785; *Later Correspondence,* iii, 227, n. 10. For their reactions to the emancipation bill see chapter 2, 37-8.

3 *Malmesbury Diaries,* iv, 1-5; R.E. Willis, 'William Pitt's Resignation in 1801: Re-examination and Document', *BIHR,* xliv (1971), 239-57.

4 For examples of George's direct applications for support see *Later Correspondence,* i, no. 14; *Cornwallis Correspondence,* i, 154-5.

communicate with some directly, by letter, or count upon various agents to relay his desires, but often peers had nothing to guide them but rather vague rumours. Thus, in 1795, a Mr Arnott informed the earl of Ailesbury

> that the Inhabitants of a certain Castle in that Neighbourhood, warmly oppose the [Datchet Canal] Bill, and that all the Bed-chamber will vote against it. . .If that is really the Case, & You have no particular, or personal Interest in the Bill, may it not be worth the Consideration whether, under these Circumstances, You will think it proper to vote, or not.

So casual a mode of canvassing was not likely to be very thorough or effective. Certainly it does not reveal the existence even of an embryonic organizational structure, and it is consequently difficult to classify this group of men as a party.[1]

It is further evident that the king's friends were not drawn exclusively from the ranks of groups which were supposedly beholden to the crown. In 1785 and 1795 about a quarter of these men had not received any of the honours nor held those offices usually associated with membership in the 'party of the crown'.[2] More importantly, an analysis of the individuals within its supposed constituent groups reveals that they were not invariably or uniformly attached to the king's government.

The inclusion of all Pitt's new peers in this group is particularly questionable. Shelburne, for example, did not enter the court party on being elevated to the marquisate of Lansdowne, nor did twenty-six of Pitt's other creations who subsequently opposed his government.[3] It is not even permissable to consign to its ranks all those who did support that minister. Lords Mulgrave, Liverpool and Selsey were each elevated to the peerage by Pitt, and each stood by him to 1801. However, their

1 Ailesbury Papers, M. Arnott to Ailesbury, 6 June 1795. To justify their claims that the late eighteenth-century whigs did constitute a party several historians have cited its improved organization and coherent leadership. See D. E. Ginter, *The Whig Organization at the General Election in 1790* (Berkeley and Los Angeles, 1967), xiv-lii; O'Gorman, *Whigs and the French Revolution*, 12-31.

2 During the 1780s this group included: Ancaster, Brooke and Warwick, Chesterfield, Darlington, Digby, Delawarr, Gage, Hamilton, Harborough, Hardwicke, Harrington, Leeds, Macclesfield, Middleton, Milton, Poulett, Rochford, Sandys, Sussex and Wentworth. During the 1790s it contained: Ancaster, Berwick, Brooke and Warwick, Courtenay, Darlington, Ducie, Heathfield, Hillsborough, Macclesfield, Middleton, Pembroke, Sandys, Sussex, Manchester, Poulett, Pomfret, Clinton and Dynevor.

3 Buckingham, Lansdowne, Townshend, Abercorn, Bute, Leicester, Lonsdale, Fortescue, Carnarvon, St. Vincent, Carteret, Queensberry, Shannon, Malmesbury, Fife, Grenville, Auckland, Upper Ossory, Dundas, Yarborough, Rous, De Dunstanville, Cawdor, Minto, Hobart, Ormonde and Carysfort.

motives for doing so varied considerably. Mulgrave was an enthusiastic Pittite, prepared even to follow his leader into opposition. Liverpool, on the other hand, was the foremost man of business in the lords, a peer devoted to the idea of smooth, efficient administration. And Selsey was a courtier who supported any government because of his devotion to George III and his thirst for patronage.[1]

Of course it might be reasonably asked whether the new peers can be equated with the Scots, the bishops and the courtiers whose very positions depended upon the good will of the government. Supposedly, the crown's hold over the Scottish representative peers derived from its control of peerage elections. Yet the available evidence shows that the administration's authority was absolute only for a brief period in the 1790s. In 1770 a party within the Scottish nobility set out to challenge the government's right to dictate the composition of the sixteen, and by 1790 it was sufficiently strong to elect six of its adherents. Ministerial control was temporarily restored after 1794 as Henry Dundas consolidated his power in Scotland, but if this process resolved difficulties for Pitt, it only created additional problems for his successors. As Addington learned in 1804, the Scots obeyed 'Harry IX' before they listened to representatives of the crown, and at the election of 1806 Dundas carried six of his candidates against the Talents. The Scottish representative peers were, in fact, more critical than their theoretically more independent countrymen who possessed British peerages: seventeen of the thirty-seven representative peers in our period opposed the government at least briefly during their parliamentary careers.[2]

If the Scots supposedly bowed to the crown because of the latter's control of peerage elections, the bishops required the support of the government to rise through the episcopal hierarchy. One of the anomalies of the eighteenth-century church was the wide diversity of episcopal incomes: the bishops of Bristol were often penurious while their princely brothers of Durham enjoyed incomes which rivalled those of

1 Mulgrave told Pitt in 1801 that 'I have not been in the Habit of differing from you on political Subjects for the last seventeen or eighteen Years. . . .' Dacres Adam Papers, PRO 30/58/4, Mulgrave to Pitt, 4 Oct. 1801. See also *ibid.*, PRO 30/58/4, Mulgrave to Pitt, 19 Oct. 1803; Newcastle Papers, NeC 2580, 2582, J. Peachey to Newcastle, 24 June [1790], 16 June [?].

2 For a fuller discussion of the peerage elections and the political loyalties of the representative peers see M. McCahill, 'The Scottish Peerage and the House of Lords in the Late Eighteenth Century', *SHR*, li (1972), 178-86. The seventeen representative peers who opposed governments were: the third earl of Aberdeen, Aboyne, Breadalbane, tenth and eleventh earls of Cassilis, ninth earl of Dalhousie, Dumfries, eleventh and twelfth earls of Eglintoun, twelfth Lord Elphinstone, Hopetoun, Kinnaird, Lauderdale, Lothian, fourth earl of Selkirk, Stair and Stormont. Only one Scot with a British peerage, the tenth earl of Kinnoul, opposed the government for any length of time between 1784 and 1801.

even the greatest landed magnates. Inevitably the variations in the wealth and importance of their respective dioceses stimulated the prelates' upwardly mobile aspirations: between 1783 and 1806 seventeen of them secured at least one translation.[1] Because those clerics received their appointments from the crown, the more cynical of their lay contemporaries concluded that they naturally gravitated to the source of patronage, shedding their political principles in the process.[2]

Yet again, the bishops were not uniformly submissive to the crown's will. The politics of seven prelates are obscured by the brevity of their tenure or their irregular parliamentary attendance.[3] Of the remaining forty-four, twenty-seven were undoubtedly the king's friends: six were former royal tutors or chaplains who owed their elevations to the king; nine others followed the lead of lay patrons who were themselves loyal partisans of the crown.[4] Six, however, were genuinely independent, and ten followed lay patrons at least briefly into opposition.[5] In fact, the most remarkable political feature of these men was their loyalty to their various patrons.

The true bastion of royal influence was the court. Fifty-five peers held court offices during our period: aside from the nine men who supported the Coalition's India Bill, only two of them directly opposed the king on a question of primary importance before 1801.[6]

1 Bagot, Barrington, Beadon, Butler, Cleaver, Cornwall, Courtenay, Douglas, Halifax, Horsley, Madan, Manners-Sutton, Porteous, Smallwell, Stuart, Thurlow, Warren.

2 *Courts and Cabinets,* ii, 14-6; *Lady Bessborough and Her Circle,* 87-8.

3 Ashburnham, Beauclerk, Lowth, Law and Egerton attended very infrequently. I have no information on the parliamentary careers of Yonge or Horne of Norwich. The bishops' participation may have been somewhat stifled by a rule of the house which demanded that they appear garbed in lawn sleeves. In 1800 proceedings in committee on a minor bill were interrupted by a debate on whether Tomline of Lincoln could vote without his prescribed habit: the chancellor and two other members argued that the order only applied to sittings of the full house, but other peers differed. In the end Tomline offered to withdraw, and the matter was referred to the committee of privileges. *The Times,* 24 July 1800.

4 *Royal Protogees:* Beadon, Hurd, Majendie, Manners-Sutton, Moss, Thomas. *Patrons:* Bagot (Bagot), Bathurst (Bathurst), Cornwallis (Cornwallis), Harley (Oxford), Moore (Marlborough), Murray (Atholl), Pelham (Chichester), Ross (Weymouth), Thurlow (Thurlow).

5 *Independents:* Horsley, Madan, Shipley, Watson, Wilson and J. Yorke. *Patrons:* Bruckner (Richmond), Burgess (Sidmouth), Butler (North), Cleaver (Buckingham), Halifax (North), Hinchcliffe (Grafton), Hungerford (Sidmouth), North (North), Smallwell (Portland) and Tomline (Pitt). Butler, Halifax and Smallwell received translations from Pitt during the 1780s. The first two thereafter supported his administration. According to *The Times,* Smallwell voted in opposition in 1788, the year after his translation to Oxford. Between 1789 and the outbreak of the war, when he supported the government, there is no evidence to show he took part in politics.

6 Cholmondeley, Dartmouth, Guildford, Hertford, Jersey, Onslow, Oxford,

Though the king maintained his right to choose his servants, ministers were able to make many of the court appointments. Writing to William Grenville, Pitt inquired:

> if the post of the Master of the Horse to the Queen is better than the Bedchamber it would be a good way of taking Lord Fauconberg off our hands. If not, Lord Delawarr seems the most likely person to be fixed upon, and either will make an opening for Lord Wentworth. . .For the other vacancy in the Bedchamber I see no candidate with any strong pretensions; and as Lord Macclesfield has taken it into his head to apply for some office, in consequence of Lord Parker's [Macclesfield's son] being turned out by the Prince, I think he would do as well as any, unless Lord Thanet could be prevailed upon to take it.

Given the fact that this letter was written shortly after the king's recovery in 1789, when Pitt's reputation was at its highest, the situation it describes is not typical. Nevertheless, ministers were probably able to control as many as half the appointments to court offices during our period.[1]

Pitt's ability to determine the composition of the household foreshadows but is not identical to the nineteenth-century system where each government automatically put its own nominees in important court posts. Eighteenth-century ministers lacked the means to insure that their appointees would remain loyal to them. With the exception of Thanet, for example, all the lords Pitt considered for vacancies in 1789 were already adherents of the crown: such men would have regarded their appointments as the just reward for past services to the king and probably have felt little obligation to Pitt.[2] Ministers found room for their friends at court; but only a few. Twelve court officers between 1783 and 1806 were genuine political appointees — men who were prepared to surrender their posts if rival politicians took power.[3]

The preceding discussion must raise doubts about the crown's capacity to insure the loyalty of peers by the careful application of its patronage resources. By and large the king's friends were not politically ambitious men, nor did most rely on the crown to provide them

Rivers and Willoughby de Broke supported the Coalition, at least initially, on the India Bill. Queensberry and Lord Lothian opposed the government's regency plan on 26 Dec. 1788. For a list of those peers who held court offices see Appendix C.

1 *HMC, 13th R.,* iii, *Fortescue MSS,* i, 535-6. For a more thorough discussion of this topic see Large, 'The Party of the Crown', *EHR,* lxviii, 685-90.

2 Fauconberg revealed his own, the earl of Macclesfield his father's attachment to the king in several letters. *Later Correspondence,* i, no. 5, iv, no. 2896. Wentworth's political views are discussed below.

3 Albermarle, Carnarvon, Chandos, Cholmondeley, second earl of Dartmouth, first and second marquises of Hertford, Jersey, Leicester, Montrose, St John and Westmorland.

164

with a livelihood. In so far as many of these peers were dependent on the crown's patronage, it was to provide them with the status which they could not achieve through the exercise of their own abilities. Important as status was to many, it was not, perhaps, as all-consuming a passion as the ambition of a politician or the desperation of a bankrupt. New peers and Scots, bishops and courtiers proved that they were not the crown's political bondsmen.

Logic alone suggests the implausibility of a theory which insists that patronage shaped the political conduct of these men. Why should a magnate like the duke of Queensberry surrender the greater part of his legislative independence for an inconsequential post and a small salary while men of lower rank and lesser fortune were fiercely independent? Is it reasonable to suppose that so substantial a portion of the nobility could be driven by one simple motive while the more independent or political peers, men who presumably shared many interests in common with the king's friends, were influenced by a much wider variety of factors?

What made the nobility society's leaders in the first place was the extent of its properties. The second duke of Northumberland, rapacious as he was, correctly perceived that

> my own Situation in this Country is much above what any office in the Kingdom can give me. I have an ample fortune & the general good opinion of my County to satisfy me, if I wish to be quiet; an anxious & hardy Race of men, my tenantry, to back me & support me in troublesome times; & so far from wishing to seek for office, it would require much persuasion indeed to prevail upon me to accept of any.[1]

Since their extensive properties made the peers substantial patrons in their own right, what government could offer them only supplemented their personal resources. It was not the foundation of their political interests. Even after Northumberland broke with the ministers in 1788, his political empire remained intact.

It is also notable that eighteenth-century magnates had a remarkably proprietary attitude towards government. If in some cases they recognized an obligation to the minister who conferred favours upon them,[2] in many instances they assumed that they had a right to pick at will from among the choicest plums in the ministerial larder. Pitt was repeatedly plagued by dukes who implied that they might as well attend the king's levees naked as come without a blue ribbon adorning their

[1] Percy Family Papers, 1viii, fos. 199-200, Northumberland to Davison, 22 May 1797 (copy).

[2] *Harcourt Papers*, iv, pt. 1, 91-2; Mann (Cornwallis) Papers, U24/C1, Cornwallis to J. Cornwallis, 12 Aug. 1789.

bosoms. When the lucrative vice-treasurership of Ireland was abolished, the earl of Mount Edgecumbe, though only weeks from death, summoned sufficient strength to write a short, emphatic note demanding to know what Pitt proposed to grant his family in its place. Again, the duke of Hamilton, after complaining to Pitt about his inattention to the duke's requests, explained:

> I have my interest to consult, & I am sure you must feel your well-fare was ever my interest. Therefore do not treat a person who wishes you most sincerely well in a manner, he does not like, & try to diminish that interest which he wishes to maintain for your prosperity, & I will add, the hapiness of this Country![1]

Because these and other peers identified their interests with those of the nation, they naturally presumed they had a right to receive the offices or favours they desired.[2]

In any case, the presumption that offices or honours made their recipients beholden to the crown is perversely unreasonable. Rewards were conferred upon men of proven loyalty, and ministerial supporters quickly protested to a minister whose patronage policies seemed aimed more at winning over enemies than caring for old friends. Even George III told Pitt that 'if due attention is not shewn to the pretensions those who have long served the Crown that either attachment or fidelity are not reasonably [rewarded?] . . . .'[3]

Typical of the men the king had in mind was the second Viscount Wentworth. Although he readily admitted that he cared little and knew less about politics, Wentworth did have strong political prejudices. Innovation of any kind was abhorrent to him, and he was equally convinced that opposition to the king's government not only aided England's enemies but also weakened the position of the landed interest. In 1782 he was forced out of financial necessity to apply for an office at court, which he eventually received in 1790. It would be absurd, however, to argue that Wentworth only became a king's friend at that point. Aside from being somewhat more diligent in his parliamentary attendance while his application was pending, Wentworth's conduct

1 Pitt Papers, PRO 30/8/130, fos. 45-8, Dorset to Pitt, 20 Oct. 1786; *Correspondence of the Prince of Wales*, iv, 63, n. 1; Pitt Papers, PRO 30/8/161, fo. 238, Mount Edgecumbe to Pitt, 5 Dec. 1795; *ibid.*, PRO 30/8/141, fo. 121, Hamilton to Pitt, 26 May 1791.

2 Many independents demanded all sorts of local patronage including the lieutenancies of their respective counties without, apparently, seeing any contradiction in their applications. See Pitt Papers, PRO 30/8/170, fos. 10-11, Radnor to Pitt, 2 Oct. 1791; L. Namier, *The Structure of Politics at the Accession of George III* (London, 1957), 17.

3 Pitt Papers, PRO 30/8/174, fos. 98-9, J. Rous to Pitt, 3 Aug. 1794; *Later Correspondence*, i, no.602.

remained perfectly consistent; long before he applied for a post, he had already been a natural ally of George III.[1]

Finally, it is evident that the peerage had a code of political ethics which included several articles governing the acceptance of ministerial favours. Even the most extravagantly rapacious nobleman understood that he would open himself to public attack and ridicule if he abandoned his friends in order to secure some prize from the administration. The first marquis of Hertford was astonishingly acquisitive; all his life he sought favours for himself and his large family. The great object of his ambition was a dukedom or at the very least a marquisate, and in 1788 William Grenville was cynically confident that the earl and his sons could be brought into the government camp the moment the new peerage was offered. Grenville's prognostication was, however, inaccurate: he failed, perhaps understandably, to perceive that Hertford had scruples. Though he was no politician, the earl had served as Lord North's lord chamberlain and under the Coalition he was lord steward. Honour compelled him to resign with his colleagues after the defeat of the India Bill, and honour also prevented him from accepting the marquisate from Pitt in 1788. As long as he could not advance and at the same time maintain his ties with his old friends, he preferred to remain an earl.[2]

The king's friends were the crown's natural allies. To a greater degree than the rest of the members of the house of lords they assumed that their steady adherence to the king and his government would help to insure political stability. Stability was their overriding concern: they did not, like the whigs, believe that the executive had destroyed the constitution's balance, and they could only perceive the dangers, not the possible advantages of such reforms as Catholic emancipation. Patronage, family tradition and friendship reinforced their attachment to the crown, but it is impossible to isolate even one peer who was influenced exclusively by one of these factors. Theories which seek to explain the behaviour of the king's friends solely in terms of patronage are consequently simplistic and misleading: not one but a multiplicity of factors governed the conduct of these men, and among them conservative political principles, not patronage, was the most important.

It was the central contention of chapter 2 that a majority in the house of lords shared a coherent view of that body's constitutional

1   *The Noels and the Milbankes,* 144, 184, 208-9, 233-4, 262.
2   A. Audrey Locke, *The Seymour Family* (Boston, 1914), 278; Hertford Papers, Eg. 3262, fos. 118-9, 133-6, Hertford to Beauchamp, 30 Jan., June 1788.

responsibilities and uniformly acted to uphold their interpretation throughout the period. At the core of that majority stood the king's friends. Their conservative ideas, not their dependence on the crown, set the tone of the house. Unless we recognize the intimate connection between their conservatism and the manner in which they acted in the house, we shall fail to understand any aspect of the lords' personality.

8

CHANNELS OF INFLUENCE

Edmund Burke once wrote that without their close association with the monarch and their extensive influence in the lower house the peers' chamber would not have existed for a single year.[1] Whether soundly based or not, this statement shows at least that one keen observer did not regard the legislative function of the house of lords as a primary source of the nobility's political power. But Burke's declaration poses questions. Whence derived the close association with the monarch, the extensive influence in the lower house? To what uses were they put? How greatly did they affect the formation and implementation of public policy?

The answer to the question of derivation is land. In a landlord-tenant society members of the peerage were the greatest landlords. It was from their acres that they derived their close association with the monarch, their extensive influence in the lower house and much else besides. With land went authority, tangible and intangible. Their estates gave the lords financial independence − a necessary qualification for those who would serve as the nation's constitutional arbiters. Property and the influence derived from property also created a web of dependence which transformed the landlord into a territorial magnate and often a borough proprietor. Without his co-operation public policy could not be implemented in the countryside, and he often determined the outcome of parliamentary elections.

Armed with this authority, the peer was a force to be reckoned with. In his own country he could organize the expression of public opinion in support of or in opposition to government measures, and his influence, moral or material, on members of the lower house was immense. In his own person he could intercede directly with ministers of the crown, who naturally gave weight to the opinions of one who spoke for so many. Year in and year out the noble lord found it more effective and less troublesome to exert his influence through the channels of public opinion, direct intercession with ministers and intervention in the lower house than through the proceedings of his own chamber. It is with these informal channels of influence that this chapter will be concerned.

---

1 *The Works of the Right Honourable Edmund Burke* (London, 1855), iii, 500.

The public to which the peers occasionally appealed was not the people in general; democracy had no sympathizers among the peerage. Their public was the small political nation — gentlemen, professional and business men, freeholders. With these elements certain members of the peerage did work closely. Often they joined together to support or oppose some local project, a road, a canal or an enclosure.[1] In the mid 1780s the earl of Hopetoun, Viscount Stormont and Lord Kinnaird joined with their countrymen to protest against the iniquitous laws that restricted the production of Scottish distilleries, and in 1795 the fifth duke of Bedford encouraged his Bedfordshire neighbours to raise petitions against the Seditious Assemblies Bill.[2] Most notably the peers rallied their neighbours in support of the royal family, the government and its policies: during the 1790s, for example, noblemen initiated and passed addresses proclaiming variously the country's inalterable opposition to sedition, its willingness to bear the costs of defeating France, its joy at the marriage of the Prince of Wales and its exultation at hearing of the monarch's escape from a series of assassins.[3]

These and other fulsome testaments of the nation's loyalty were rarely spontaneous. Before raising a petition at Birmingham in support of the American war, Matthew Boulton had received considerable prodding from the second earl of Dartmouth, the lord privy seal. Members of Pitt's new administration also encouraged and assisted their noble followers in organizing the addresses that poured in from all parts of the country during the early months of 1784. In 1789, during the Regency Crisis, the attempts of opposition peers to raise their own addresses foundered for lack of popular support. On the other hand, relatively inactive noblemen, such as Lords Coventry and Fortescue, had little difficulty in uniting local opinion in support of Pitt's regency proposals.[4]

During the early phases of the crisis provoked by the French Revolu-

---

1   See the petitions presented against the Cromford Canal Bill, *LJ*, xxxviii, 443, 8 June 1789; Birmingham Canal Bill, *ibid.*, xxxix, 108, 116-7, 174, 179, 180, 190, 197, 8, 11, 12 Apr., 9, 10, 11, 16, 20 May 1791.

2   *Scots Magazine*, xlvi (1784), 551-2; *ibid.*, xlvii (1786), 95-6; *LJ*, xl, 558, 560, 10, 11 Dec. 1795. Helston, the duke of Leeds's pocket borough, also sent an opposing petition. *Ibid.*, xl, 564, 14 Dec. 1795.

3   *HMC, 13th R.*, iii, *Fortescue MSS*, ii, 282, 284; Verulam Papers, D/EV F35, fo. 280, Grimston to J. Cope, 12 Mar. 1798; *ibid.*, D/EV F27, J. Cowper to Grimston, 20 May, 1795; Percy Family Papers, 1v, fo. 262, Northumberland to Sheriff of Northumberland [no date].

4   Boulton Papers, Dartmouth to Boulton, 19 Jan. 1775. For a discussion of addresses in the 1784 crisis see above, chapter 2, 33-4. Wentworth Woodhouse MSS, F34(h)/168, J. Dixon to Fitzwilliam, 24 Dec. 1788; Derry, *The Regency Crisis*, 129; Pitt Papers, PRO 30/8/126, fo. 137, Coventry to Pitt, 17 Jan. 1789.

tion the peers again rallied the country in support of ministerial policy. Following the issuing of a royal proclamation against sedition, ministers openly solicited supporting addresses. In Cambridgeshire Charles Yorke advised his brother, the third earl of Hardwicke, to proceed slowly, following the leading property owners rather than attempting 'to lead or force them ourselves and perhaps fail, or raise another kind of spirit'. Nevertheless, as soon as a county meeting was scheduled, Yorke advised the earl to settle in advance the course of procedure as a means of stifling any opposition. A meeting called for the same purposes in Buckinghamshire was permitted even less scope for spontaneous action. All arrangements, including the preparation of the address, were overseen by the marquis of Buckingham in conjunction with his brother, Lord Grenville. The latter not only suggested ways in which the proposed address should be improved and eventually carried; he even advised that Lord Loughborough, in whose judicial circuit Buckinghamshire fell, might 'prepare the way for it by his charge'[1]

Appeals to popular opinion were weapons which peers could use to good effect on some occasions. In support of a local grievance that did not infringe on political alignments such action could remedy genuine inequities.[2] However cynically we may regard some of the loyal addresses, they too had important consequences in certain instances: those raised to support Pitt in 1784 helped to bring him into power as well as office, and during the Regency Crisis in 1788-9 the government used similar manifestations of public adherence to counteract the negative impact of the defections within the ranks of its parliamentary supporters.[3] But the Bedfordshire petitions against the Seditious Assemblies Bill, although a tribute to the territorial influence and moderate radicalism of the duke of Bedford, did not prevent the passage of the bill. 'Formed opposition', especially if expressing itself through public opinion, was neither natural nor congenial to the peers of the realm[4]

Direct intercession with the king's ministers was an essentially confidential procedure. In 1798 and 1799 the marquis of Buckingham

1 Hardwicke Papers, Add. MS 35392, fos. 236-8, C. Yorke to Hardwicke, 24, 26 June 1792; *HMC, 13th R.*, iii, *Fortescue MSS*, ii, 282, 284; *Courts and Cabinets*, ii, 211-2.

2 The grievances of the Scottish distillers were somewhat assuaged by the Distillery Act of 1785 (25 Geo. III, c. 22).

3 J. Cannon, *The Coalition*, 185-9; Derry, *The Regency Crisis*, 127-32.

4 At most, the whigs were able to introduce a few modifications into this bill. See *PH*, xxxii, 257-8, 11 Nov. 1795; Grafton Papers, 423/734, Lauderdale to Grafton, 12 Nov. 1795.

relied on a series of letters to convince his brother that the militia's flank corps should not be placed under the command of regular army officers. He could not bear, he confessed, 'the thoughts of being forced. . .into discussions in Parliament which must be highly dangerous. . .' Similarly, after noting that Pitt did not like his friends to propose alterations to government bills unless 'in some manner suggested by himself', the earl of Exeter appealed to a friend to secure the minister's approval of an amendment which he wished to make in a window tax bill.[1] By means of a letter or a short conversation with a friend in the government these and other peers hoped to settle disputes without having publicly to criticize their political leaders.

Direct intercession with ministers was also the most efficient means of offering advice. The duke of Richmond, who considered his criticisms of Lord Hobart's militia bills to be evidence of his friendship, was able to be far more detailed and precise in a letter than he was on the floor of the house. Moreover, if his case was sufficiently persuasive, he might convince the ministers to alter their plans without ever budging from Goodwood where he usually had innumerable pressing matters to attend to.[2]

To measure the effect of the nobility's direct appeals, we shall briefly examine some of their efforts to shape the government's militia policies. After 1793 there was a substantial amount of militia legislation in which many peers took an interest: seventy-seven were either lords lieutenant, colonels of the militia or both, and many others were deputy lieutenants or officers in the volunteer corps. Experience enabled most of these men to become reasonably competent in their posts,[3] but they also came to share certain prejudices. Both these characteristics left their imprint on the militia, primarily because the government found that it could not implement its policies without the approval and support of these men.[4]

Lord Grenville claimed on one occasion that the principal advantages to be gained from the periodic meetings which ministers held with the lieutenants and militia colonels were the rallying of support for new

1 *HMC, 13th R.*, iii, *Fortescue MSS*, iv, 177-8; Pitt Papers, PRO 30/8/121, fos. 130-1, Exeter to Carysfort, 3 Apr. 1798.

2 Buckinghamshire Papers, D/MH I 13, Richmond to Hobart, 26 July 1801; Chichester Papers, Add. MS 33111, fos. 277-8, Richmond to Pelham, 17 July 1803.

3 J. W. Fortescue, *The County Lieutenancies and the Army, 1803-14* (London, 1909), 35.

4 Western, *The English Militia*, 225-9.

measures and the arrangement of details. Certainly it was in this last respect that individual peers made their most remarkable contribution. In some instances the noble lords' criticisms were narrowly interested. Lord Rous, himself an officer in the volunteers, petitioned Pitt to include a clause in a pending gamekeepers bill that would exempt from its strictures all those men already enrolled in volunteer companies.[1] More often, however, the peers' suggestions reflect a detailed knowledge of the problems involved in organizing such forces and a genuine concern for their well-being.

Militia officers complained again and again that responsible ministers framed their military policies without being properly informed of varying local conditions. 'Why', asked the duke of Buccleuch, 'will not the Ministers consult with those, who know something of Scotland?' Sir Charles Grey's plans for the defense of the southern counties against a possible invading army provoked a more stinging attack from Lord Sheffield: 'a more compleat example of ignorance of the County & of the absence of common sense & common abilities, cannot be conceived'.[2]

To improve measures proposed by such poorly informed men the peers forwarded their own highly detailed suggestions. The marquis of Buckingham hoped in 1796 that keepers of royal forests and parks would be included in the bill to enrol gamekeepers into special companies of sharpshooters. Two months later he recommended several additions to the Supplementary Militia Bill, including the appointment of a clerk to pay the troops, the introduction of a requirement that one-third of the serjeants be locally resident and the creation of a more equal system of levies. In 1803 the duke of Richmond proposed that lords lieutenant be empowered to appoint deputies who could act in their stead in case of temporary incapacity, and the duke of Montrose submitted some very sensible recommendations on how the government might go about raising a militia in Scotland with greater success.[3]

1 *Courts and Cabinets*, ii, 255-6. Lord Cornwallis, as perhaps befitted a soldier, tolerated less dissent. In 1795 he told Windham that the colonels had been assembled and told they must supply an efficient force to build up the corps of artillery. *Cornwallis Correspondence*, ii, 290; Pitt Papers, PRO 30/8/174, fos. 115-6, Rous to Pitt, 26 Nov. 1796.

2 Liverpool Papers, Add. MS 38237, fos. 121-2, Buccleuch to R. Dundas, 28 Aug. [1807]; Buckinghamshire Papers, D/MH I 18, Sheffield to Hobart, 2 Aug. 1801. See also Grenville Papers, Add. MS 41851, fos. 81-2, Buckingham to T. Grenville, 11 Mar. 1798.

3 Pitt Papers, PRO 30/8/117, fos. 94, 108-9, Buckingham to Pitt, 30 Oct. 1796, 23 Dec. [1796]; Buckinghamshire Papers, D/MH I 96, Richmond to Hobart, 27 June 1803; Pitt Papers, PRO 30/8/160, fos. 269-70, Montrose to Pitt, 15 Dec. 1794.

Through their direct intercessions these and other peers also hoped to correct the more glaring errors in pending legislation. Buckingham found Dundas's Yeomanry Bill of 1798 in sore need of tidying: the allowances for the yeomen were inadequate as presently established, and the period during which recruits were to be exempted from the horse tax would have to be extended. If Pitt wished to frame truly effective legislation, Buckingham added, he should consult with the earls of Dorchester and Winchelsea, men who had extensive experience with yeomanry companies.[1]

In 1804 Lord Dynevor pointed out an especially serious flaw in the government's Volunteer Bill. According to one clause in that measure farmers were permitted to receive compensation from their own labourers for the time the latter had lost while attending drill sessions. This compensation, Dynevor claimed, would take most of the pay that the troops received for their military service, and he expected that many would withdraw from their regiments rather than make such payments.[2]

Often the nobility's suggestions were incorporated into the pertinent legislation, and the errors which they noted were corrected. A harried Dundas told Lord Buckingham that those parts of the Militia Bill of 1799 'which Your Lordship and Lord Powis particularly adverted to, as admitting the intrigues of Recruiting officers into the quarters of your Regiment, are omitted in the state into which it is now amended'. On Dynevor's letter, cited above, there is a note indicating that his complaint would be 'attended to in the H. of Lords'. During preliminary discussions on the Militia Bill of 1795 the earls of Darlington and Poulett expressed concern that the measure as drafted would deprive them of full control over the management and staffing of any fencible companies which they might raise: within three weeks, however, Darlington was supporting the bill, for in the meantime a clause had been introduced guaranteeing to the colonels full power over these regiments. Again in 1796, when Pitt proposed to treble the size of the militia, various commanders including Lords Hertford, Radnor, Berkeley and Fortescue bluntly informed the minister that his plan was 'impracticable'. Then, according to Charles Yorke, they made changes which they believed were necessary to insure the bill's operational efficiency.[3]

1 *Ibid.*, PRO 30/8/117, fos. 126-8, Buckingham to Pitt, 15, 16 Apr. 1798.
2 Liverpool Papers, Add. MS 38240, fos. 266-7, Dynevor to C. Yorke, 24 Mar. 1804.
3 Home Office Papers, HO 50/30, Dundas to Buckingham, 25 June 1799 (copy); Pitt Papers, PRO 30/8/168, fo. 250, Poulett to Pitt, 24 Apr. 1795; *ibid.*, PRO 30/8/128, fo. 140, Darlington to Pitt, 10 May 1795; Hardwicke Papers, Add.

The more active and enthusiastic officers did not, of course, always restrict themselves to commenting upon the details of government proposals. In the fall of 1796 Buckingham anxiously wrote to his brother Tom to inquire whether the final plan for the augmentation of the militia had been devised: 'I shall expect it very impatiently', he added, '& the more so because I have a plan which I only keep back from the D of York least it should militate as far as it goes with theirs'.[1] Individuals did in some instances exercise a decisive influence in shaping the general form as well as the details of military policy, but normally even the determined marquis of Buckingham was unable singlehandedly to make the war office revise the basic principles of its plans.[2] Such triumphs required the united, concerted action of a substantial body of militia officers.

Confronted with the possibility of a French invasion early in 1798, the duke of York ordered that the militia's elite flank companies should in the future be commanded by regular army officers. Though a number of lieutenants and colonels at once acquiesced to this proposal, Dundas told Lord Grenville that the latter's brother along with Lord Berkeley and other militia officers questioned its legality.[3]

Its opponents believed, in fact, that the plan struck at the very heart of the militia system. According to Buckingham the militia was founded 'upon the principle of preserving the local connexion between the officers & the men'. Gentlemen entered the service, not out of professional ambition, but to become 'Members of a Provincial Society composed of their friends and their connexions, even with the Soldiers as far as is proper, and are encouraged to a perseverance in the same routine of Duty by a Spirit of Emulation and County rivalry from which the Service ultimately reaps advantage'. The introduction of regular army officers would not only stifle this healthy competition; many gentlemen would probably resign their commissions because of the new procedure.[4]

MS 35393, fos. 3-4, C. Yorke to Harkwicke, 15 Oct. 1796; Western, *The English Militia*, 221.

1 Grenville Papers, Add. MS 42058, fos. 36-7, Buckingham to Grenville, 17 Sept. (1796).

2 Buckinghamshire Papers, D/MH I 121, Eldon to Hobart [no date].

3 Home Office Papers, HO 50/30, 'Resolutions of a Meeting at the Thatched House Tavern', 23 Apr. 1798; *HMC, 13th R.*, iii, *Fortescue MSS*, iv, 169-70.

4 Grenville Papers, Add. MS 41851, fos. 81-2, Buckingham to T. Grenville, 11 Mar. 1798; HO 50/30, Buckingham to Lt. Col. Hope, 22 Mar. 1798; Fitzwilliam Papers, Box 54, J. Savile Foljambe to Fitzwilliam, 2 Oct. 1798. Buckingham proposed to assign one of his companies under its major to the army's service. The plan was rejected for reasons which Cornwallis explained to a friend.

Faced with the prospect of mass resignations or worse, an outright refusal to obey orders, the government temporized. An appeal to parliament on this issue was impossibly dangerous as Dundas made clear to Grenville.

> You are well aware of the disagreeable state in which Government is placed by any measure in Parliament relative to the militia, when perhaps the one half of the respectable officers would hold one language, and the other half an opposite language, tending to inspire doubts in the minds of the militia privates that the faith of the land was not kept to them.

The best that Dundas could hope for was that the opponents would respect the judgment of the law officers in favour of the plan's legality.[1]

Even this tepid optimism was misplaced. By the fall of 1798 defenders of the militia's purity had organized themselves into a committee, presided over by Earl Fitzwilliam. At a meeting at the Thatched House Tavern on 15 December, the colonels instructed Fitzwilliam to inform the duke of York that they regarded the separation of the flank companies as being inconsistent with the principles on which the militia rested. Some were later disheartened when the duke ignored this missive, but the enthusiasts remained adamant: Lord Radnor pressed eagerly for an appeal to parliament and a fuller judgment from the law officers, and the earl of Carnarvon, who feared that this invidious project only marked the first step in the duke's campaign to reform the militia according to his Germanic tastes, urged Fitzwilliam to mobilize the whole body of militia officers.[2]

This last dramatic gesture proved to be unnecessary. Throughout the early months of 1799 belligerent declarations from the Horse Guards and the reiterated opinions of the law officers only provoked more negative resolutions from the Thatched House officers, who were seemingly immune to all reason. The government, in fact, had been checkmated. After a series of meetings with Dundas in early April, Carnarvon triumphantly reported that the enemy was on the retreat. Although the duke of York insisted that the army proceed with the

---

'If Lord B had been the only wrongheaded, absurd, Colonel of the Militia, I think the Duke [of York] might have consented, but as the brotherhood are numerous, he was right to check these follies in the bud'. *HMC, 13th R.*, iii, *Fortescue MSS*, iv, 179-81; *Cornwallis Correspondence*, ii, 332.

1 *HMC, 13th R.*, iii, *Fortescue MSS*, iv, 169-70; Home Office Papers, HO 50/30, J. Scott and J. Mitford to Dundas, 6 Apr. 1798.

2 *Ibid.*, HO 50/30, 'Resolutions of a Meeting at the Thatched House Tavern', 15 Dec. 1798; Fitzwilliam Papers, Box 54, Downe to Fitzwilliam, 23 Dec. 1798; *ibid.*, Box 55, Radnor to Fitzwilliam, 8, 10 Jan. 1799; *ibid.*, Box 55, Carnarvon to Fitzwilliam, 9, 11 Jan., 1 Feb. 1799.

plan, the war office was fully aware that many militia officers would refuse to co-operate with any expansion of the army's control over their regiments. Thus, on 22 June 1799, Dundas announced to Fitzwilliam and his allies that he would recommend that the flank companies rejoin their respective militia regiments. Without ever raising this issue directly in parliament, the outraged portion of the militia officers were thus able to force basic changes in war office policies.[1]

Because eighteenth-century government relied upon the co-operation of major landowners to implement and uphold their measures, the latter were bound to have a voice in formulating policy. Some of their advice was ridiculous. Much reflected the interests and prejudices of the correspondents. Yet, much legislation was also improved as a result of the nobility's interventions. By means of their intercessions ministers, who otherwise might have remained ignorant, gained valuable insights into local conditions. The peers' willingness to carry the concerns of their neighbours to Westminster and to communicate to the ministers the results of their own experiences as managers of estates and leaders of local government undoubtedly helped to accommodate the process of legislation to divergent communities and interests.

The most concrete manifestation of the power which the nobility derived from its vast properties was the ability to determine the outcome of an ever greater number of parliamentary contests. Fifty-six of them nominated or exercised a decisive influence in securing the return of 115 MPs at the general election of 1780, and four years later sixty returned 127 members from English, Welsh and Scottish boroughs.[2] Oldfield, who analysed the interests in each borough following the elections of 1790 and 1796, assigned an even larger degree of weight to aristocratic patrons. According to his calculations eighty peers nominated or influenced the return of 167 MPs from British boroughs in 1790, and at the next election eighty-six chose 181 MPs

---

1 Home Office Papers, HO 50/30, Dundas to Fitzwilliam, 26 Mar. 1799; Fitzwilliam Papers, Box 55, Carnarvon to Fitzwilliam, 2 Apr. 1799; Home Office Papers, HO 50/30, Duke of York to Dundas, 10 May 1799; Fitzwilliam Papers, Box 56, Dundas to Fitzwilliam et al., 22 June 1799. The Militia Act of 1799 (39 George III, c. 1) reduced the size of the militia and encouraged the disembodied troops to enlist in the regular army. It infuriated such diehards as Fitzwilliam, Carnarvon, Berkeley or Radnor, but was accepted by the vast majority of militia commanders. Western, The English Militia, 236.

2 Figures for 1780 and 1784 are based on the histories of county and borough constituencies in History of Parliament: The House of Commons, 1754-1790, ed. Sir L. Namier and J. Brooke (London, 1964), i. For a list of these peers and their respective borough interests, see Appendix D.

from these seats.[1] Nor was the nobility's electoral influence confined to the boroughs. Though no peer absolutely controlled the return of a county member, twenty-three of the members sitting for an English, Welsh or Scottish county in 1780 and twenty-eight of these MPs in 1784 owed their selection primarily to the local territorial interest of a particular noble magnate.[2]

The growth in the size of the peerage during this period accounts in part for its expanding influence over electoral politics. Twenty of the peers created between 1784 and 1801 controlled a total of forty-one seats.[3] In fact, a peerage was small recompense for the advantages a minister derived from a borough magnate's support. During the unsettled months of 1784 Pitt elevated five borough patrons to the upper house:[4] two of these, Sir James Lowther and Edward Eliot, controlled between them eleven borough and three county seats.

However, several peers of more ancient standing were assiduously expanding their interests during this period. Within three or four years the first marquis of Buckingham inherited one seat at St Mawes, purchased another there and began to establish his control over a third in the venal borough of Aylesbury.[5] In 1780 the electors of Helston rebelled against their patron, Lord Carmarthen, who later became fifth duke of Leeds: yet, by 1786 Carmarthen had regained sufficient influence to elect one member, and Oldfield claims that he returned both members in 1790 and 1796.[6] The most spectacular accomplishments, however, belong to the eleventh duke of Norfolk. His father took no part in electoral politics, but the son, as Lord Surrey, returned three members in 1784 in addition to securing his own election at Carlisle. Six years later Oldfield estimated that Norfolk controlled five seats, and in 1796 his interest had grown to nine.[7]

Noble interests were important in the first place because they provided ministers and, to a lesser extent, opposition leaders with the means of returning important supporters to parliament. Throughout our period the government influence over boroughs which it had once

1 The results of Oldfield's analyses are concisely presented in *English Historical Documents, 1783-1832*, ed. A. Aspinall and E. A. Smith (New York, 1959), xi, 224-36.

2 See Appendix E.

3 See Appendix F.

4 In addition to Lowther and Eliot, Lord Bulkeley, Sir J. Cocks and Thomas Pitt received English peerages.

5 *History of Parliament*, i, 215, 239; *English Historical Documents*, xi, 225.

6 *Ibid.*, xi, 224.

7 *History of Parliament*, ii, 645; *English Historical Documents*, xi, 225.

controlled was declining, and Pitt understandably leapt at the opportunity of returning useful friends when vacancies occurred in the seats of his noble allies.[1] Many of the law officers in these years, including Pepper Arden, Erskine, Kenyon, Archibald Macdonald, John Mitford and Scott sat for a nobleman's pocket borough as did such leading men of business as Eden, Mornington, Mulgrave, Rose and Steele. Opposition leaders always had fewer seats at their disposal, but by the late 1780s they had established a fund to aid the candidacies of their less affluent supporters.[2]

Important as their lordships' ability to return able men to parliament was, the political influence which they exercised through their members in the house of commons was of still greater significance. Most peers chose the candidates to fill their seats and paid at least a portion of the election expenses. Many endeavoured to control the parliamentary conduct of their nominees. But the relationship between patrons and their members varied widely. Before defining the extent of the nobility's influence in the lower house, we must, therefore, establish the degree to which peers controlled the conduct of men they returned to parliament.

Many of these MPs claimed for themselves considerable political independence. Before standing for election some candidates demanded that patrons guarantee their right to pursue an independent line in the house.[3] More troublesome were those members who discovered once they reached Westminster that they could improve their personal prospects by transferring their allegiance to another political faction. Lord Bulkeley only avoided such a breach with his member, John Parry, by using his own influence to secure for the latter a Welsh judgeship. The less fortunate Earl Spencer had no choice, on the other hand, but to accept the defection of Humphrey Minchin, a member who transferred his support to Pitt because his main object in parliament was to get things done for his family.[4]

---

[1] *History of Parliament*, i, 55-6; Pares, *George III and the Politicians*, 196-8; *HMC, 13th R.*, vii, *Lonsdale MSS*, 152. Many peers offered their seats to ministers without demanding any recompense. See Pitt Papers, PRO 30/8/123, fo. 176, Clinton to Pitt, 17 June 1795; *ibid.*, PRO 30/8/112, fo. 213, Beaufort to Pitt, 11 Mar. 1796; *ibid.*, PRO 30/8/173, fo. 86, Rolle to Pitt, 15 Oct. 1799.

[2] *Whig Organization*, ed. D. Ginter, xxx-i; Wentworth Woodhouse MSS, F 115 (a)/7, Derby to Fitzwilliam, 18 July 1789; *ibid.*, F 115(a)/64, Devonshire to Fitzwilliam, 11 June; *ibid.*, F 115(a)/65, Lord R. Spencer to Fitzwilliam, 2 Aug.

[3] Twiss, *Eldon*, i, 144-5; *HMC, 14th R.*, iv, *Kenyon MSS*, 516; *Colchester Diaries*, i, 130.

[4] *Courts and Cabinets*, i, 360-3; Pitt Papers, PRO 30/8/117, fo. 183, Bulkeley to Pitt, 28 Apr. 1788; Spencer Papers, Box 5, H. Minchin to Spencer, 9 Dec. 1787; *ibid.*, Box 5, Spencer to Minchin (copy).

Even the most cordial partnerships were occasionally disrupted during severe political upheavals. In such circumstances a few MPs chose to resign their seats.[1] Others stayed away from the house temporarily in order to avoid a public breach with their patrons.[2] Most, however, continued in the course they had chosen, acknowledging at the same time that they would not be returned by the same patron at a subsequent election.[3]

A range of considerations bound members to their patron. For a man like James Hare, who sought a seat only to escape arrest for debt, the duke of Devonshire was the only one of his constituents who mattered.[4] A number of members were the political disciples of those who gave them their seats. One such person, Dr French Laurence, Lord Fitzwilliam's member for Peterborough, told the earl:

> your opinion upon all subjects — I speak most sincerely from the very bottom of my heart — is so correct, wise, & upright, that I should be very inattentive to my own benefit & improvement, independently of every feeling of gratitude, if I were not desirous of consulting it whenever I have an opportunity. Indeed your Lordship cannot confer upon me so great a favour, as by doing me the honour of communicating your sentiments in the fullest manner as the occasions arise.

However obsequious Laurence's language may seem, he was sincere; when Pitt offered him a post, he declined because he knew how much Fitzwilliam disapproved of that minister.[5]

Other members were parts of family rather than political machines. Because their object in maintaining a parliamentary interest was to advance the prosperity of their respective families, Lords Hardwicke and Hertford demanded absolute loyalty from their members.[6] The second earl of Radnor dispatched to his son, Lord Folkestone, lengthy advice on every possible topic. Folkestone was apparently amendable to parental prodding: Lord Herbert, on the other hand, found his position painfully constricting.

I have lately discovered what has long been known, that in this

1 Pitt Papers, PRO 30/8/152, fos. 157-8, Hawkesbury to Pitt, 10 Dec. 1788.

2 Fitzwilliam Papers, Box 46, W. Milner to Fitzwilliam, 25 Sept., 18 Nov. 1794; Dacres Adam Papers, PRO 30/58/4, Lord C. Lennox to Pitt, 7 June 1802.

3 *History of Parliament*, ii, 409; *HMC, 14th R.*, i, *Rutland MSS*, iii, 68.

4 *History of Parliament*, ii, 585.

5 Fitzwilliam Papers, Box 50, Dr French Laurence to Fitzwilliam, 17 Dec. 1796; *ibid.*, Box 54, Fitzwilliam to Laurence, 24 Sept. 1798. See also *ibid.*, Box 48, Lord Milton to Fitzwilliam, 7 Apr. 1795.

6 Hardwicke Papers, Add. MS 35381, fo. 240, Hardwicke to P. Yorke, 3 Feb. 1784; Hertford Papers, Eg. 3260, fos. 104-6, Hertford to Lord R. Seymour Conway [no date].

blessed country nobody sits on principle, being all biassed by connexions, either friendly or family interest etc. For my part I have been on three divisions in the House and out of those three times have only voted once according to my opinions, and did that *en cachet* for fear my *family connexions* should get hold of it. And after all this the world are pleased to call me a free Englishman and a member of a free Parliament.[1]

The steady adherence which the Herbert family demanded of its eldest son was no more than what many patrons expected from their clients in the house of commons. According to these men the borough proprietor had a right to set the line of political conduct for the partnership. The most notorious of this breed of patron was the first earl of Lonsdale, a disagreeable martinet who expected his 'ninepins' to respond even to the most contradictory orders. Yet other peers were equally, if less spectacularly highhanded. Lord Buckingham informed Sir Alexander Hood that in case they should differ on public questions, '. . .I am persuaded that the same fair & honourable impulse which has hitherto guided you would induce you to surrender your seat. . .'[2] The second duke of Newcastle forced Charles Mellish, a supporter of the Coalition, to retire early in 1784, and in the subsequent parliament at least four MPs resigned because of irreconcilable differences with their patrons.[3]

Most borough proprietors were less dictatorial. They endeavoured to return MPs who shared their political sentiments; as the duke of Leeds told Charles Abbot, there was little sense in going to the trouble and expense of nominating a member if he then took an entirely different line in the house of commons. They never hesitated to advise their clients, telling them when to attend, how to vote and even offering their services to ministers at debates.[4] Moreover, other peers as well

---

1 Radnor Papers, D/EPb 028, 6, 10, Radnor to Folkestone, 24 Apr. 1801, 21 Apr. 1804; *History of Parliament*, ii, 611.

2 Sir William Lowther apologized to Pitt for voting against the government on the regency but said that his patron left him no choice. Pitt Papers, PRO 30/8/153, fo. 146, Lowther to Pitt, 19 Jan. 1789; Bridport Papers, Add. MS 35202, fos. 154-5, Buckingham to Hood, 6 Dec. (1790).

3 Those who resigned because of disagreements with their patrons were: R. Cunninghame, East Grinstead, E. Leeds, Reigate, C. Rainsford, Bere Alston and G. Rose, Launceston. See Hardwicke Papers, Add. MS 35382, fos. 103-4, Hardwicke to P. Yorke, 29 May 1784.

4 *Colchester Diaries*, i, 127; Leeds Papers, Add. MS 28060, fo. 56, Northumberland to Carmarthen, 1 Jan. 1784; Sydney Papers, Box I, Ailesbury to Sydney, 5 Feb. [1784]; Granville Papers, PRO 30/29/6/4, fo. 530, Duchess of Beaufort to G. Leveson Gower, 29 Dec. 1806; Olson, *The Radical Duke*, 222-4; *HMC*, *13th R.*, iii, *Fortescue MSS*, iii, 402, 403-4; Ailesbury Papers, E. Hyde to Ailesbury, 25 June 1792; *Minto Papers*, iii, 318-9; Fitzwilliam Papers, Box 50, Laurence to Fitzwilliam, 31 Dec. 1796; Pitt Papers, PRO 30/8/122, fo. 48, Chandos to Pitt, 30 Apr. 1787.

as politicians and royalty assumed these members were politely abject: again and again patrons were asked to instruct their MPs to attend and vote for specific bills or motions![1]

Nevertheless, this type of patron tolerated some independence. Leeds and Abbot differed publicly on a tax bill. Lord Camelford, the proprietor of Old Sarum, protested that it was a 'whimsical thing' for a member of that most rotten of boroughs to vote for Pitt's reform bill in 1785. Yet, neither lord attempted to remove his misguided member. Even when their differences occurred on the most fundamental issues, these patrons refrained from replacing obstreperous members. Some claimed to respect an MP's right to form his own opinions. Most disliked replacing a man before a parliament had run its course: special elections were expensive and troublesome, and peers who summarily dismissed independent members often received considerable criticism.[2]

There was finally a small group of peers which surrendered all influence over their nominees. Patrons who put their interests at the disposal of their political leaders forfeited their right to direct the conduct of the members returned from their boroughs. Ministers or their opposition counterparts selected the suitable candidates, who usually paid their own expenses. Some patrons, in fact, sold their seats, collecting as much as £3,000 apiece after 1780.[3] Having paid over his money, the new member was free to vote as he wished or as his political leaders instructed him.[4]

A few other patrons found the management of their boroughs to be an annoying, tiresome burden. One of these, Lord Cornwallis, told his brother 'never look to my conduct in the political line, but act entirely

1 *HMC, 15th R.,* vii, *Ailesbury MSS,* 280; *Correspondence of the Prince of Wales,* i, no. 215; Granville Papers, PRO 30/29/5/4, fos. 793-4, Countess of Sutherland to Marchioness of Stafford, Saturday; Campbell, *Lord Chancellors,* vi, 386.

2 *Colchester Diaries,* i, 124-31; *History of Parliament,* iii, 587; Spencer Papers, Box 5, Spencer to H. Minchin (copy); *History of Parliament,* iii, 129.

3 John Robinson arranged the purchase of seats at the election of 1784. *The Parliamentary Papers of John Robinson, 1774-84,* ed. W. R. Laprade (London, 1922), 107-8, 128. Among those whig peers to sell their seats was the earl of Cholmondeley. See Holland House Papers, Add. MS 51584, fo. 20, Tierney to Holland, Saturday, 1802; *ibid.,* Add. MS 51823, fo. 124, Cholmondeley to Holland, 16 Oct. 1806.

4 At the general election of 1780 Edward Eliot returned four members on the recommendation of Lord Rockingham. Despite the fact that Eliot supported Pitt after December 1783, those members remained in opposition and were replaced at the subsequent general election. *History of Parliament,* ii, 389. On the other hand, the duke of Newcastle. a supporter of Pitt's government, sold one of his seats at Boroughbridge to Lord Palmerston. a coalitionist, who continued to oppose the government for the duration of the 1784 parliament. *Ibid.,* iii, 520.

for yourself, and consider yourself, as you really are, as independent as any member in the House of Commons'. Other magnates, such as the third duke of Marlborough, cared little about politics and were not sufficiently forceful to impose a line of conduct on their members.[1]

After acknowledging the uniqueness of each relationship between a peer and his members, it remains true that even relatively independent members took care to maintain harmonious relations with their patrons. The figures embodied in Table IV demonstrate that the overwhelming majority of MPs voted with their patrons on three of the most crucial

TABLE IV

Voting Patterns of MPs
Returned by the Nobility

	Peace Prelims. 13 Feb. 1783	2nd Reading India Bill, 27 Nov. 1783	Motion on Regency, 16 Dec. 1788
	%	%	%
MPs voting like their patrons	66	67	88
MPs voting on opposite sides from their patrons	9	10	9
Unsure	25	23	3

Note: The large number of members classified as unsure in the first two divisions is the result of two factors: first, there is no list of the peers' division on the peace preliminaries, and second, some of the lords who favoured the India Bill on 27 November changed their minds by mid-December. Their opinions were in flux, and it is consequently impossible to tell where many stood before the first division in the house of lords on 15 December.

---

1 *HMC, Various Collections,* vi, *Cornwallis Wykeham-Martin MSS,* 333; Mann (Cornwallis) Papers, U24/C4, Cornwallis to J. Cornwallis, 27 Sept. 1804. Marlborough told William Eden in 1785 that 'I certainly can not desire you to act in Parl[t] inconsistently with your former Conduct' even though he hoped the latter would support Pitt. In 1789 the duke refused to ask his members to vote for the repeal of a bill which they had previously supported. Auckland Papers, Add. MS 34419, fo. 459, Marlborough to Eden, 12 Jan. 1785; *ibid.,* Add. MS 34452, fo. 427, Marlborough to Auckland, 5 May.

divisions of the 1780's. Moreover, the results presented in this table only vary marginally when the relationships 'between peers and their MPs are analysed over a longer period. Using Stockdale's list of MPs and our own analysis of the peerage's political affiliations, we find that seventy percent of the peers' members stood by them during the early months of 1784 and that fifteen percent took opposing positions.[1] Similarly, during the Regency Crisis seventy-seven percent of the MPs in this category voted on the same side as their noble mentors, and twelve percent differed from them.[2]

Among the most loyal of these MPs was Daniel Pulteney who told his patron, the duke of Rutland, that he was invariably ready 'to execute all the minor business your Grace will direct me to do'. Rutland was only one of many patrons who gained surrogates in the lower house. French Laurence, Fitzwilliam's member for Peterborough, communicated regularly with the earl about the progress of a bill relating to the government of that town and solicited his advice on how to proceed with it. Similarly, Thomas Bucknall, Lord Grimston's member for St Albans, urged his patron to inform him immediately 'should there be any Clause you would wish to introduce, for regulating, or to inforce the intended alterations, in the Poor Laws; and let me know the respective Clauses, I will do my best to bring them before the Committee'.[3]

It was seen in chapter 5 that Grimston, Ailesbury and innumerable other peers called upon friends and dependents in order to insure the passage of private and local bills in which they were interested.[4] Similar tactics were used to pass or defeat certain public bills. When his neighbours in the West Riding protested against a bill which would have permitted the export of raw wool, Earl Fitzwilliam not only mobilized his own members against it; he used his influence with Portland and Fox to commit the whig party against the measure as well.[5]

---

1 Stockdale, *Parliamentary Debates*, i, Appendix 1-15. In this list Stockdale catagorized members according to their political affiliations just prior to the general election.

2 The peers' sentiments on the regency question can be ascertained from the division on 26 Dec. 1788 and the protest of 23 Jan. 1789. *PH*, xxvii, 890-1; *LJ*, xxxviii, 339-40. Debrett has a list of 'the majority and minority on the questions respecting the Regency'. *Parl. Reg.*, xxv, 289-96.

3 *History of Parliament*, iii, 337-9; Fitzwilliam Papers, Box 50, Laurence to Fitzwilliam, 9 Dec. 1796; Verulam Papers, D/EV F28, T. Bucknall to Grimston, 23 Jan. 1797.

4 See above chapter 5.

5 Fitzwilliam Papers, Box 38, Pemberton Milnes to Fitzwilliam, 9 Nov. 1786; *ibid.*, Box 38, Portland to Fitzwilliam, 3 Feb. 1787.

At major political confrontations the impact of the individual patron's interest varied according to the closeness of the division. During the early phases of the regency crisis both Pitt and the Prince of Wales courted the powerful earl of Lonsdale. Yet, when the first division on that question took place, the fact that Lonsdale's members had transferred their support to the opposition was of relatively little importance; Pitt's majority, even without the 'ninepins', was overwhelming. On the other hand, the results of especially close divisions, such as that on Shelburne's peace preliminaries, did depend on the conduct of men like the earl of Sandwich who controlled eleven or twelve votes.[1]

However, it was as a body, not as individuals, that the nobility made its most substantial impact on the commons' character and proceedings. In the first place the peers' MPs reinforced the conservatism of the lower house. Many peers had been distressed, even appalled by Pitt's seemingly rash determination to proceed with his measure of parliamentary reform in 1785.[2] Suspecting their patrons' unease, some MPs requested instructions on how to proceed, and others received emphatic, if unsolicited advice.[3] In the end MPs sitting for nobly controlled boroughs deserted Pitt in droves. A minister who could normally count upon the support of eighty, even ninety such members saw his following halved on this occasion: only forty-three of the 127 such members voted with Pitt, and six of these sat for seats dominated by whig patrons.[4]

A second consequence of the nobility's extensive electoral interests was a strengthening of the government's political position in the house of commons. In general noble borough proprietors supported the king's government. Of the sixty who returned MPs at the election of 1784 only seventeen, controlling thirty borough seats, opposed Pitt.

1 *HMC, 13th R.,* vii, *Lonsdale MSS,* 141-3; I. R. Christie, *The End of Lord North's Ministry, 1780-82* (London, 1958), 203-6. Since the peace preliminaries were only lost by sixteen votes (224-208) large interests such as Sandwich's were extremely important in this instance.

2 Hardwicke Papers, Add. MS 35623, fo. 265, Northumberland to Hardwicke, 2 Apr. [1785].

3 *HMC, 14th R.,* i, *Rutland MSS,* iii, 97, 169; Hardwicke Papers, Add. MS 35382, fos. 266-7, 312-3, Hardwicke to P. Yorke, 2 Feb., 27 Mar. 1785; Auckland Papers, Add. MS 34419, fo. 459, Marlborough to Eden, 12 Jan. 1785. One of Lord Fitzwilliam's members, P. Heywood, wrote in 1789 to inquire whether his patron would support another controversial reform, the repeal of the Test Act as it applied to dissenters. Fitzwilliam Papers, Box 40, Heywood to Fitzwilliam, 31 Oct. 1789.

4 Burgoyne (Derby), H. Cecil (Exeter), P. Clerke (Bolton), R. Fitzpatrick (Bedford), J. Hare (Devonshire) and W. Sloper (Spencer). Two of Lord Lansdowne's members, Barré and Mahon, also supported Pitt.

Pitt's creations and the political realignment produced as a result of the French Revolution weighted the balance even more heavily in the government's favour. Each of the fifteen men with borough interests who was ennobled between 1790 and 1801 initially supported Pitt, and only two — Dundas and Yarborough — publicly opposed the policies of his first government after receiving their peerages.[1] Moreover, eleven of the seventeen whigs who had returned MPs for boroughs in 1784 transferred their allegiance to Pitt by 1794, and in the meantime Fox only gained three new noble borough mongers — Grafton, Lansdowne and Norfolk.[2]

Like their patrons the great body of MPs within this group supported the king's administration. On 27 November 1783, they divided 55-34 in support of the Coalition's India Bill. Yet, within four months the majority were adherents of Pitt's new administration: according to Stockdale's calculations sixty-four supported the new administration, fifty-one opposed it. Four years later their adherence to Pitt's government was even more decisively expressed. On 16 December 1788, they upheld the ministry's plan for a regency by a margin of 80-39.

MPs returned by members of the peerage were, in fact, more attached to the government than the house of commons as a whole. While the majority of the lower house stood by Fox during the early months of 1784, the peers' members, as we shall see, gradually moved into Pitt's camp. On 16 December 1788, 268 MPs (56.7% of those voting) supported the government; the nobility's members, however, gave Pitt a majority of over two to one.[3] Only at the second reading of the India Bill on 27 November were the peers' MPs less forthcoming in their support for the government than the house as a whole, a fact which may indicate that a portion of the peerage disliked the bill even before George made his famous pronouncement.[4] Normally, however, the nobility's nominees strengthened a government's hold over the house of commons.

This was particularly the case in periods of political flux. Between November 1783, and the following March there was a decisive political

1 See Appendix F.

2 Carlisle, Devonshire, Exeter, Fitzwilliam, Hertford, Pelham, Powis, Spencer, Townshend, and Walpole. The fourth earl of Sandwich, who died in 1792, was succeeded by a Pittite son.

3 *Parl. Reg.*, xxv, 90-5, 16 Dec. 1788. 204 members voted against the government.

4 The Coalition carried the second reading by a majority of 229 (65.6%)-120 (34.4%). Of the eighty-nine members sitting for peers' seats, fifty-five (61.7%) supported the government. *Ibid.*, xiii, 308-15, 27 Nov. 1783.

realignment of parties in the house of commons. On the day after the lords rejected the India Bill, the Coalition's supporters carried a motion condemning the king's intervention by a majority of seventy-three. A month later when they asked for Pitt's resignation, that majority had sunk to twenty-one, and by early March Fox and his cohorts could only muster pluralities of seven, nine and finally one.[1]

Within the broad context of this realignment, the nobility's MPs stand out. According to a list compiled by Edmund Burke fifty-four Northites voted for the India Bill and subsequently switched to Pitt's side of the house in 1784.[2] Since two of the men on this list did not then hold seats in parliament, and at least four others whom Burke says changed sides, had opposed the India Bill on its second reading, the list is not an unimpeachable source.[3] Still, it enables us to demonstrate the extensive influence which the peerage could exert in the lower house. Over half of the members who changed sides between November 1783, and the following spring were dependent in one way or another on a peer: among the fifty-two sitting members on Burke's list twenty-one sat for seats controlled by Pittite peers, and seven others were near relations or political minions of such noblemen.[4]

A more accurate measure of the nobility's influence can be made by comparing the results of the division at the second reading of the India Bill with Stockdale's analysis of political allegiances in the spring of 1784. As we have noted, the peerages' MPs supported the Coalition on 27 November by a majority of 55-34. Over the next months, however, three factors combined to alter the balance markedly in Pitt's favour. Ten of those MPs who voted with the Coalition on 27 November transferred their allegiance to Pitt by April 1784; only one opponent of the India Bill within this group then supported Fox and his allies.[5] More significantly, thirty-one MPs who had not voted at the second reading were, often at the instigation of their patrons, in their seats

---

1 Cannon, *The Coalition,* 141, 170, 198, 201-2.

2 L. G. Mitchell, *Fox and the Whigs,* 91.

3 Neither Ilay Campbell nor Sir C. Furnaby are listed in *The History of Parliament* as having seats in the house of commons during the proceedings on the India Bill. A. Herbert, G. Medley, Lord Hyde and N. Wraxall all voted against the bill on its second reading. *Parl. Reg.,* xiii, 308-15.

4 Ambler, Bayntun, J. Calvert, F. Campbell, Caswell, Cockburn, Coghill, Cox, Edmonstone, Egerton, Gideon, W. Gordon, A. Herbert, Laurie, Lincoln, Medley, Morris, J. Murray, Percy, Pitt and Stephenson owed their seats to peers. H. Boscawen, N. Curzon, A. Gordon, Lord Hyde, G. Rodney, Ward and Wraxall were closely related to or associated with Pittite peers.

5 Ambler (Newcastle), Campbell (Argyll), Caswall (Bridgewater), Cockburn (Hamilton), Cox (Northumberland), Edmonstone (Argyll), Egerton (Bridgewater), J. Murray (Atholl), Stephenson (Falmouth) and Gideon (Montague).

by the following January. Of these thirty-one members, twenty-two supported Pitt, nine Fox.[1] Finally, four MPs — a Pittite and three coalitionists — who had voted in November were absent throughout the early months of 1784. A coalitionist, Hugh Palliser, refused to follow his patron, Lord Sandwich, into opposition, and one of the duke of Newcastle's members stayed away rather than offend the sensibilities of his grace.[2] As a result of these switches and new arrivals — phenomena which were in many instances dictated by the noble patrons — Pitt enjoyed the support of a majority of the peers' MPs in the house of commons.

The political realignments of 1783-4 drove the whigs from office; those of 1792-4 nearly destroyed the party. Dr O'Gorman estimates that seventy-seven whig MPs changed sides in 1793 and 1794.[3] Among the twenty-six opposition MPs, who, as members of the third party, formed an alliance with Pitt in 1793, ten sat for boroughs in which the influence of a peer friendly to the government predominated.[4] Fifty-one Portland whigs in the house of commons broke with Fox in 1794: twenty were the nominees of peers who shared their new allegiance to the government, and two were closely related to such peers.[5] Indeed, MPs sitting for constituencies dominated by a lord comprise 41.5% of all the whigs who transferred their support to the government in these years.

In presenting these figures we do not mean to imply that party affiliation was invariably dictated by noble patrons. Periods of political

1 The twenty-two Pittites included: Calvert, Coghill, Cornwallis, Courtown, Drummond, Euston, Feilding, Flood, Fluyder, Hamilton, Laurie, Lincoln, Mulgrave, A. Murray, Norton, Bayntun Rolt, Trentham, Tyrconnel, Morris, Wilmot and Woodley. J. Gally Knight, a Pittite, was returned by the duke of Newcastle for Aldborough in place of its Foxite member, C. Mellish.
    The nine coalitionists included: Foley, Honywood, Michel, Shuldam, Sloper, Strahan, Stuart, Weddell and J. Yorke.
    For examples of the pressures applied by peers on these men see Leeds Papers, Add. MS 28060, fo. 56, Northumberland to Carmarthen, 1 Jan. 1784; Sydney Papers, Box 1, Ailesbury to Sydney, 5 Feb. [1784].

2 *History of Parliament,* ii, 223, iii, 129. As we noted earlier Charles Mellish was forced by the duke of Newcastle to resign his seat and was replaced by a Pittite.

3 O'Gorman, *The Whigs and the French Revolution,* 250-3.

4 Anstruther, Ashley, Beauchamp, Burke, Erskine, Grey, C. Townshend, Downe. County members: Hartley, Pierrepont.

5 Benyon, Bingham, Clinton, G. Damer, L. Damer, Duncannon, A. Foley, F. Grigg, T. Grenville, W. Keene, Lee, H. Pelham, Payne, W. Seymour-Conway, J. Stewart, H. Walpole. County members: E. Bentinck, G. A. Cavendish, T. Pelham, C. Spencer. Relatives: J. Campbell, Titchfield.

upheaval were bound to have a disruptive effect on partnerships which hitherto had been entirely cordial. At least seven of the whig MPs who went over to the government in 1793-4 deserted their patrons in the process; conversely, ten Foxite MPs owed their seats to lords who adhered to Pitt.[1] Some of those who rallied to Pitt in 1784 and later during the French Revolution would have done so without receiving any pressure from their benefactors. Yet, having made these concessions, we must still insist that the influence exerted by a Bridgewater or a Newcastle in 1784 or a Fitzwilliam in 1794 helped to shape the conduct of a substantial number of MPs.

The peers were local magnates. Their influence was most felt when they were dealing from positions of strength, the strength an individual exercised in his own country where he could appeal to the intangible loyalties that grew out of his possession of land and, to be sure, out of his position as a lord. From his acres and his status derived his ability to arouse and direct local opinion, his ability to gain and affect the ear of the minister, his ability to influence the lower house.

Regardless of his personal talents, the well-endowed peer was a man of great importance. Politicians courted his favour and weighed his every move carefully. A borough proprietor, fortunate enough to return a rising political star, shared in his protege's glory.[2] More tangibly, he was likely to reap the fruits of ministerial favour. The obliging patrons who sold their seats to the government not only received hard cash: Eliot was made a baron and his son went to the treasury board. Edgecumbe became an earl and supported his new rank with the ample revenues of the vice-treasurership of Ireland, and Falmouth received several lucrative sinecures. Ailesbury, as we have seen, was a royal favourite who held a succession of court offices; in 1786 he, an Englishman, was invested with the Scottish Order of the Thistle. Though these and similar rewards may seem excessive, they were also probably justified. The nobility's extensive political resources at once shaped the character of the house of lords and contributed to the smooth functioning of the government and the constitution.

Throughout our period the house of lords was restrained, even quiescent. Its members were conservative, anxious to preserve order and insure the stable functioning of government. As legislators they were

1 Pro-government MPs with Foxite patrons: T. Stanley, F. North, T. Gascoigne, J. Scudamore, J. Walwyn, J. Webb, and J. H. St. Leger. Foxites with pro-government patrons: G. A. H. Cavendish, J. Courtenay, J. Hare, J. Harrison, D. Long, J. Rawdon, M. Robinson, J. Townshend, P. C. Windham.

2 Sir James Lowther received fulsome congratulations on the initial performance of William Pitt. *HMC, 13th R.*, vii, *Lonsdale MSS*, 140.

aroused only by measures which offended their political instincts or touched directly on their diverse territorial or economic interests. With great public issues they were content to accept the recommendations of the king's ministers, and differences were generally composed behind the scenes. Because they possessed such enormous resources and influence, they were able to secure their political objectives while maintaining their restrained pose in the house of lords.

These resources were integral to the functioning of the entire political system. Ministers were influenced and in some instances restrained by the knowledge that they often had to depend upon these enormously powerful men. A house of commons in which a quarter to a third of the membership depended to some degree on these men was likely to give careful consideration to their concerns. Certainly, the chance of its clashing with the crown or the lords was diminished by the peers' powerful interest. But the house of lords' normal passivity made conflict between the two houses unlikely in any case. Because they possessed other means of molding policy, the noble lords often did not need to jeopardize the government's position in their house or to offend the commons by criticizing legislation or policy as a body. Their house was consequently able to remain what the majority intended it should be — the bulwark of the king's government.

9

THE PEERS, PATRONAGE AND THE
NATIONAL COMMUNITY

In an age in which patronage provided an essential reinforcement for the vertical loyalties of the British community, members of the peerage were active, effective patrons. The breadth of the noble lords' interests enabled them to establish contacts in diverse communities and with disparate groups; even the most successful pioneers of the industrial revolution sought out aristocratic patrons to watch over their interests in London. For these and other clients peers laboured directly in the house of lords or indirectly through public opinion, sympathetic ministers and dependents in the commons to frame legislation or to modify policy.

Most peers acknowledged some responsibility to attend in London to the needs of their friends and dependents, but two types among the nobility were particularly active as patrons. A nobleman with wide-ranging economic interests in mines or canals as well as landed estates normally established contacts in neighbouring manufacturing or commercial communities; the extent of his economic activities insured him a large and varied clientage. Similarly, the possession of an electoral interest increased the likelihood of a peer's assuming this role. Those seeking a benefactor in London naturally turned to men whom they perceived to have sufficient power to secure their objects, and the preservation of his political hegemony depended not a little on the lord's speedy delivery of such services.

Close scrutiny in fact demonstrates that the nobility's efforts in behalf of less powerful groups sprang more from practical and self-interested motives than from disinterested paternalism. A substantial portion of the peerage recognized that its economic well-being and political preeminence depended upon the prosperity and contentment of the important groups within the nation. In advancing the projects of varied clients and communities, these peers strengthened directly or indirectly their economic position and their traditional status as social and political leaders.

Through its patronage the nobility provided access to the inner circles of power for those who lacked a strong political voice at Westminster. That groups continued to rely on noble patrons attests to the deference which eighteenth-century society accorded to its traditional leaders. It also illustrates the degree to which the tiny political nation continued to provide for the essential needs of important segments of the community. In an age of fundamental economic and social transformation when the threat of political upheaval hung over Westminster and dampened politicians' enthusiasm for change, the peers' patronage at least permitted certain groups to exercise indirectly some influence over the shape of legislation and public policy.

Either because of personal interest of family tradition most peers had special clients who looked to them for aid and support. When, for example, the officers of the Indian army learned of a plan to introduce a new military system in India, they turned naturally to the son of the great Clive to help them guard against 'those pernicious Innovations which the grasping Hand of Power or Want of Information lay them open to'.[1]

A relatively small number of peers included among their clients the poor of their neighbourhoods. The marquis of Buckingham, as noted in an earlier chapter, pressed during the 1790s for less burdensome militia levies. During the food shortages of 1800-1 he also urged Pitt to move vigorously to alleviate hardships, partly because he wished to prevent food riots. In 1792 the organizer of sick clubs in the West Riding of Yorkshire petitioned for the support of Earl Fitzwilliam, a peer whose family, he said, had always taken 'an active part in the business of the Riding'. True to his family's tradition, Fitzwilliam responded with good advice and promises of assistance once the necessary legislation reached London.[2]

Mainly, however, peers promoted legislation that embodied the economic or political needs of the propertied classes. Of particular concern were the projects of the landed interest. Many lords applied their energies to securing the passage of estate, enclosure or drainage bills for their fellow landlords.[3] Promoters of roads or canals called upon neighbouring noblemen to help them carry the necessary legislation.[4] Some noble patrons also endeavoured to modify national

1 Clive MSS, Eur. MSS G37/Box 69, E. Montague to Clive, 7 Mar. 1794.

2 Pitt Papers, PRO 30/8/117, fos. 108-9, Buckingham to Pitt, 23 Dec. [1796]; Dacres Adam Papers, PRO 30/58/3, Buckingham to Pitt, 14 Oct. 1800; Wentworth Woodhouse MSS, F47(f)/28, J. Beckett to Fitzwilliam, 8 June 1792; ibid., F47(f)/29, 31, Fitzwilliam to Beckett, 15 June, 25 Dec. 1792 (copies).

3 Radnor Papers, D/EPb/E66; Spencer Papers, Box 11, Spencer to Dowager Countess Spencer, 15 May 1792; Hardwicke Papers, Add. MS 35687, fos. 72, 80, C. Pemberton to Hardwicke, 8 Jan., 24 Aug. 1800; ibid., Add. MS 35685, fos. 113 ff; ibid., Add. MS 35686, fos. 5-169.

4 Ibid., Add. MS 35686, fos. 240-1, T. Jordan to Hardwicke, 16 Mar. 1796;

policies according to the needs of their rural neighbours: Viscount Townshend insisted that a pending corn bill should not discriminate against counties such as Norfolk which exported barley, and noblemen from wool-growing counties tried in 1788 to loosen the restrictions placed on the export of raw wool by its manufacturers. Again, during the last years of the century the duke of Bedford along with Lords Carrington and Hobart pressed actively for a broad general enclosure act. Though their more extensive plans never passed into law, these men were able through their agitation to lay the groundwork for the modified act of 1801.[1]

As was noted in chapter 5 peers also assisted borough or county officials in securing or modifying a range of legislation. At the behest of town elders they sponsored measures to permit the lighting and paving of streets. When the vestrymen of St Peter's in St Albans introduced bills to raise money for a new church tower and chancel, they naturally appealed to the town's leading aristocratic potentates, Lords Grimston and Spencer. Peers gave voice to their neighbours' opposing views on pending reforms in county government and militia policy; they took a special, if intermittent interest in bills for the relief of the poor; and they enthusiastically advocated legislation to finance the construction of new county buildings.[2]

However, the eighteenth-century peerage extended its patronage beyond the agrarian community to include projects emanating from the worlds of commerce and industry.[3] The transport requirements of industry and the land, for example, often intertwined: thus, Wedgwood, Boulton and other industrialists commenced a long, fruitful partnership with Lord Gower and his more famous brother-in-law,

Harrowby Papers, cdxxxv, S/H Series, Document 54, fos. 6-7; Wentworth Woodhouse MSS, F68(b)/2, Fitzwilliam to F. Edmunds, 3 Jan. 1800; Verulam Papers, D/EV F27, D/EV F34, *passim.*

1 Pitt Papers, PRO 30/8/186, fo. 170, Townshend to Walsingham, 13 Mar. 1787; *The Times,* 11, 12, 14 June 1788; J. H. Ramage, 'The English Woollen Industry', 229-48. For Carrington's activities in support of general enclosure see, R. Mitchison, 'The Old Board of Agriculture', *EHR,* lxxiv (1959), 57-9. For Hobart's see Buckinghamshire Papers, D/MH 191, Eldon to Hobart [no date]; *ibid.,* D/MH C337, Hobart to Eldon, 23 May 1801 (copy). For Bedford's see *The Times,* 4, 12 July 1800.

2 Harrowby Papers, cdxxxv, S/H Series, Document 55, fo. 9; Hardwicke Papers, Add. MS 35682, fos. 243-4, P. Peckard to Hardwicke, 8 Feb. 1785; Spencer Papers, Box 50, J. N. Boys to Spencer, 26 Feb., 10 Dec. 1803; Verulam Papers, D/EV F36, fo.141, Grimston to T. Kinder, 28 Mar. 1801; *ibid.,* D/EV F29, T. Kinder to Grimston, 30 Mar. 1801; Delaval [Waterford] MSS, 2/DE 49/1, Magistrates of Lancaster to Delaval, 5 Feb. 1798.

3 For a more extended discussion of the nobility's patronage of industrialists, see M. McCahill, 'Peers, Patronage and the Industrial Revolution', *Journal of British Studies,* xvi(1976).

Francis, third duke of Bridgewater, when in 1765 those magnates consented to lobby for the passage of the Trent and Mersey Canal Bill.[1] Politics also influenced such interventions. During the 1790s, the town of Hull divided on the question of whether additional dock space was needed. Those citizens who desired new facilities enlisted the support of the duke of Leeds, while the proprietors of the existing dock — men who were also his foremost political allies in the town — recruited Earl Fitzwilliam to oppose the measure.[2]

For whatever reasons, peers took up the whole range of questions pertinent to the interests of merchant or industrial capitalists in a rapidly developing economy. They sponsored or oversaw the passage of legislation regulating the conduct of certain mercantile occupations.[3] They endeavoured to arrange the details of national policies to suit the commercial interests of their particular clients whether they be fishermen of the Scottish Highlands or corn merchants of East Anglia. And they pressed for 'every relief, consistent with public service' when wartime administrations implemented policies which, by inhibiting the free movement of goods, adversely affected local industries.[4]

Occasionally noble patrons went beyond such details to present their protegé's broader criticisms of national commercial policies. The most substantial opposition to Pitt's scheme for expanding commerce between England and Ireland came, of course, from the manufacturing community whose discontents the whigs skillfully exploited to score a minor victory over the government. Yet, the party did not exploit the manufacturers merely to further its own political ends. Whig magnates from several of the industrial counties were obliged, by virtue of their territorial pre-eminence, to oppose the propositions. Many of the

---

1 E. Meteyard, *The Life of Josiah Wedgwood* (London, 1865), i, 412-13, 425-26. At a meeting on 30 Dec. 1765, Gower explained why he agreed to support the proposed canal. It was, he claimed,

> of the utmost consequence to the manufacturers of that and adjacent counties, and to the kingdom in general; that ever since he had heard of the scheme, it had been his determination to support it with all his interest, both provincial and political; for he was satisfied that the landed and trading interest were so far from being incompatible, that they were the mutual support of each other.

J. Phillips, *A General History of Inland Navigation, Foreign and Domestic* (London, 1795), 156.

2 Fitzwilliam Papers, Box 46, *passim;* Egerton MSS, Eg. 3506, fos. 39-54.

3 Delaval [Waterford] MSS, 2/DE 49/1, Mr Shawe to Delaval, 21 May 1788.

4 Auckland Papers, Add. MS 34419, fo. 359, Gordon to Eden, 8 Jan. 1786; Hardwicke Papers, Add. MS 35392, fos. 197-8, 201, 205, Yorke to Hardwicke, 16, 22 Jan., 7, 9 Feb. 1791; Pitt Papers, PRO 30/8/142, fo. 63, Hardwicke to Pitt, 10 Feb. 1791; *ibid.*, PRO 30/8/131, fo. 117, de Dunstanville to [?], 25 May 1798.

petitions which poured in from Lancashire were, for example, presented by the earl of Derby. In Yorkshire the woollen manufacturers sought Earl Fitzwilliam's advice on how best to present their case against the propositions and later pressed him to introduce an amendment which would bar the export of raw wool to Ireland. Both of these men vigorously opposed the resolutions in the house of lords. The excellence of Derby's performance was noted even by his opponents, and Fitzwilliam, after carefully sifting the evidence presented by the manufacturers against the plan, delivered an able, critical speech at the final debate.[1]

Noblemen were equally adept at representing industrialists on issues which related directly to problems of production. In 1773 Matthew Boulton waited upon forty noble lords to solicit their support for a bill which would establish assay offices at Birmingham and Sheffield, but he found himself particularly indebted to the earl of Dartmouth whose good advice and skilful lobbying were instrumental in carrying the measure. Anxious to obtain a special clay from South Carolina for his potteries, Josiah Wedgwood appealed to Lord Gower for assistance: because Gower had secured his position for the current attorney general of the colony, he was able through the latter to attend to Wedgwood's needs. Similarly, Samuel Garbett, the indefatigable lobbyist for Birmingham manufacturers, recommended to Pitt that he discuss possible means of restraining the emigration of skilled labour with the earl of Dunmore, a peer who, Garbett claimed, was particularly knowledgeable on that topic.[2]

No act of government was more likely to provoke manufacturers during the early phases of the industrial revolution than a proposal to tax the raw materials they used. Here again, members of the peerage proved themselves to be invaluable intermediaries. Brewers from the north of England complained to Lord Delaval that additional duties on malt or malt liquor would further inhibit their ability to compete with their Scottish counterparts. Thus, they called upon Delaval to secure legislation which would prevent Scottish malt from being brought into England 'without paying an Additional Duty so as to make the same equal to the English Malt Duty. . . .' Watt, who in the 1780s interested himself in the manufacturer of fossil alkali, happily reported

1 *The Times*, 2, 15 July 1785; *PH*, xxv, 836-8, 8 July 1785; Wentworth Woodhouse MSS, F65/26, R. Parker to Fitzwilliam, 4 June 1785; *ibid.*, F65/27, Fitzwilliam to R. Parker [draft]; *PH*, xxv, 869-73, 18 July 1785; Ashbourne, *Pitt*, 132-4; *HMC, 14th R., Rutland MSS*, iii, 226-7, 229-30.

2 A. Westwood, *The Assay Office at Birmingham, Part I* (Birmingham, 1936), 25; Boulton Papers, Notebook 10, fos. 7-8; *Wedgwood Letters*, 55-6; Pitt Papers, PRO 30/8/138, fos. 63-4, Garbett to Pitt, 27 Sept. 1786.

to Joseph Black that Lord Dudley had spoken to North about removing the duty from salts used in that process and had found the minister agreeable on the condition that he could find alternate sources of revenue.[1] Colliery owners and ironmasters also found themselves in need of potent allies when Pitt revealed in 1784 that the government intended to lay a tax on coals. Among the leaders of the campaign to block this imposition was Richard Reynolds, a former manager of the great works at Coalbrookedale and tenant of Lord Gower's at Donnington Wood. Relying on his connection with that nobleman and Gower's own interest as a foundry owner, Reynolds addressed his complaints to the earl in hopes that he would use his influence with Pitt to block the tax.[2]

Even on such highly complicated and contentious issues as patents manufacturers were able to enlist noble support. Wedgwood and other Staffordshire potters relied upon Lord Gower and the marquis of Rockingham to arrange a satisfactory compromise when a proposal to extend the patent of Richard Champion threatened their own enterprises. Professor Robinson has demonstrated that Boulton carefully cultivated sympathetic peers in the course of his successful campaign to extend Watt's patent in 1775. Seventeen years later, when a Cornishman named Hornblower applied to take out a patent on an engine similar to Watt's, both Boulton and Garbett again called upon their friends in the peerage to oppose this petition.[3]

Obviously then, noblemen extended their patronage to widely varying clients and causes. Solicitous of the needs of property owners, they nevertheless gave voice, if intermittently, to the concerns of more humble citizens. Rural neighbours could command but not consume their attention, for merchants and industrialists received invaluable support from a number of peers. The breadth of their activities and the efforts which they exerted in behalf of clients are, in fact, testaments to the peerage's vitality, its enterprise and its resourcefulness.

1 Delaval [Waterford] MSS, 2/DE 49/1, Committee of Brewers to Delaval [no date] ; *Partners in Science; Letters of James Watt and Joseph Black*, ed. E. Robinson and D. McKie (Cambridge, Mass., 1970), 99.

2 T. S. Ashton, *Iron and Steel in the Industrial Revolution* (Manchester, 1951), 164-6; H. M. Rathbone, *Letters of Richard Reynolds with a Memoir of His Life* (London, 1852), 279-82.

3 *Wedgwood Letters*, 177-80; E. Robinson, 'Matthew Boulton and the Art of Parliamentary Lobbying', *Historical Journal*, ns. vii (1964), 209-29; Boulton Papers, S. Garbett to Boulton, 21 Mar., 10 Apr. 1792; *ibid.*, Garbett to Rawdon, 22 Mar. 1792 (copy).

In order to define fully the impact and importance of the nobility's patronage it is essential to make some estimate of the proportion of peers who actually advanced the projects discussed above. We know specifically from our research of fifty-seven lords who espoused such causes.[1] This group, which reflects available manuscript collections more truly than eighteenth-century realities, certainly does not include all those peers who were active patrons during this period. Nevertheless, it provides some clues as to the types of noblemen who were likely to undertake such responsibilities.

An analysis of the characteristics of men within our group indicates that it represents a fairly broad spectrum of the nobility. Included within its ranks were many of the nation's greatest magnates, men such the dukes of Devonshire, Marlborough and Northumberland or the earls of Derby, Egremont and Fitzwilliam. The majority, however, were more modest proprietors, and several were professional politicians or men of business who were not endowed with large properties. If the group contains representatives of the various economic levels of the peerage, it also embraces whigs, Pittites and courtiers from all sections of the country; neither political affiliation nor place of residence seems to have been a determinant. Nor did potential clients turn only to the most active members in the house of lords: assiduous participants, such as Liverpool, Auckland or Harrowby, as well as the relatively inert dukes of Devonshire and Marlborough were effective patrons. The last two simply relied upon dependent MPs and their influence with the king's ministers to carry their objectives.

The nobility's general willingness to serve as patrons is further demonstrated by the lists which industrial lobbyists compiled when attempting to carry legislation through parliament. In 1773 Matthew Boulton appealed to forty noble lords for help in passing the bill to establish assay offices at Birmingham and Sheffield. While there is no evidence to show that all responded to his applications, it is clear that he addressed himself to politicians of all persuasions, courtiers and bishops, magnates and peers of more limited means. Two years later Boulton again lobbied among the peerage, this time in support of the bill to extend the patent on Watt's steam engine. On this occasion his

---

1 Ailesbury, Argyll, Atholl, Auckland, Bathurst, Beaufort, Bedford, Bridgewater, Brownlow, Buckingham, Buccleuch, Carnarvon, Carrington, Chandos, Clive, Dartmouth, Delaval, Derby, Devonshire, Dudley, Dundas, de Dunstanville, Dunmore, Effingham, Egremont, Falmouth, Fitzwilliam, Gordon, Grimston, Harborough, Hardwicke, Harrowby, Hertford, Hobart, Hopetoun, Huntingdon, Kinnaird, Lansdowne, Leeds, Liverpool, Marlborough, Moira, Newcastle, Norfolk, Northumberland, Portland, Radnor, Romney, Sheffield, Spencer, Stafford, Stamford, Stanhope, Stormont, Townshend, Uxbridge, Warwick.

requests were directed more specifically to noblemen from his own locality and to those who, on account of their mines, might have had a practical interest in the steam engine. However, he did not attempt to recruit only the greatest magnates or members of one particular party; instead, he again appealed to any peer who might possibly be of assistance.[1]

If a variety of peers accepted the calls to advance the legislative business of clients or friends, it is also apparent that some were far more active than others. Our group of fifty-seven noblemen, encompassing as it does a variegated mixture of the peerage, still has distinctive qualities. At least thirty-six derived some of their income from mineral or other non-agricultural sources.[2] Thirty invested in or were directors of canal companies.[3] Most significantly, thirty-nine maintained powerful electoral interests.[4]

While such men were not typical of their order, a large segment of the peerage shared at least one of these attributes. According to Oldfield eighty-six peers returned members to the house of commons in 1796. At least thirty and probably many more of the families that did not possess extensive electoral interests did derive a substantial portion of their income from non-agricultural sources, and over one hundred peers contributed to the construction of the canal system in the late eighteenth century.[5] Thus, at the opening of the parliament of

1 Boulton Papers, Notebook 10, fos. 7-8; Robinson, 'Boulton and Parliamentary Lobbying', *Historical Journal*, ns. vii (1964), 220-4.

2 Ailesbury, Argyll, Bathurst, Beaufort, Bedford, Bridgewater, Buccleuch, Carrington, Chandos, Clive, Dartmouth, Delaval, Derby, Devonshire, de Dunstanville, Dudley, Dundas, Dunmore, Effingham, Egremont, Falmouth, Fitzwilliam, Hopetoun, Huntingdon, Leeds, Moira, Newcastle, Norfolk, Northumberland, Portland, Radnor, Stafford, Stamford, Stanhope, Stormont, Uxbridge.

3 Ailesbury, Argyll, Beaufort, Bedford, Bridgewater, Brownlow, Buccleuch, Buckingham, Carnarvon, Clive, Dartmouth, Devonshire, Dudley, Dundas, Egremont, Fitzwilliam, Grimston, Harborough, Harrowby, Huntingdon, Marlborough, Moira, Newcastle, Sheffield, Spencer, Stafford, Stamford, Stanhope, Uxbridge, Warwick.

4 Ailesbury, Argyll, Atholl, Bathurst, Beaufort, Bedford, Bridgewater, Brownlow, Buccleuch, Buckingham, Carrington, Chandos, Clive, Derby, Delaval, Devonshire, de Dunstanville, Dundas, Harrowby, Hertford, Lansdowne, Leeds, Marlborough, Newcastle, Norfolk, Northumberland, Portland, Radnor, Spencer, Stafford, Townshend, Uxbridge, Warwick, Egremont, Falmouth, Fitzwilliam, Gordon, Grimston, Hardwicke.

5 Abergavenny, Ashburnham, Balcarres, Breadalbane, Bute, Cadogan, Darlington, Dartmouth, Ducie, Dudley, Dynevor, Effingham, Elgin, Eglintoun, Ferrers, Glasgow, Grey de Wilton, Hamilton, Lothian, Macclesfield, Mansfield, Middleton, Moira, Newark, Pomfret, Shrewsbury, Stamford, Strafford, Strathmore, Talbot. A number of other peers — Bradford, Cardigan, Cawdor, Elphinstone, Hawke, Plymouth, Ribblesdale, Scarborough and Scarsdale — held properties from which minerals were extracted during the nineteenth century. The estimates of the

1796 well over half the 257 lay members of the house of lords had one or all of the qualifications which distinguish our active group of patrons.

That political potentates or active entrepreneurs should be assiduous patrons is entirely understandable. Because they had to nurse their constituencies, because they had a formidable array of power, peers with electoral interests were likely to be inundated with applications for assistance. Likewise, a peer whose economic activities radiated out from his estates was bound to establish contacts in an ever wider range of communities: whereas the diligent landlord supported the enclosure, drainage, road or canal bills forwarded by his rural neighbours, Lords Gower and Dudley advanced the projects of Garbett or Boulton, Watt or Wedgwood. To maintain or expand their empires magnates were in fact compelled to espouse the causes of business partners, neighbours and dependents.

Almost without exception these noble patrons would have explained that their efforts in behalf of diverse clients sprang from a desire to promote the well-being of their neighbours and dependents. Lord Spencer agreed to serve on the committee of the Grand Junction Canal because of the project's obvious 'General Utility'. The third earl of Hardwicke actively supported the controversial Eau Brink Drainage Bill, a project which was 'likely to prove in its consequences the most effectual plan that has been suggested for the improvement of the Fens since their original drainage in the last century by the Earl of Bedford'. In a similar vein the earl of Dartmouth told Boulton that 'the pleasure of assisting my neighbours, & the satisfaction I have in contributing in any degree to the success of their designs is ample recompense for any trouble I may have [had] occasion to take. . . .' in advancing the passage of the Birmingham Assay Bill.[1]

These statements were not mere rhetorical flourishes. Garbett told Boulton in 1765 that 'these old county familys look upon themselves as the Patrons of the Trade of the Neighbourhood and realy have great inclination to serve us when they distinctly understand the subject. . . .'[2] Certainly no parliamentary lobbyist appreciated the wisdom

---

number of peers participating in the construction of canals is based on the references to their activities in Hadfield's volumes on English canals.

[1] Spencer Papers, Box 11, Spencer to E. Gray and A. Chaplin, 13 Nov. 1792; H. C. Darby, *The Draining of the Fens* (Cambridge, 1956), 133; A. Westwood, *The Assay Office*, 25.

[2] E. Robinson, 'Boulton and Parliamentary Lobbying', *Historical Journal*, ns. vii (1964), 221; cf. J. Norris, 'Samuel Garbett and the Early Development of Industrial Lobbying in Great Britain', *EcHR*, 2nd Ser., x (1958), 450-60.

of this statement more than Boulton: that adept manoeuvrer invariably looked for support from the neighbouring nobility and gentry when he had measures pending in parliament.

Nevertheless, very tangible factors usually underlay the peerage's public-spirited patronage. Ricardo notwithstanding, the economic interests of landowners did not exist in isolation from or in opposition to those of the commercial or manufacturing segments of the economy. Improvements in local transportation opened entire regions to the national market, and profits taken from steadily rising rents helped to spawn a modern banking system.[1] Nor, of course, were all estates strictly agricultural enterprises. Many noblemen had the good fortune to possess lime, slate, coal, iron or copper deposits on their properties, and certain peers were proprietors of manufacturing establishments. Lord Delaval owned the largest bottle works in England, Gower the greatest share in the Lilleshall iron works. The earl of Ashburnham married the heiress of the Crowley's. As early as 1786 Lord Ducie had installed a steam engine in his forge, while Rockingham and Shrewsbury both operated blast furnaces.[2]

So closely interwoven were the economic interests of noblemen with those of the surrounding countryside that it is often impossible to determine precisely whether a peer supporting enclosure, drainage or canal bills acted in his own behalf or for his neighbours. In 1790 the freeholders of Malton informed Lord Fitzwilliam, the largest landowner of the parish, that they wished to enclose their fields and commons. Was the earl, in attempting to reconcile all parties to this proposal and push it rapidly through parliament, responding to his own needs or to those of the parish? The same blend of motives is evident in Hardwicke's espousal of the Eau Brink Drainage Bill. Hardwicke believed that the project would promote prosperity in the area, but the solicitor for the bill also noted that drainage would increase the earl's cultivable property. Probably in this instance, the proposed measure was beneficial to its sponsor and the community: the construction of a channel would enable Hardwicke to drain his land; it would also permit the authorities of the Bedford Level Corporation to control the Ouse, there-

---

[1] L. S. Pressnell, *Country Banking in the Industrial Revolution* (Oxford, 1965), 246-8.

[2] Francis Askham, *The Gay Delavals* (New York, 1955), 149, 284; Granville Papers, PRO 30/29/2, fos. 240-5, 'John Kite's Account, 1799'; M. W. Flinn, *Men of Iron: the Crowleys in the Early Iron Industry* (Edinburgh, 1962), 87-9; G. E. Mingay, *English Landed Society in the Eighteenth Century* (London, 1963), 194; J. T. Ward, 'Landowners and Mining' in *Land and Industry: The Landed Estate and the Industrial Revolution*, ed. J. T. Ward and R. G. Wilson (New York, 1971), 70.

by preventing floods which regularly destroyed lives and property.[1] Hardwicke and others could honestly protest that their seemingly self-seeking activities were designed to promote regional prosperity, but it is evident that a keen awareness of their own needs often heightened, if it did not precipitate the noble lords' anxiety for the well-being of their neighbours.

In many instances public-spiritedness gave way completely to undisguised self-interest. It was entirely logical for Lord Delaval, himself the owner of coal mines and a bottle works, to try and adjust pertinent legislation to the tastes of neighbouring coal merchants and bottle manufacturers. When Boulton set out to secure support for the extension of Watt's patent, he sought not only local magnates but noble colliery owners who might at some time have use for a steam engine. We have already noted that the Cornish copper industry relied heavily on the parliamentary lobbying of two of its leading figures, Lords de Dunstanville and Falmouth. When iron masters organized to oppose Pitt's coal tax in 1784, they addressed their complaints to Lords Dudley and Gower both of whom happened to have large foundries.[2]

John, second Viscount Dudley was, in fact, one of the most active of the late eighteenth-century aristocratic entrepreneurs. The fortunate proprietor of estates that contained large deposits of limestone, coal and iron ore, Dudley personally took a lead in exploiting his resources. Under his direction new pits were opened, and he also became a principal shareholder in four canal companies. Of special importance to this peer was the Dudley Canal, which opened the growing markets of the Black Country and Birmingham to the coal and iron extracted from his mines. Acting on behalf of the other shareholders, most of whom were local businessmen and manufacturers, Dudley applied his energy and time to carrying successive bills through parliament, thereby earning the board's gratitude for 'his unremitted Attention to the Interests of this Company and for his very powerfull and successfull Exertion in Parliament in support of the Extension of the Canal'.[3]

1 Wentworth Woodhouse MSS, F73(a)/12, 28, Fitzwilliam to Lambert, 19 Nov. 1790 (draft), J. Cleaver to Fitzwilliam, 31 Oct. 1792; Hardwicke Papers, Add. MS 35685, fo. 297, W. Creasey to Hardwicke, 21 Aug. 1792; *ibid.*, Add. MS 35686, 132-3, Hardwicke to M. Gardner, 19 Feb. 1799.

2 Delaval [Waterford] MSS, 2/DE 49/1, Mr Shawe to Delaval, 21 May 1788; Pitt Papers, PRO 30/8/129, fo. 85, Delaval to Pitt, 23 Feb. 1794; E. Robinson, 'Boulton and Parliamentary Lobbying', *Historical Journal*, ns. vii (1964), 222; *Reynolds Letters*, 279-82.

3 C. Hadfield, *The Canals of the West Midlands* (Newton Abbot, 1966), 73-7, 109; T. J. Raybould, 'The Development and Organization of Lord Dudley's Mineral Estates', *EcHR*, 2nd Ser., xxxi (1968), 529.

The range and importance of Dudley's economic interests is again illustrated during the proceedings on Pitt's Irish trade propositions. Dudley, normally a supporter of the government, told the house in a speech against this measure 'that he should be ashamed to meet any person in his own neighbourhood, if he did not give them every opposition in his power'. No doubt as Baron of Birmingham he may have felt some obligation to represent local opinion on the subject, but Samuel Garbett noted that Dudley was also concerned by the reaction of his tenantry, many of whom were nail workers. These men envisaged immediate ruin the moment under-taxed, cheaply produced Irish products flooded the English market. Thus, the neighbours whose opinions carried so much weight with Dudley were probably his tenants on whose prosperity his own partially depended.[1]

Where Dudley acted singlemindly to promote the prosperity of his estates, political as well as economic considerations influenced other peers. Josiah Wedgwood and Earl Gower were drawn together in the first instance by their common support for the Trent and Mersey Canal, a project from which both men hoped to reap financial advantages. Thereafter Gower's patronage of Wedgwood was designed to enlist political support from that formidable figure. By securing clay from South Carolina for Wedgwood's potteries, by blocking the renewal of an inconvenient patent, Gower was demonstrating to Wedgwood and his associates the degree of his power and usefulness.

The political considerations which induced Gower and other members of the nobility to take parliamentary clients were explicitly defined by the duke of Portland. In a letter to Earl Fitzwilliam, the duke stressed the advantages which that peer would derive from taking office under Pitt.

> If I am [?] in my Supposition that our acceptance of office will be the means of rallying & reuniting & incorporating the old whigs & of setting up & fairly establishing the standard of true Aristocracy will not that apply equally to the West Riding of Yorkshire, & with more effect there, with more effect in a manufacturing or commercial Part of the Kingdom, than any where else. If you are not a Principal, if you do not place Yourself in that Situation in which it is evident to the Landed Commercial & Manufacturing Interest of Yorkshire that in addressing themselves to you they address themselves to a person capable of giving them a direct answer without any intervention whatever, they will not be brought to look up to you as they ought, & you will not have that [?] that Influence that Authority which is so very desireable at all times & so peculiarly essential in the present.[2]

1 *PH*, xxv, 835, 8 July 1785; Lansdowne-Garbett Correspondence, i, fos. 131-2, Garbett to Lansdowne, 9 Feb. 1785; Boulton Papers, Garbett to Boulton, 8 June 1785.

2 Wentworth Woodhouse MSS, F31(b)/19, Portland to Fitzwilliam, 19 June 1794.

At stake here were two factors: the political power of a great magnate and the preservation of a political system dominated by the aristocracy. What is interesting is Portland's explicit assumption that both would be strengthened and perpetuated by the community's willingness to rely on men such as Fitzwilliam to uphold its interests in London.

Peers who maintained political empires were bound, in fact, to secure the speedy passage of legislation presented from the ranks of their political supporters. Thus, when Lord Grimston told a correspondent that he was always eager to promote legislation likely to enrich St Albans and its environs, he was probably being less than frank. For over thirty years a member of the Grimston family had sat for St Albans, and his lordship's diligence in support of local bills was one means of insuring further electoral triumphs. Lord Harrowby, who nominated one of the members for Tiverton, admitted his obligation to promote a paving bill presented by the borough, and Earl Spencer only agreed to undertake the time-consuming sponsorship of the Finch Hatton Enclosure Bill because he was bound by 'county obligations' to its promoter. Conversely, Charles Yorke warned his brother that the latter's wholehearted endorsement of the Eau Brink Drainage Bill might endanger the Yorke interest in Cambridgeshire, and Hardwicke did eventually mediate disputes before submitting the enacting legislation.[1]

If some peers regarded such patronage as a means of underpinning their political interests, others naturally sought out clients who might help them to establish political empires. Having seen his interest in Yorkshire collapse at the general election of 1784, Earl Fitzwilliam wasted no time in moving to restore his family's former eminence. In the process he demonstrated the enormous importance of serving the needs of potential constituents. For example, one of the first indications of his renascent political authority in the county came in 1790 when his candidate, Lord Burford, was returned for Hull. A major source of the earl's support in the town was its dock company. He had in 1787 earned the gratitude of the chairman and directors by 'protecting us against a most wicked attempt to deprive us of our Rights most solemnly vested in us by Parliament'. This he did by instructing his brother-in-law, Sir Thomas Dundas, to put off the second reading of an offensive bill for three months. The bond once established proved long lasting. Burford was elected with the company's

---

1 Verulam Papers, D/EV F35, fo. 32, Grimston to W. Donnville, 7 Apr. 1794; *History of Parliament*, i, 307-10; Harrowby Papers, cdxxxv, S/H Series, Document 55, fo. 9; Spencer Papers, Box 11, Spencer to Dowager Countess Spencer, 15 May 1792.

support. In turn Fitzwilliam and Burford helped to thwart an attempt on the part of the town's merchants to extend dock facilities, a plan which the existing company strongly opposed.[1]

A more important source of potential support was the woollen industry of the West Riding. In 1785 Fitzwilliam supported woollen manufacturers in their opposition to the export of wool to Ireland, and two years later he helped to postpone a bill, sponsored by the manufacturers of the southwest, which would have prohibited the movement of raw wool by coastal vessels. This measure, which was theoretically designed to prevent smuggling, enraged certain of Fitzwilliam's allies who regarded it as part of a plot by their southern rivals to destroy their prosperity by increasing the costs of transporting raw wool. When the bill was reintroduced in 1788, Fitzwilliam ineptly and unsuccessfully moved to postpone it again, but in spite of his failure, Leeds and Halifax manufacturers applied to him three years later to refute the government's assertion that England's wool trade with Russia was of negligible importance.[2]

Most noblemen acknowledged some obligation to advance projects put forward by their neighbours. Their zeal was sharpened in many instances by the prospect of personal financial gain, and because the range of their economic interests was so broad, those interests sometimes coincided with the needs of fellow landlords, sometimes with new captains of industry. Of course, noblemen also looked to gain political advantages as a result of their endeavours. In furthering the needs of local clients peers expected to enlist new allies and strengthen established allegiances, thereby solidifying their political machines. A number also expected that the fulfillment of their paternal responsibilities would reinforce the social and political position of the aristocracy and buttress the political system that bestowed upon their lordships such a disproportionate amount of political power. And while they pursued their own political and economic goals, peers could point to the fact that their endeavours in many instances contributed to the public's well-being: what enriched the nobleman and strengthened his

1 Fitzwilliam Papers, Box 34, W. Hammond to Fitzwilliam, 5 May, 1787; *ibid.,* Box 45, H. Ker to Fitzwilliam, 30 Jan. 1793; *ibid.,* Box 45, Fitzwilliam to Ker, 8 Feb. 1793 [draft]; *ibid.,* Box 46, Burford to Fitzwilliam, 12 Feb. 1794; *ibid.,* Box 46, H. Ethrington to Burford, 15 Sept. 1794.

2 Wentworth Woodhouse MSS, F65/26-7, R. Parker to Fitzwilliam, 4 June 1785, Fitzwilliam to Parker [draft]; Fitzwilliam Papers, Box 38, Pemberton Milnes to Fitzwilliam, 1 Aug. 1786, 10 Jan. 1787; *The Times,* 12 June 1788; Wentworth Woodhouse MSS F65(e)/70, Pemberton Milnes to Fitzwilliam, 29 Apr. 1791. The electoral importance of the woollen industry was particularly apparent in 1806 and 1807. See J. Ramage, 'The English Woollen Industry', 344-6; E. A. Smith, 'The Yorkshire Elections of 1806 and 1807: A Study in Electoral Management', *Northern History,* ii (1967), 67-83.

political interest often enriched the surrounding community and contributed to its contentment.

While their patronage may have helped to enrich noble lords or to strengthen their political interests, it is less clear to what extent such activity reinforced the standard of 'true' aristocracy and the political system which the peerage dominated. This last is a broad question, of which the resolution depends on factors whose relative weight and impact cannot be precisely measured. Still our evidence is sufficient to demonstrate several pertinent points on the basis of which it is possible to formulate some conclusions.

It is obvious in the first place that lords performed valuable services for a variety of individuals and groups. Earl Fitzwilliam, for example, offered sound, practical counsel to innumerable petitioners for private bills. Though parliament was generally hostile to working-men's organizations, he told the organizer of Yorkshire sick clubs that members would approve legislation designed to encourage so beneficial a society. On at least one occasion he urged sponsors of a private bill to enlist the services of the clerk of parliament in carrying their measure through that body, and in order to avoid losing their bills for lack of time, he and other peers encouraged potential applicants to prepare their measures for submission at the opening of the session.[1]

It was seen in chapter 5 that peers performed a variety of services once private bills reached parliament. When such measures provoked controversies, noble lords endeavoured to mediate among opposing parties. They sponsored measures in their own house, took the chair at committees and used their influence to secure favourable rulings from the small number of peers who dominated private bill proceedings. Most notably, the nobility provided the political support which enabled these clients to arrange the details of their measures and carry contested bills through parliament.[2]

This ability to marshal support for various projects, public as well as private, was the noble patron's most substantial asset. 'Lord Derby', wrote Matthew Boulton in 1773, 'took me about with him yesterday in his Chariot to several ministerial Members pressing them to serve us. He

1 Wentworth Woodhouse MSS, F47(f)/29, 31, Fitzwilliam to J. Beckett, 15 June, 25 Dec. 1792 (copies); *ibid.*, F73(a)/12, Fitzwilliam to Lambert, 19 Nov. 1790 [draft]; *ibid.*, F68(d)/18, Fitzwilliam to T. Beaumont, 18 Mar. 1793; Harrowby Papers, cdxxxv, S/H Series, Document 53, fo. 33.

2 See above chapter 5.

says he has talked much to the King in my favour'.[1] Derby's political influence was not exceptional, but like other members of his order he enjoyed access to all points in the political hierarchy. Because of his territorial power kings and cabinet ministers as well as local justices and MPs attended to his applications.

Often, in fact, clients asked nothing more of their patrons than that they enlist ministerial support for their projects. Arguing that North's approval was in itself sufficient to guarantee the success of the bill to extend Watt's patent, Boulton urged the earl of Dartmouth to discuss the matter with that statesman immediately. During the canal boom of the 1790s noblemen, apparently operating on the same premise, called upon Pitt again and again to support their measures. In a more unusual case, Lord Liverpool told Boulton in 1799 that once he had secured the king's blessing, most of the opposition to a bill for the enclosure of lands in the duchy of Lancaster would vanish.[2]

Indeed, where clients wished to embark on any substantial departure from established national policies, it was essential for patrons to conduct preliminary negotiations with his majesty's ministers. Thus, Viscount Dudley approached North about removing duties from salt for James Watt. Samuel Garbett, a consistent critic of the government's treatment of manufacturers, relied upon five powerful noble intermediaries — the marquises of Lansdowne and Stafford, the earls of Liverpool and Warwick and Lord Moira — to convince Pitt of the benefits which would accompany an end to the East India Company's monopoly. Even they were unsuccessful, but Matthew Boulton later received very effective service from Liverpool. By relating current copper prices to the difficulties involved in introducing a copper coinage, he was able to induce Liverpool, the father of the latter project, to advocate steps which would break the monopoly of Thomas Williams and reduce the price of copper.[3]

In parliament noble patrons proved themselves at once to be able advocates and canvassers for their clients' views. Pemberton Milnes, agent for certain of the West Riding woollen manufacturers, repeatedly urged Earl Fitzwilliam to get his friends to attend crucial divisions on the bill to prohibit the export of raw wool. In fact, the bill probably

1 Westwood, *The Assay Office at Birmingham*, 25.

2 Boulton Papers, Boulton to Dartmouth, 21 Feb. 1775; Pitt Papers, PRO 30/8/156, fo. 37, Marlborough *et al.* to Pitt, 29 Dec. 1792; *ibid.*, PRO 30/8/314, fo. 43, Ailesbury *et al.* to Pitt [no date]; Boulton Papers, N. Edwards to Boulton, 12 July, 19 Nov. 1800.

3 *Partners in Science*, 99; Pitt Papers, PRO 30/8/138, fo. 112, Garbett to Pitt, 31 Oct. 1791; J. Harris, *The Copper King*, 116-7.

lapsed in 1787 because Fitzwilliam was able to convince the whig leadership to commit the party's forces against it.[1] Several years earlier, in 1784, Samuel Garbett was distressed by his inability to defeat in the commons a bill which would permit the export of brass. Shortly before the measure went up to the lords, however, he was introduced to Lord Rawdon, who, after mastering the details of the question, 'in his first Speech in the House of Lords overset the Bill that had passed the lower House by a great Majority. . . .' Two months later the same peer again intervened to protect the interests of Birmingham manufacturers; after the Sheffield Plate Bill was carried in the commons without amendment, Rawdon successfully canvassed support for the Birmingham position and secured the modifications which Garbett and other local manufacturers desired.[2]

The nobility's proficiency as patrons is revealed not only in their actions, but also through the obsequious, though apparently genuine expressions of gratitude sent by clients to their noble benefactors. Thus, Boulton thanked the earl of Dartmouth for 'the kindness of effectual good offices your Lordship did myself, & this part of the country in the affair of the Assay Bill'. After ably representing Samuel Garbett's interests on two occasions, Lord Rawdon was informed by Garbett that 'it would be a happy Circumstance for Britain if a few such Characters as your Lordship would endeavor to know the Importance of its Manufactures. . . .'[3]

Men of far less ability than Rawdon or Dartmouth proved themselves to be equally adept patrons. The earl of Warwick's talents were applauded by the committee of the Warwick and Birmingham Canal Company in a minute which stated that 'the obtaining of the [canal] Act . . .was owing to his Lordship's great Exertions in support of it'. Lord Auckland, whose judgment reflected a wide political experience, informed a friend in 1797 that '. . . Ld Egremont is become a most useful Character in His Country; & is exercising His Mind & His Property in a way that does more Good to Mankind than all the Politicks & pretended Philosophers, are capable of doing.'[4]

Statements such as Auckland's have some validity. Men who benefited from the nobility's patronage responded with support which at

1 Fitzwilliam Papers, Box 38, Portland to Fitzwilliam, 3 Feb. 1787.

2 Garbett-Lansdowne Correspondence, i, fos. 64-5, Garbett to Lansdowne, 2 Oct. 1784.

3 Boulton Papers, Boulton to Dartmouth, 26 June 1773 (copy); Garbett-Lansdowne Correspondence, i, Garbett to Rawdon [no date].

4 C. Hadfield, *Canals of the East Midlands* (Newton Abbot, 1966), 165; Auckland Papers, Add. MS 35728, fos. 294-5, Auckland to Sheffield, 23 Nov. 1797.

once enhanced the fortunes of their patrons, strengthened the king's government and helped even to shore up the eighteenth-century political system. In 1782 Garbett requested his friend, Lord Shelburne, to support a canal bill in whose success the earl of Dartmouth was deeply interested. Seven years earlier Earl Gower had queried Wedgwood on local reactions to the calling out of the militia; though cool, Wedgwood's response also contained a firm and important promise of support. In the same year Boulton earned the gratitude of his patron, Lord Dartmouth, by raising a petition in support of the necessary but unfortunate American war. Again, in 1792, Boulton performed equally valuable services for another patron, Lord Gower, who in 1786 had been elevated to the marquisate of Stafford. Not only did Boulton emasculate certain local proposals for reform; he also rallied all segments of the Birmingham manufacturing community in support of king and constitution.[1]

It is impossible, however, to conclude as Auckland or Portland did that a responsible aristocracy was sufficient to preserve the traditional political order. At the end of their lives both Richard Reynolds and Josiah Wedgwood, men who had benefited frequently from the peers' patronage, advocated various political reforms. Even while he attempted to rally Birmingham for king and country, Boulton told Stafford that substantial changes would be required to completely pacify the Birmingham industrial community. Samuel Garbett, while commending Rawdon for his understanding of the intricacies of an industrial economy, simultaneously decried a government which could enter into extensive commercial negotiations with foreign powers without first ascertaining the status of England's industries.[2]

Viewed from the perspective of these men, the patronage system was a stop-gap. Lacking direct access to parliament and the cabinet, Boulton, Garbett and others had to rely on intermediaries. Yet, such a situation could not be prolonged indefinitely, and only the cataclysm of the French Revolution spared Portland's 'true' aristocracy from witnessing a prolonged, forceful campaign for parliamentary reform. Until reform came, the patronage system served as a safety valve, permitting Norfolk squires but also industrial manufacturers to secure at least a portion of their legislative or political needs. By sustaining

1 Garbett-Lansdowne Correspondence, i, fos. 33-4, Garbett to Shelburne, 30 Jan. 1783; *Correspondence of Josiah Wedgwood: 1781-1794*, ed. Lady Farrer (London, 1906), 185-6; *HMC, 14th R.*, x, *Dartmouth MSS*, ii, 257-9; Boulton Papers, Dartmouth to Boulton, 19 Jan. 1775.

2 *Wedgwood Correspondence*, 126-7; *Reynolds Letters*, 201-2; Boulton Papers, Boulton to Stafford, 11 Dec. 1792; Garbett-Lansdowne Correspondence, i, Garbett to Rawdon [no date].

these and other groups, the peers endowed the unreformed parliament with a certain vitality by giving access to power to the nation's under-represented regions and propertied interests.

CONCLUSION

Once the house of lords is accorded the status of an active, independent branch of the constitution, the nature of its interaction with the house of commons becomes a matter of great importance. Interaction did, as we have seen, exist at a number of levels. It is useful in concluding this work to draw together points made throughout the text in order to define more precisely the relationship which existed between lords and commons.

In both houses the questions which preoccupied members were primarily local or particularistic ones.[1] Because the commons' membership was more diverse than the lords', because members of the lower house had constituents to serve and satisfy, the range and extent of their endeavours and discussions was far broader than those of the upper house.[2] Yet peers like MPs watched over the enclosure or estate, paving or lighting bills forwarded by their neighbours or political allies; they too took a lively interest in legislation relating to local government and the militia; and certain of them effectively exploited their influence in behalf of a clientage more broadly diverse in its composition than that of all save the most assiduous MPs.

The passage of legislation which concerned the average member required an intimate degree of co-operation between the two houses. Often the preparation of bills was a joint effort, involving consultations between local advocates and their allies in both houses. Initiators of bills in one house needed sponsors to carry measures through the other as well as allies to form the quorums in committees. By the end of the century the commons was even sending copies of private and local bills it received to the lord chairman and adding the amendments which he proposed. In so doing it recognized that officer's paramount authority; the commons' restraint also helped to rationalize and simplify the private bill procedure.

The necessity of careful calculation and interaction was all the greater when organizing the passage of reform bills. The conservative house of lords, while never rigidly opposed to all change, required skilful handling. Thus, reformers took care to placate the appropriate lords before

---

1   Thomas, *The House of Commons,* 231, 240.

2   Hardwicke Papers, Add. MS 35381, fo. 157, Hardwicke to P. Yorke, 16 Nov. 1783; *PH,* xxiv, 1215-6, 7 July 1784; Fitton and Wadsworth, *The Strutts and the Arkwrights, 1758-1830* (Manchester, 1958), 70-1; P. Mathias, *The Brewing Industry in England, 1700-1830* (Cambridge, 1959), 330-1; R.G. Wilson, *Gentlemen Merchants: The Merchant Community in Leeds, 1700-1830* (Manchester, 1971), 166-7.

proceeding with their bills: bishops were often consulted on matters relating to the church, judges on a much wider range of measures. Their lordships' opinions were not binding, of course, but sensible reformers often heeded advice, particularly if offered by the powerful and prestigious law lords. Advocates of reform also had to be sensitive to the institutional pride of the upper house. Rather than risk losing a bill to abolish privileges of members of parliament in equity suits, Samuel Romilly exempted the lords from the strictures of the bill: he hoped that some peer would move an amendment including the nobility but correctly discerned that their lordships would regard such a clause in the commons' bill as an abridgement of their independence.[1]

It was the passage of the bill to abolish the slave trade that most clearly revealed the necessity for careful preparation before bringing on a great reform in the lords. Pitt was able to carry Dolben's Slave Trade Regulation Bill by threatening his recalcitrant colleagues with dismissal, but all his personal prestige and lobbying were insufficient to secure the passage of more radical measures in the upper house. Grenville, on the other hand, devised a more complex strategy which avoided the necessity of making a direct assault on their lordships' conservative sentiments. Moving first for the abolition of the trade with enemy colonies, he then convinced members in both houses that abolition of the British trade would be a prelude to worldwide abolition. After muting the arguments of those who believed that the trade was essential for the nation's commercial well-being and isolating the West Indians, he and his allies could then effectively bring the influence of government to bear on peers and MPs alike.[2]

On great public issues members of both houses tended to stand aside while their leaders conducted the business and dominated the debates. Observers remarked upon the pervasive indifference within the house of lords during proceedings on measures of the greatest import. Yet, the peers were not perpetually moribund nor were their lapses into somnolence unique. Fox told Lord Holland in 1803 that 'there seems to be a sort of deadness in the House of Commons, worse than even the worst times of the House of lords', and several days later he complained to Grey that 'the insipidity of the House of Commons is beyond conception'.[3] While rejecting the lords' attempts to alter money bills, members of the house of commons themselves exhibited little knowledge or understanding of financial matters. They rarely bothered to

1 *The Life of Sir Samuel Romilly*, ed. by his sons (London, 1842), ii, 66-7.
2 Anstey, *The Atlantic Slave Trade*, 364-402.
3 *Memorials and Correspondence*, iii, 216, 396.

scrutinize the expenditure of monies voted in previous sessions and only infrequently questioned the new estimates presented by ministers[1]. Amateurishness and inattention permeated both houses. Politicians and men of business were left to arrange and debate the great matters of state.

The preponderance of the politician and the professional further served to intertwine the proceedings of the lords and commons. These men dominated the course of business in both houses. Thus, when problems arose in the lords, leading ministers naturally turned to Pitt for advice. Grenville and Hawkesbury were strong leaders because, being members of the inner circle of government, they could speak authoritatively. The inability of Thurlow and others to obtain similar access in the late 1780s and their consequent spurts of critical independence only emphasized the necessity for close co-operation between leading ministers in the two houses.

'As in the House of Lords, Lord Grenville must inevitably be the person to take the lead', Fox wrote of the Grenvillite opposition in 1803, 'I should think T. Grenville, Wyndham and others, would have some plan of acting in the House of Commons conformable to his'. The standards Fox set for the Grenvilles were not always enforced on his own party. Still, if somewhat haphazardly , the whigs endeavoured to plan strategies and define positions on important public issues. When, for example, the government introduced its Treasonable Practices and Seditious Meetings Bills in November 1795, Fox not only recruited supporters among the lords and MPs, but in consultation with colleagues he organized a campaign of opposition in both houses and in the country.[2]

Over the course of the late eighteenth century relations between the two houses of parliament remained harmonious. The ability of politicians and advocates of pending measures to co-ordinate their strategies certainly gave a coherence to the proceedings in the two assemblies. More importantly, governments normally enjoyed sizeable majorities in the commons as well as the lords, and the number of issues which might have divided the two bodies was small. It is further notable that respective jurisdictions, particularly on private and local legislation, were defined with a precision that at once ensured efficient scrutiny and precluded confrontation. Finally, the lords' reluctance to provoke upheavals that might jeopardize the orderly process of government led them to adopt a relatively passive posture on most issues.

1 J.E.D. Binney, *British Public Finance and Administration, 1774-92* (Oxford, 1958), 253-4.

2 *Memorials and Correspondence*, iii, 411; *ibid.*, iii, 124.

This harmony did not betoken an equality between the two houses: the commons was unquestionably the stronger branch of government. It represented, at least virtually, the nation. In comparison to the lords, its members were diverse in terms of their social background, economic interests and ideological orientations. Its richer, more varied membership endowed the house of commons with a dynamism which was reinforced by the institution's history and traditions. For centuries the commons had been the aggressive partner of the constitution, the critic, the innovator. Contemporary political realities reinforced its historic importance and vigour. For nineteen years Pitt oversaw the formulation of public policy; even after 1793 he remained the driving force in national life. His presence in the house augmented its stature, all the more because the political struggles of these years remained so closely linked to his own personality and that of Charles Fox. Attention naturally focused on their duels in the house of commons. It was there that the principal arguments and potential modifications in important policies were set out and debated. Very often the house of lords was left in the unhappy position of merely rehashing points already raised in the commons.[1]

Yet, four factors combined to elevate the house of lords to a place of importance within the constitution and thereby prevent the house of commons from becoming the dominant house. In the first place, the house of lords was particularly efficient or expert in performing certain legislative chores. The house effectively discharged the first duty of any second chamber: its members, and especially the law lords, regularly, sometimes skilfully corrected drafts of legislation which had been sent up from the house of commons. Most importantly, the house of lords devised a cogent, equitable procedure for private and local legislation and recruited competent men to implement it. As a result, the lords came to dominate proceedings on measures which comprised two-thirds of the total amount of legislation passed by parliament in any session. In assuming these functions the house of lords insured that it would make its impact on the legislative process.

The political talents and stature of its members also augmented the prestige and importance of the house of lords. The peerage produced individuals of ability and understanding: Holland, King, Lansdowne, Moira, Spencer or Stanhope raised important points and sponsored motions which at once enlivened and gave a distinctive quality to the proceedings of their house. But to a remarkable degree it was the former house of commons men — lawyers such as Eldon, Loughborough or Thurlow, administrator-politicians such as Auckland,

1   See, for example, Derry, *The Regency Crisis,* 91-3, 112-4, 148.

Grenville, Hawkesbury or Liverpool — who dominated the house during this period. The lawyers by right of their offices, personalities and prestige, the politicians by right of their access to the inner circles of power and a professionalism which distinguished them from their colleagues spoke with an authority and force which strengthened the ministerial position in the house of lords and enhanced the stature of that body.

This steady flow of able MPs into the house of lords forms one of the more interesting and revealing aspects of the interaction between the two houses. Peerages automatically accompanied appointment to high judicial office; they provided ministers with the means of retiring inconvenient allies; many were actively solicited as testaments of royal approval for past services. Yet, Pitt was always aware of the need to enlarge the thin ranks of men of business in the lords. The peerage during these years did not produce leading politicians or men who aspired to master the complexities of administration and important national questions. Thus, the two most formidable and effective government politicians — Grenville and Hawkesbury — were sent specifically to fill a dangerous vacuum in the government leadership. In so far as these appointments betoken a recognition of the need for able spokesmen in the upper house, they reveal Pitt's and Addington's implicit assumption that the proceedings in the upper house were of importance, that the peers did participate in the national political process.

Their lordships' enormous political resources further strengthened the position of their house. These resources enabled peers to modify policy according to their own needs and to those of a varied clientage. No government could ignore the demands of men who possessed such vast territorial authority, and in accepting their proposals it often accommodated policies and legislation to diverse needs and interests. More importantly, the growth of the peerage's clientage in the house of commons enabled the former group to exercise considerable influence in the lower house. Through their members noblemen could determine the outcome of proceedings on legislation. Their interests served to reinforce the position of the king's government in the commons, particularly in periods of political upheaval. As a bloc the peers' MPs formed a conservative, restraining political influence within the house of commons.

Finally, the lords shared a conservative political point of view — one to which they adhered with remarkable consistency. What pre-occupied the nobility was a concern for order and a belief that order required the existence of strong government. In pursuit of this object their lordships supported administrations in which the king expressed his confidence. They uniformly and successfully upheld the royal prerogative against challenges from the commons and from ministers who dominated the commons. Yet they did so without being blind to the existence of incompetence or crippling political weakness. In 1783 and 1804 they joined with the commons in attacking governments even while the leaders of those administrations retained the confidence of the king. They did so as conservatives, however: weak or incompetent administrations were incapable of ensuring that steady operation of government which they deemed to be so essential.

The two houses of parliament possessed distinctive personalities, responsibilities and objectives. The commons was the dynamic aggressive partner: its role was a dramatic and, in the long term, a pivotal one. But the realities of eighteenth-century life were shaped at least in part by the interacting of the two houses. The peers made their own special contributions. Sometimes those were achieved in conjunction with the house of commons. On other occasions the lords was able to dictate to the lower house.

APPENDICES

Appendix A

Public bills defeated in the
house of lords, 1783-1805

1783-4   *East India Company Bill*
Scotch Protestant Oaths Bill
Scotch Protestant Oaths Bill

1785   Insolvent Debtors Bill
Phillips Reward Bill
Election Voters Bill
Bankrupts Creditors Bill

1786   *Pawnbrokers Bill*
Ecclesiastical Court Bill
St. Eustatius Prize Bill
Criminals Bill
Election Bill
Lottery Bill

1787   American Debts Bill
Bankrupts Bill
Insolvent Debtors Bill
British Fisheries Bill

1788   Insolvent Debtors Bill
Scotch Election Bill

1789   Church of England Relief Bill
Humane Society Bill
Bakers Company Bill
Election Bill
Ecclesiastical Tithes Bill
Scotch Ministers Relief Bill
Corn Regulation Bill
Trees Preservation Bill
Bill to commemorate the Revolution
Cocoa Nut Duty Bill
Poor Relief Bill

1790   *Lottery Bill*
Tobacco Duty Bill
Cocoa Nut Duty Bill
Coasting Trade Bill

1791   Libel Juries Bill
              Bill to prevent the counterfeiting of certificates of servants.

1792   New Forest Timber Bill
              Soldiers and Mariners Bill
              Debtors and Creditors Bill

1793   Debtors Relief Bill
              Patentees Rights Bill
              Bankrupts Bill

1794   *Hessian Troops Indemnity Bill*
              Foreign Slave Trade Abolition Bill
              Roman Catholic Attornies Bill

1795   Parochial Settlements Bill
              Hemp and Flax Bill

1796   Debtor and Creditor Bill
              Quakers Relief Bill
              Bill to Suspend the Legacy Duty Act
              Misdemeanors Costs Bill

1797   Vagrant Laws Bill
              Catholics in the Army Bill
              Wasteland Cultivation Bill

1798   Election Expenses Bill
              Shipowners Bill
              Bill to reduce holidays in public offices
              Misdemeanors Expenses Bill
              Attornies Indemnification Bill
              Bill to regulate indentures of attornies' clerks

1799   Sheriffs Indemnity Bill
              Militia Reduction Bill
              Slave Trade Immunity Bill
              Ribbon Manufacturers Bill
              Millwrights Bill

1800   Adultery Prevention Bill
              Papists Bill
              Enclosure Consolidation Bill

1801   Insolvent Debtors Bill
              General Enclosure Bill

Masters and Servants Bill

1802   Election Expenses Bill
Manure Bill
County Bridges Bill
Debtors Relief Bill
Irish Bankrupts Bill
Poor Badges Bill

1803   Insolvent Debtors Bill
Woollen Manufacturers Bill
Curates Residence Bill
Irish Chalkers Bill
Irish Small Debts Bill
Bill to punish those who destroy ships

1804   Slave Trade Abolition Bill
Chimney Sweepers Bill
Irish Clergy Bill
Bill to exempt clergy from arrest

1805   *English Army to Repeal Bill*
Local Oaths Correction Bill
Irish Distillery Bill
Church Land Planting Bill
Partition of Land in Ireland Bill
Revenue Regulation Bill
Trust Monies Security Bill
Customs Offices Fees Bill
First Fruits (Ireland) Bill

(Italic indicates bills initiated by governments or likely to be of particular interest to them).

Appendix B

Peers occupying cabinet, high government
or judicial offices, 1783-1806

Cabinet

Lord President of the Council

Earl Gower (Dec. 1783-Nov. 1784)
Lord Camden (Nov. 1784-Apr. 1794)
Earl Fitzwilliam (July-Dec. 1794)
Earl of Mansfield (Dec. 1794-Sept. 1796)
Earl of Chatham (Dec. 1796-June 1801)
Duke of Portland (July 1801-Jan. 1805)
Lord Sidmouth (Jan.-July, 1805)
Earl Camden (July, 1805-Jan. 1806)

Lord Privy Seal

Duke of Rutland (Dec. 1783-Mar. 1784)
Earl Gower [cr. Marquis of Stafford, 1786] (Nov. 1784-July 1794)
Earl Spencer (July-Dec. 1794)
Earl of Chatham (Dec. 1794-Sept. 1796)
Earl of Westmorland (Feb. 1798-Jan. 1806)

Lord Chancellor

Lord Thurlow (Dec. 1783-June 1792)
Lord Loughborough (Jan. 1793-Feb. 1801)
Lord Eldon (Apr. 1801-Jan. 1806)

Home Secretary

Lord Sydney (Dec. 1783-June 1789)
W. W. Grenville (June 1789-June 1791) [received peerage, Nov. 1790]
Duke of Portland (July 1794-July 1801)
Lord Pelham (July 1801-Aug. 1803)
Lord Hawkesbury (May 1804-Jan. 1806)

Foreign Secretary

Marquis of Carmarthen [Duke of Leeds, Mar. 1789] (Dec. 1783-Apr. 1791)
Lord Grenville (June 1791-Feb. 1801)

Lord Hawkesbury (Feb. 1801-May 1804) [took seat in house of lords by right of his father's barony, Nov. 1803]
Lord Harrowby (May 1804-Jan. 1805)
Lord Mulgrave (Jan. 1805-Jan. 1806)

Secretary of State for War and Colonies

Lord Hobart (Mar. 1801-May 1804)
Earl Camden (May, 1805-July 1805)

First Lord of the Admiralty

Viscount Howe (Dec. 1783-July 1788)
Earl of Chatham (July 1788-Dec. 1794)
Earl Spencer (Dec. 1794-Feb. 1801)
Earl of St. Vincent (Feb. 1801-May 1804)
Viscount Melville (May 1804-Apr. 1805)
Lord Barham (Apr. 1805-Jan. 1806)

Master General of Ordinance

Duke of Richmond (Jan. 1784-Feb. 1795)
Marquess Cornwallis (Feb. 1795-1801) [ceased to hold a seat in the cabinet after his appointment to the lieu-tenancy of Ireland, June 1798]
Earl of Chatham (June 1801-Jan. 1806)

President of the Board of Trade

Lord Hawkesbury [cr. earl of Liverpool, 1796] (1791-May 1804)
Duke of Montrose (June 1804-Jan. 1806)

Commander-in-Chief of Army

Lord Amherst (Jan. 1793-Dec. 1794)

Ministers without Portfolio

Earl Camden (June 1798-Feb. 1801)
Duke of Portland (Jan. 1805-Jan. 1806)
Lord Harrowby (Jan.-July 1805)

Chancellor of Duchy of Lancaster

Lord Hawkesbury (1791-May 1804)
Lord Mulgrave (June 1804-Jan. 1805)

Earl of Buckinghamshire (Jan.-July 1805)
Lord Harrowby (July, 1805-Jan. 1806)

Non-Cabinet Offices

Chancellor of Duchy of Lancaster

Earl of Clarendon (1784-6)
Lord Pelham (Nov. 1803-May 1804)

Postmasters General

Earl of Tankerville (1784-6)
Lord Carteret (1784-9)
Earl of Clarendon (Sept.-Dec. 1786)
Lord Walsingham (1787-94)
Earl of Westmorland (Sept. 1789-Mar. 1790)
Earl of Chesterfield (1790-8)
Earl of Leicester (1794-9)
Lord Auckland (1798-1804)
Earl Gower (1799-1801) [called to the house of lords by
right of his father's barony, 1799]
Duke of Montrose (1804-6)

President of the Board of Control

Earl of Dartmouth (July 1801-July 1802)

Master of the Mint

Earl of Effingham (1784-9)
Earl of Chesterfield (Sept. 1789-Feb. 1790)
Earl of Leicester (1790-4)
Earl Bathurst (1804-6)

Lord Lieutenant of Ireland

Duke of Rutland (1784-7)
Marquis of Buckingham (1787-9)
Earl of Westmorland (1790-4)
Earl Fitzwilliam (Dec. 1794-Mar. 1795)
Earl Camden (1795-8)
Marquis Cornwallis (1798-1801)
Earl of Hardwicke (1801-6)

Judicial Offices

Lord Chief Justice

Earl of Mansfield (1756-88)
Lord Kenyon (1788-1802)
Lord Ellenborough (1802-18)

Chief Justice of the Common Pleas

Lord Loughborough (1780-93)
Lord Eldon (1799-1801)

Appendix C

Noble members of the households of
George III and Queen Charlotte
December 1783-January 1806

King's Household

Lord Steward

Duke of Chandos (1783-9)
Duke of Dorset (1789-99)
Earl of Leicester (1799-1802)
Earl of Dartmouth (1802-4)
Earl of Aylesford (1804-12)

Lord Chamberlain

Earl of Salisbury (1783-1804)
Earl of Dartmouth (1804-10)

Groom of the Stole

Viscount Weymouth (1783-96) [cr. marquis of Bath, 1789]
Duke of Roxburghe (1796-1804)
Earl of Winchelsea (1804-12)

Master of the Horse

Duke of Montagu (1780-90)
Duke of Montrose (1790-5)
Earl of Westmorland (1795-8)
Earl of Chesterfield (1798-1804)
Marquis of Hertford (1804-6)

Captain of the Yeomen of the Guard

Earl of Aylesford (1783-1804)
Lord Pelham (1804)
Earl of Macclesfield (1804-1830)

Captain of the Band of Gentlemen Pensioners

Earl of Leicester (1783-1790)
Viscount Falmouth (1790-1806)

Lords of the Bedchamber

Duke of Queensberry (1760-1789)

Earl of Oxford (1760-90)
Lord Willoughby de Broke (1761-1816)
Earl of Denbigh (1763-1800)
Duke of Roxburghe (1767-1796)
Earl Fauconberg (1777-1802)
Earl of Winchelsea (1777-1804)
Lord Onslow (1780-1814)
Lord Boston (1780-1825)
Lord Rivers (1782-1803)
Earl of Essex (1782-99)
Earl of Galloway (1783-1806)
Lord Delawarr (1789-95)
Viscount Wentworth (1790-1815)
Earl Poulett (1795-1819)
Earl of Macclesfield (1797-1804)
Lord Somerville (1799-1817)
Lord Sydney (1800-10)
Second Lord Amherst (1802-4; 1804-13)
Lord St. Helens (1803-1830)
Second Lord Rivers (1804-19)
Lord Arden (1804-12)

Colonels of the Guard Regiments

First Troop

Marquis of Lothian (1767-89)
Lord Dover (1789-92)
Earl of Harrington (1792-1829)

Second Troop

Lord Amherst (1779-97)
Lord Cathcart (1797-1814)

Comptroller of the Household

Earl of Macclesfield (1791-97) [Macclesfield succeeded his father in 1795]

Master of the Robes

Lord Brudenell (1760-90) [Brudenell was raised to the peerage in 1780; he succeeded his brother as fifth earl of Cardigan in 1790]

Lord Selsey (1792-1808) [Selsey was raised to the peerage in 1794]

Master of Buckhounds

>Earl of Sandwich (1783-1806) [succeeded his father in 1792]

Queen's Household

Lord Chamberlain

>Earl of Ailesbury (1780-92)
>Earl of Morton (1792-1818)

Treasurer

>Earl of Guildford (1774-90)
>Earl of Ailesbury (1792-8)

Master of the Horse

>Earl of Waldegrave (1784-9)
>Earl of Harcourt (1790-1809)

Comptroller

>Earl of Effingham (1781-1814) [succeeded his brother as earl in 1791]

Appendix D

Parliamentary interests
of the peerage

	1780	*1784*
Ancaster	Boston-1	Boston-1
Argyll	Ayr Burghs-1[a]	Ayr Burghs-1
Beaufort	Monmouth-1	Monmouth-1
Bedford[b]*	Okehampton-1 Tavistock-2	Okehampton-1 Tavistock-2
Bolton*	Totnes-1	Totnes-1
Bridgewater	Brackley-2	Brackely-2
Chandos	Winchester-1	Winchester-1
Devonshire*	Derby-1 Knaresborough-2	Derby-1 Knaresborough-2
Grafton	Bury St. Edmunds-1 Thetford-2	Bury St. Edmunds-1 Thetford-2
Marlborough	Heytesbury-1 Oxford-1 Woodstock-2	Heytesbury-1 Oxford-1 Woodstock-2
Newcastle	Aldborough-2 Boroughbridge-2 East Retford-1 Newark-1	Aldborough-2 Boroughbridge-2 East Retford-1 Newark-1
Northumberland	Bere Alston-2[c] Launceston-2 Newport-2	Bere Alston-2 Launceston-2 Newport-2

Note: This list was composed on the basis of the short histories of each borough for these years in *History of Parliament: The House of Commons, 1754-1790,* ed. Sir Lewis Namier and John Brooke (London, 1964), i.

a. This list includes Scottish and Welsh as well as English boroughs controlled by peers.

b Bedford was a minor during these years. His electoral interests in 1780 were controlled by his grandmother and the associates of his late grandfather who stood on opposite political sides. Christie, *The End of North's Ministry,* 54. In 1784 the entire Bedford interest went to Coalition candidates.

c. On the death of the first duke of Northumberland in 1786 Bere Alston passed to his second son, Lord Louvaine. The other two constituencies passed to the second duke.

* Indicates peers who opposed Pitt's government in 1784.

Portland*	Wigan-1	
Queensberry	Dumfries Burghs-1	
Richmond	Chichester-2	Chichester-1
Rutland[d]	Bramber-1	Bramber-1
	Grantham-1	Grantham-1
	Newark-1	Newark-1
Buckingham[e]	Buckingham-2	Buckingham-2
Lansdowne	Calne-2	Calne-2
	Chipping Wycombe-1	Chipping Wycombe-1
Rockingham	Higham Ferrers-1	
	Malton-2	
Abingdon	Westbury-2	Westbury-2
Ailesbury	Great Bedwyn-2	Great Bedwyn-2
	Marlborough-2	Marlborough-2
Bathurst	Cirencester-1	Cirencester-1
Carlisle*	Morpeth-2	Morpeth-2
Cornwallis	Eye-2	Eye-2
Derby*	Preston-1	Preston-1
Exeter*	Stamford-2	Stamford-2
Fitzwilliam[f]*	Peterborough-1	Higham Ferrers-1
		Malton-1
		Peterborough-1[g]
Gower	Lichfield-1	Lichfield-1
	Newcastle-under-Lyme-2	Newcastle-2
Grosvenor	Chester-2	Chester-2
Guildford*	Banbury-1	Banbury-1
Hardwicke	Reigate-1	Reigate-1
Hertford*	Orford-2	Orford-2
Lonsdale		Appleby-1
		Cockermouth-2
		Haslemere-2

d. Rutland died in 1787 leaving a minor heir. His electoral interest was managed by his widow and her father, the duke of Beaufort, who served as the new duke's guardian.

e. Buckingham inherited control of one seat at St Mawes from his father-in-law, Lord Nugent, and purchased another from the Boscawens in 1788. *Ibid.*, i, 239. He also began to establish an interest in the venal borough of Aylesbury in the late 1780s. *Ibid.*, i, 215.

f. Fitzwilliam inherited Higham Ferrers and Malton from his uncle, the marquis of Rockingham, in 1782.

g. In 1786 Fitzwilliam captured the second seat at Peterborough.

* Indicates peers who opposed Pitt's government in 1784.

Orford	Ashburton-1 Callington-2[h] Castle Rising-1	Ashburton-1 Castle Rising-1
Oxford	New Radnor-1	New Radnor-1
Pembroke	Wilton-2	Wilton-2
Portsmouth	Andover-1	Andover-1
Poulett	Bridgewater-1	Bridgewater-1
Powis*	Montgomery-1	Montgomery-1
Radnor	Salisbury-1	Salisbury-1
Sandwich*	Huntingdon-2	Huntingdon-2
Spencer*	Okehampton-1 St Albans-1	Okehampton-1 St Albans-1
Thanet	Appleby-1	Appleby-1
Warwick	Warwick-1	
Westmorland	Lyme Regis-2	Lyme Regis-2
Bolingbroke*	Wootton Basset-2	Wootton Basset-2[i]
Falmouth	Tregony-2 Mitchell-1 St Mawes-1	Tregony-2[j] Truro-2
Montague	Midhurst-2	Midhurst-2[k]
Mount Edgecumbe	Bossiney-1 Fowey-1 Lostwithiel-2 Plympton-1	Bossiney-1 Fowey-1 Lostwithiel-2 Plympton-1
Sackville		East Grinstead-2[l]
Townshend*	Great Yarmouth-1 Tamworth-1	Tamworth-1
Weymouth	Tamworth-1 Weobley-2	Tamworth-1[m] Weobley-2

h. The editors of the *History of Parliament* are unable to determine whether Orford nominated one member for Callington in 1784. *Ibid.*, i, 226-7.

i. After the election of 1784 the St Johns conceded one seat at Wootton Basset to the earl of Clarendon. *Ibid.*, i, 422-3.

j. Falmouth sold his interest at Tregony to Sir Francis Bassett in 1788. *Ibid.*, i, 241-2.

k. Montague sold Midhurst to the earl of Egremont in 1787, who in turn sold it to Lord Carrington in 1797. *Ibid.*, i, 395-6; H. A. Wyndham, *A Family History*, 240-1.

l. The Sackville interest at East Grinstead was inherited at the viscount's death in 1785 by his nephew, the third duke of Dorset.

m. Weymouth sold his seat at Tamworth to Sir Robert Peel in 1790. *History of Parliament*, 376-7.

* Indicates peers who opposed Pitt's government in 1784.

Brownlow	Grantham-1	Grantham-1
Bulkeley		Beaumaris-1
Camelford		Old Sarum-2
Eliot		Grampound-2
		Liskeard-2
		St Germans-2
Foley*	Droitwich-1	Droitwich-1
Grantley		Guildford-1
Harrowby	Tiverton-1	Tiverton-1
Onslow	Guildford-1	Guildford-1
Pelham*	Lewes-1	Lewes-1
Sommers		Reigate-1
Sydney		Whitechurch-1
Walpole*	Great Yarmouth-1	King's Lynn-1
	King's Lynn-1	

*   Indicates peers who opposed Pitt's government in 1784.

Appendix E

Counties in which one or
more peers chose a member

1780	*1790*
Argyllshire (Argyll-1)	Argyllshire (Argyll-1)
Bedfordshire (Bedford-1)	Anglesey (Uxbridge-1)
Buckinghamshire (Temple-1)	* Bedfordshire (Bedford-1)
Cambridgeshire (Hardwicke-1)	Buckinghamshire (Buckingham-1)
(Rutland-1)	Cambridgeshire (Hardwicke-1)
Derbyshire (Devonshire-1)	(Rutland-1)
Dorsetshire (Rivers-1)	Carnarvonshire (Bulkeley-1)
Dumfriesshire (Queensberry-1)	Cumberland (Lonsdale-1)
Gloucestershire (Beaufort-1)	* Derbyshire (Devonshire-1)
(Berkeley-1)	Dorsetshire (Rivers-1)
Huntingdonshire (Manchester-1)	Dumfriesshire (Queensberry-1)
(Sandwich-1)	Gloucestershire (Beaufort-1)
Lanarkshire (Hamilton-1)	(Berkeley-1)
Lancashire (Derby-1)	* Huntingdonshire (Manchester-1)
Northumberland (Northumber-land-1)	* (Sandwich-1)
Nottinghamshire (Newcastle-1)	Lanarkshire (Hamilton-1)
(Portland-1)	* Lancashire (Derby-1)
Oxfordshire (Marlborough-1)	Northumberland (Northumber-land-1)
Peeblesshire (Queensberry-1)	Nottinghamshire (Newcastle-1)
Perthshire (Atholl-1)	* (Portland-1)
Rutland (Exeter-1)	Oxfordshire (Marlborough-1)
(Gainsborough-1)	Peeblesshire (Queensberry-1)
Staffordshire (Gower-1)	Perthshire (Atholl-1)
	* Rutland (Exeter-1)
	(Gainsborough-1)
	Staffordshire (Gower-1)
	Westmorland (Lonsdale-2)

* denotes peers in opposition to Pitt at the time of the general election.

Appendix F

Peers created during Pitt's first
administration with parliamentary interests
at the time of their creation.

Bolton	Totnes-1
Bradford (2)	Wenlock-1
	Wigan-1
Midleton	Whitchurch-1
Bulkeley	Beaumaris-1
Calthorpe (2)	Bramber-1
	Hindon-1
Camelford (2)	Old Sarum-2
Carrington (4)	Midhurst-2
	Wendover-2
Clive (4)	Bishop's Castle-2
	Ludlow-2
Curzon	Clitheroe-1
De Dunstanville (2)	Penryn-2
Dundas (2)	Richmond-2
Eliot (6)	Grampound-2
	Liskeard-2
	St Germans-2
Grimston	St Albans-1
Harewood	Northallerton-1
Lonsdale (5)	Appleby-1
	Cockermouth-2
	Haslemere-2
Lyttleton	Bewdley-1
Northwick	Evesham-1
Ribblesdale	Clitheroe-1
Sommers	Reigate-1
Yarborough (2)	Great Grimsby-2

BIBLIOGRAPHY

A. Manuscript Sources
B. Printed Primary Sources
C. Secondary Sources
D. Articles

A. *Manuscript Sources*

Alnwick Castle	Percy Family Papers, 1iv-1viii.
Althorp	Spencer Papers
Berkshire Record Office	Braybrooke Papers Radnor Papers
Assay Office, Birmingham	Boulton Papers
Birmingham Reference Library	Boulton-Watt Papers Garbett-Lansdowne Correspondence (copies from the Lansdowne MS at Bowood)

British Library

> *Additional Manuscripts*
> Auckland Papers, Add. MSS 34419, 34452-6, 45728-9, 46490-1, 46519
> Bridport Papers, Add. MSS 35202
> Chichester Papers, Add. MSS 33090-3, 33099, 33101, 33106-11, 33128-30
> Fox Papers, Add. MSS 47561, 47563-74, 47579
> Grenville Papers, Add. MSS 41851-6, 42058
> Hardwicke Papers, Add. MSS 35381-3, 35390-4, 36541-4, 35622, 35682, 35686-7, 45030
> Holland House Papers, Add. MSS 51467, 51530, 51533, 51566, 51571-2, 51577, 51584-5, 51593, 51595, 51598, 51660-1, 51682-6, 51691-4, 51794, 51802-3, 51818-23, 51845
> Leeds Papers, Add. MSS 27915, 27918, 28059-67
> Liverpool Papers, Add. MSS 38190-2, 38218-41, 38259, 38473, 38567
> Melville Papers, Add. MSS 40102
> Morley Papers, Add. MSS 48218-26, 48244-6

Northington Papers, Add. MSS 38716
Robinson Papers, Add. MSS 37835
Rose Papers, Add. MSS 42772-4
Dropmore Papers, Add. MSS 58863, 58874, 58884-5, 58906-9, 58932, 58935-8, 58946, 58935, 58987-93, 59255, 59311, 59378-81, 59388-91

Egerton Manuscripts
Hertford Papers, Eg. 3060-2
Leeds Papers, Eg. 3498, 3505-6

BL Facsimiles
Abergavenny Papers, BL Facs 340(2)
Buckinghamshire Record Office:
    Buckinghamshire Papers
Chatsworth: Chatsworth Papers, Fifth Duke's Group
Essex Record Office
    Braybrooke Papers
    Sperling Papers
Hatfield House
    Salisbury Papers
Hertfordshire Record Office
    Cowper Papers
    Verulam Papers
Hopetoun House
    Linlithgow Papers
House of Lords Record Office
    'The Roll of the Standing Orders of the House of Lords'
    Committee Books, 1783-1806
    Proxy Books, 1783-1806
Kent Record Office
    Camden Papers
    Mann (Cornwallis) Papers
    Sackville Family Papers
    Waldeshare Papers
University of Leeds, Brotherton Library
    Sidney Papers
Northamptonshire Record Office
    Fitzwilliam Papers
Northumberland Record Office
    Delaval [Waterford] MSS (Property of the Newcastle Central Library)
University of Nottingham Library
    Newcastle Papers
    Portland Papers

Oxford University, Bodleian Library
    Clarendon Papers
    North Papers
Public Record Office
    Chatham Papers, PRO 30/8
    Cornwallis Papers, PRO 30/11
    Dacres Adam Papers, PRO 30/58
    Granville Papers, PRO 30/29
    Manchester Papers, PRO 30/15
Sandon Hall
    Harrowby Papers
National Library of Scotland
    Lynedock Papers
    Melville Papers
Scottish Record Office
    Breadalbane Papers GD 112
    Buccleuch Papers, GD 224
    Dalhousie Papers, GD 45
    Melville Castle MSS, GD 51
    Morton Papers, GD 150
    Minutes of Peerage Elections, 1784-1802. SRO PE/8
Sheffield Public Library
    Wentworth Woodhouse MSS
East Suffolk Record Office
    Pretyman-Tomline Papers
West Suffolk Record Office
    Grafton Papers
Wiltshire Record Office
    Ailesbury Papers

Historic Manuscripts Commission

Abergavenny MSS, Tenth Report, part vi.
Ailesbury MSS, Fifteenth Report, part vii.
Bathurst MSS.
Carlisle MSS, Fifteenth Report, part vi.
Cornwallis Wykeham-Martin MSS, Various Collections, vol. vi.
Dartmouth MSS, Eleventh Report, part v; Fourteenth Report, part x.
Denbigh MSS.
Fortescue MSS, Thirteenth Report, part iii, vols. i-vii.
Kenyon MSS, Fourteenth Report, part iv.
Knox MSS, Various Collections, vol. vi.
Laing MSS, vol. ii.

Lothian MSS.
Lonsdale MSS, Thirteenth Report, part vii.
Rawdon Hastings MSS, vol. iii.
Rutland MSS, Fourteenth Report, part i, vol. iii.
Stopford Sackville MSS, vol. i.
Sutherland MSS, Fifth Report, part i.

B. *Printed Primary Sources*

Auckland, Lord, *The Journal and Correspondence of William, Lord Auckland,* ed. Bishop of Bath and Wells (London, 1861-2), 4 vols.

Banks, Sir Joseph, *The Banks Letters,* ed. W. R. Dawson (London, 1958).

Beresford, John, *The Correspondence of the Right Hon. John Beresford,* ed. William Beresford (London, 1854), 2 vols.

Bessborough, Countess of, *Lady Bessborough and Her Family Circle,* ed. Earl of Bessborough in collaboration with A. Aspinall (London, 1940).

Burke, Edmund, *The Correspondence of Edmund Burke,* ed. T. W. Copeland *et al.,* (Cambridge, 1963-70), vols. iv-ix.

———— *The Works of the Right Honourable Edmund Burke* (London, 1855), vol. iii.

Canning, George, *George Canning and His Friends,* ed. Jocelin Bagot (London, 1909), 2 vols.

Castlereagh, Lord, *Memoirs and Correspondence of Viscount Castlereagh,* ed. Marquis of Londonderry (London, 1848-51), vols. i-v.

Colchester, Lord, *The Diary and Correspondence of Charles Abbot, Lord Colchester,* ed. Charles, Lord Colchester (London, 1861), 3 vols.

Cornwallis, Marquis, *Correspondence of Charles, First Marquis, Cornwallis,* ed. Charles Ross (London, 1859), 3 vols.

Delany, Mary, *The Autobiography and Correspondence of Mary Granville, Mrs. Delany,* ed. Lady Llanover (London, 1862), 3 vols.

Devonshire, Duchess of, *Georgiana: Extracts from the Correspondence of Georgiana, Duchess of Devonshire,* ed. Earl of Bessborough (London, 1955).

Farington, Joseph, *The Farington Diary,* ed. James Greig (New York, 1923), vols. i-iii.

236

Fife, Lord, *Lord Fife and His Factor: Being the Correspondence of James, Second Lord Fife, 1729-1809*, ed. Alistair and Henrietta Tayler (London, 1925).

Fox, Charles James, *Memorials and Correspondence of Charles James Fox*, ed. Lord John Russell (London, 1853-7), 4 vols.

George III, *The Correspondence of King George the Third, 1760-1783*, ed. J. W. Fortescue (London, 1928), vols iii-vi.

———— *The Later Correspondence of George III, 1783-1810*, ed. Arthur Aspinall (Cambridge, 1962-70), 5 vols.

George, Prince of Wales, *The Correspondence of George, Prince of Wales, 1770-1812*, ed. Arthur Aspinall (London, 1963-9), vols i-vi.

Glenbervie, Lord, *The Diaries of Sylvester Douglas (Lord Glenbervie)*, ed. Francis Bickley (London, 1928), 2 vols.

Grafton, Duke of, *The Autobiography and Political Correspondence of Augustus Henry, Third Duke of Grafton*, ed. William R. Anson (London, 1898).

The Harcourt Papers, ed. Edward Harcourt (Privately Printed), 14 vols.

Holland, Lady, *The Journal of Elizabeth Lady Holland (1791-1811)*, ed. Earl of Ilchester (London, 1908), 2 vols.

Holland, Lord, *Memoirs of the Whig Party during My Time*, ed. Lord Holland (London, 1852-4), 2 vols.

———— *Further Memoirs of the Whig Party, 1807-21*, ed. Lord Stavordale (New York, 1905).

Intimate Society Letters of the Eighteenth Century, ed. 9th Duke of Argyll (London, 1910), 2 vols.

Jeringham, Edward, *Edward Jeringham and His Friends*, ed. Lewis Bettany (London, 1919).

Leeds, Duke of, *The Political Memoranda of Francis Fifth Duke of Leeds*, ed. Oscar Browning (London, 1884).

Leveson-Gower, Lord Granville, *Lord Granville Leveson-Gower (First Earl Granville): Private Correspondence, 1781 to 1821*, ed. Castalia, Countess Granville (London, 1916), 2 vols.

Malmesbury, Earl of, *Diaries and Correspondence of James Harris, First Earl of Malmesbury*, ed. Earl of Malmesbury (London, 1845), 4 vols.

Memoirs of the Court and Cabinets of George the Third, ed. Duke of Buckingham and Chandos (London, 1853-5), 4 vols.

Minto, Earl of, *Life and Letters of Gilbert Elliot, first Earl of Minto,* ed. Countess of Minto (London, 1874), 3 vols.

Miscellanies, ed. Earl Stanhope (London, 1863).

Miscellanies: Second Series, ed. Earl Stanhope (London, 1872).

The Noels and the Milbankes: Their Letters for Twenty-five Years, 1767-1792, ed. Malcolm Elwin (London, 1967).

Partners in Science; Letters of James Watt and Joseph Black, ed. E. Robinson and D. McKie (Cambridge, Mass., 1970).

Pembroke, Earl of, *Pembroke Papers, 1780-1794; Letters and Diaries of Henry, Tenth Earl of Pembroke and His Circle,* ed. Lord Herbert (London, 1950).

Pitt, William, *Correspondence between the Right Honble. William Pitt and Charles, Duke of Rutland, 1781-1787,* ed. Duke of Rutland (Edinburgh, 1890).

Reynolds, Richard, *Letters of Richard Reynolds; with a Memoir of his Life,* ed. H. M. Rathbone (London, 1852).

Robinson, John, *Parliamentary Papers of John Robinson, 1774-1784,* ed. W.T. Laprade (London, 1922).

Rose, George, *The Diaries and Correspondence of the Right Hon. George Rose,* ed. L. Vernon Harcourt (London, 1860), 2 vols.

Sheridan, Richard Brinsley, *The Letters of Richard Brinsley Sheridan,* ed. C. Price (Oxford, 1966), 2 vols.

Stuart-Wortley, Mrs. E., *A Prime Minister and His Son* (London, 1925).

Walpole, Horace, *The Letters of Horace Walpole,* ed. Peter Cunningham (London, 1866), vols. viii-ix.

———— *The Last Journals of Horace Walpole during the Reign of George III from 1771 to 1783,* ed. A. F. Steuart (London, 1910), 2 vols.

Watson, Richard, *Anecdotes of the Life of Richard Watson, Bishop of Landaff* (London, 1818), 2 vols.

Wedgwood, Josiah, *Correspondence of Josiah Wedgwood: 1781-1794,* ed. Lady Farrer (London, 1906).

———— *The Selected Letters of Josiah Wedgwood,* ed. A. Finer and G. Savage (New York, 1965).

Windham, William, *The Windham Papers; The Life and Correspondence of the Rt. Hon. William Windham, 1750-1810,* ed. Earl of Rosebery (London, 1913), 2 vols.

Wraxall, Nathaniel, *The Historical and Posthumous Memoirs of Sir Nathaniel Wraxall,* ed. H. B. Wheatley (London, 1884), 5 vols.

C. *Secondary Sources*

Adams, E. D., *The Influence of Grenville on Pitt's Foreign Policy, 1787-1798* (Washington, 1904).

Anglesey, Marquis of, *One-Leg: The Life and Letters of Henry Paget, First Marquis of Anglesey, K. G. 1768-1854* (London, 1961).

Anstey, Roger, *The Atlantic Slave Trade and British Abolition, 1760-1810* (Atlantic Highlands, N.J., 1975).

Ashbourne, Edward Gibson, Lord, *Pitt: Some Chapters of His Life and Times* (London, 1898).

Ashton, T.S., *Iron and Steel in the Industrial Revolution* (Manchester, 1951).

Askham, Francis, *The Gay Delavals* (New York, 1956).

Bagot, William, Lord, *Memorials of the Bagot Family* (Blithfield, 1824).

Beattie, J.M., *The English Court in the Reign of George I* (Cambridge, 1967).

Binney, J.E.D., *Public Finance and Administration, 1774-1792* (Oxford, 1958).

Boulton, Geoffrey, *The Passing of the Irish Act of Union* (Oxford, 1966).

Bramwell, George, *The Manner of Proceeding on Bills in the House of Lords* (London, 1831).

Briggs, Asa, *The Age of Improvement, 1783-1867* (New York, 1959).

Brock, W.R., *Lord Liverpool and Liberal Toryism: 1820 to 1827* (London, 1967).

Brooke, John, *King George III* (New York, 1972).

Campbell, Lord, *Lives of the Lord Chancellors* (New York, 1878), vols. vi-ix.

Cannon, John, *The Fox-North Coalition: Crisis of the Constitution, 1782-4* (Cambridge, 1969).

Christie, Ian R., *The End of North's Ministry, 1780-1782* (London, 1958).

———— *Myth and Realities in Late-Eighteenth Century Politics and Other Papers* (London, 1970).

Clifford, Frederick, *A History of Private Bill Legislation* (London, 1885-7), 2 vols.

E. H. Coleridge, *The Life of Thomas Coutts, Banker* (New York, 1920), 2 vols.

Derry, John W., *The Regency Crisis and the Whigs, 1788-9* (Cambridge, 1963).

English Historical Documents, 1783-1832, ed. A. Aspinall and E. A. Smith (New York, 1959), vol xi.

Ehrman, John, *The Younger Pitt: The Years of Acclaim* (New York, 1969).

Ellis, C. T., *Practical Remarks, and Precedents of Proceedings in Parliament* (London, 1802).

──────── *The Solicitor's Instructor in Parliament Concerning Estate Bills and Inclosure Bills* (London, 1799).

Ellis, Kenneth, *The Post Office in the Eighteenth Century: A Study in Administrative History* (London, 1958).

Erskine May, Thomas, *The Constitutional History of England Since the Accession of George III, 1760-1860* (New York, 1876), 2 vols.

Fergusson, Alexander, *The Honourable Henry Erskine, Lord Advocate for Scotland* (London and Edinburgh, 1882).

Finch, Pearl, *History of Burley-on-the-Hill* (London, 1901), 2 vols.

Fitzmaurice, Lord Edmond, *Life of William, Earl of Shelburne* (London, 1875-6), 3 vols.

Foord, Archibald, *His Majesty's Opposition, 1714-1830* (Oxford, 1964).

Fortescue, John W., *The County Lieutenancies and the Army, 1803-1814* (London, 1909).

──────── *British Statesmen of the Great War, 1793-1814* (Oxford, 1911).

Furber, Holden, *Henry Dundas, First Viscount Melville, 1742-1811* (London, 1931).

Ginter, D. E., *Whig Organization and the General Election of 1790* (Berkeley and Los Angeles, 1967).

Gonner, E. G. K., *Common Land and Inclosure* (London, 1912).

Gore-Browne, Robert, *Chancellor Thurlow; The Life and Times of an XVIIIth Century Lawyer* (London, 1953).

Hadfield, Charles, *The Canal Age* (Newton Abbot, 1968).

Hadfield, Charles, *The Canals of the East Midlands* (Newton Abbot, 1966).

————— *The Canals of the West Midlands* (Newton Abbot, 1966).

Halevy, Elie, *England in 1815* (London, 1961).

Harris, J. R., *The Copper King, A Biography of Thomas Williams of Llaniden* (Toronto, 1964).

Hatsell, John, *Precedents of Proceedings in the House of Commons* (London, 1818), vol. iii.

Hodgson, Robert, *The Life of the Rt. Reverend Beilby Porteous, D.D.* (London, 1811).

Holdsworth, William, *A History of English Law* (London, 1938), vols. x-xi.

Holland Rose, J., *William Pitt and the National Revival* (London, 1911).

————— *William Pitt and the Great War* (London, 1911).

————— *Pitt and Napoleon; Essays and Letters* (London, 1912).

Jackman, W.T., *The Development of Transportation in Modern England* (London, 1962).

Keir, David Lindsay, *The Constitutional History of Britain since 1485* (Princeton, 1966).

Kemp, Betty, *King and Commons, 1660-1832* (London, 1959).

Kenyon, George T., *The Life of Lloyd, First Lord Kenyon* (London, 1873).

Lambert, Sheila, *Bills and Acts; Legislative Procedure in Eighteenth Century England* (Cambridge, 1971).

Land and Industry: The Landed Estate and the Industrial Revolution, ed. J. T. Ward and R. G. Wilson (New York, 1971).

Langford, Paul, *The First Rockingham Administration, 1765-6* (Oxford, 1973).

Locke, A. Audrey, *The Seymour Family* (Boston, 1914).

Malett, Hugh, *The Canal Duke: A Biography of Francis, 3rd Duke of Bridgewater* (London, 1961).

Marshall, Dorothy, *Eighteenth Century England* (London, 1962).

Markham, David, *A History of the Markham Family* (London, 1854).

Meteyard, Elizabeth, *The Life of Josiah Wedgwood* (London, 1865-6), 2 vols.

Mingay, G. E., *English Landed Society in the Eighteenth Century* (London, 1963).

Mitchell, L. G., *Charles Fox and the Disintegration of the Whig Party, 1782-1794* (London, 1971).

Namier, Lewis, *England in the Age of the American Revolution* (London, 1963).

———— *Personalities and Powers* (London, 1955).

———— *The Structure of Politics at the Accession of George III* (London, 1957).

———— and John Brooke, *History of Parliament: The House of Commons, 1754-1790* (London, 1964), 3 vols.

Norris, John, *Shelburne and Reform* (London, 1963).

O'Gorman, F., *The Whig Party and the French Revolution* (London, 1967).

Olson, Alison, *The Radical Duke; The Career and Correspondence of Charles Lennox, Third Duke of Richmond* (London, 1961).

Pares, Richard, *George III and the Politicians* (Oxford, 1953).

Pellew, George, *The Life and Correspondence of the Right Hon. Henry Addington, First Viscount Sidmouth* (London 1847), 3 vols.

Phillips, N. C., *Yorkshire & English National Politics, 1783-84* (Christchurch, New Zealand, 1961).

Pressnell, L. S., *Country Banking in the Industrial Revolution* (Oxford, 1965).

Rowse, A. L., *The Churchills, from the Death of Marlborough to the Present* (New York, 1958).

Sainty, J. C., *Leaders and Whips in the House of Lords* (House of Lords Memorandum 31, 1964).

Sichel, Walter, *Sheridan* (Boston, 1909), 2 vols.

Soloway, R. A., *Prelates and People; Ecclesiastical Social Thought in England, 1783-1852* (London, 1969).

Spencer, Frederick, *Municipal Origins; An Account of English Private Bill Legislation Relating to Local Government, 1740-1835* (London, 1911).

Stanhope, Earl, *Life of the Rt. Honourable William Pitt* (London, 1879), 3 vols.

Stirling, A.M.W, *Coke of Norfolk and His Friends* (London, 1908), 2 vols.

Summers, Dorothy, *The Great Ouse: The History of a River Navigation* (Newton Abbot, 1973).

Sykes, Norman, *Church and State in England in the XVIIIth Century* (Cambridge, 1934).

Tate, W. A., *Parliamentary Land Enclosures in the County of Nottinghamshire during the 18th and 19th Centuries, 1743-1868* (Nottingham, Thoroton Society, 1935).

Thomas, P. D. G., *The House of Commons in the Eighteenth Century* (Oxford, 1971).

Thompson, F. M. L., *English Landed Society in the Nineteenth Century* (London, 1963).

Thorold Rogers, J. E., *A Complete Collection of the Protests of the Lords* (Oxford, 1875), vol. ii.

Turberville, Arthur S., *A History of Welbeck Abbey and Its Owners* (London, 1938), 2 vols.

———— *The House of Lords in the XVIIIth Century* (Oxford, 1927).

———— *The House of Lords in the Age of Reform, 1784-1837* (London, 1958).

Twiss, Horace, *The Public and Private Life of Lord Chancellor Eldon* (London, 1844), 3 vols.

Vivian, Comley, *The Sandys Family History: 1178-1907*, revised and edited by T. M. Sandys (London, 1907).

Vulliamy, C. E., *The Onslow Family: 1528-1874* (London, 1953).

Wake, Joan, *The Brudenells of Deene* (London, 1953).

Warwick, Countess of, *Warwick Castle and Its Earls, from Saxon Times to the Present Day* (London, 1903), 2 vols.

Westwood, Arthur, *The Assay Office at Birmingham, Part I* (Birmingham, 1936).

Western, J. R., *The English Militia in the Eighteenth Century; The Story of a Political Issue, 1660-1802* (London, 1965).

Weston, Corrine, *English Constitutional Theory and the House of Lords* (New York, 1965).

Wilberforce, R. I. and S. W., *The Life of William Wilberforce* (London, 1839), 5 vols.

Williams, O. C., *The Historical Development of Private Bill Procedure and Standing Orders in the House of Commons* (London, 1948).

Wyndham, H. A., *A Family History: 1688-1837. The Wyndhams of Somerset, Sussex and Wiltshire* (London, 1950).

Yonge, Charles D., *The Life and Administration of Robert Bankes, Second Earl of Liverpool* (London, 1868), 3 vols.

Ziegler, Philip, *Addington; A Life of Henry Addington, First Viscount Sidmouth* (London, 1965).

D. Articles

R. Anstey, 'A Re-interpretation of the Abolition of the British Slave Trade, 1806-7', *EHR*, lxxxvii (1972).

A. Aspinall, 'The Cabinet Council, 1783-1835', *Proceedings of the British Academy*, xxxviii (1952).

W. Bowden, 'The Influence of the Manufacturers on Some of the Early Policies of William Pitt', *AHR*, xxix (1924).

A. S. Foord, 'The Waning of the "Influence of the Crown" ', *EHR*, lxii (1947).

D. Large, 'The Decline of the "Party of the Crown" and the Rise of Parties in the House of Lords, 1783-1837', *EHR*, lxxviii (1963).

M. W. McCahill, 'The Scottish Peerage and the House of Lords in the Late Eighteenth Century', *SHR*, li (1972).

———— 'Peers, Patronage and the Industrial Revolution', *Journal of British Studies*, xvi (1976).

R. Mitchison, 'The Old Board of Agriculture (1793-1822)', *EHR*, lxxiv (1959).

L. B. Namier, 'Monarchy and the Party System', *Personalities and Powers* (London, 1965).

J. Norris, 'Samuel Garbett and the Early Development of Industrial Lobbying in Great Britain', *EcHR*, 2nd Series, x, (1958).

T. J. Raybould, 'The Development and Organization of Lord Dudley's Mineral Estates', *EcHR*, 2nd Series, xxxi (1968).

G. C. Richards, 'The Creations of Peers Recommended by the Younger Pitt', *AHR*, xxxiv (1928).

E. Robinson, 'Matthew Boulton and the Art of Parliamentary Lobbying', *Historical Journal*, ns. vii (1964).

J. C. Sainty, 'The Origins of the Leadership of the House of Lords', *BIHR*, xlvii (1974).

———— 'The Origin of the Office of Chairman of Committees in the House of Lords', House of Lords Record Office Memorandum No. 52 (1974).

'Abstracts of Wiltshire Inclosure Awards and Agreements', ed. R. E. Sandell, *Wiltshire Record Society*, xxv (1969).

E. A. Smith, 'The Yorkshire Elections of 1806 and 1807: A Study in Electoral Management', *Northern History*, ii (1967).

W. E. Tate, 'Parliamentary Counter-Petitions during the Enclosures of the Eighteenth and Nineteenth Centuries', *EHR*, lix (1944).

P. D. G. Thomas, 'Check List of M.P.s Speaking in the House of Commons, 1768 to 1774', *BIHR*, xxxv (1962).

R. E. Willis, 'Fox, Grenville and the Recovery of Opposition, 1801-1804', *Journal of British Studies*, xi (1972).

———— 'William Pitt's Resignation in 1801: Re-examination and Document', *BIHR*, xliv (1971).

INDEX

To avoid a plethora of cross-references peers are indexed under title. Persons appearing only in appendices or lists are not included in the index.

254

Questions, 65-6

Radnor, Jacob, 2nd earl of, 23, 28n, 79n, 80, 179, 196n, 197n, 228; and militia, 76, 173, 175, 176n
Rawdon, Lord, *see* Moira, 2nd earl of
Redesdale, John, Lord, 118, 163, 178
Regency crisis, 123, 131, 133, 169; and peers' parliamentary interests, 182-3, 185-6
Representative peers of Scotland, 2, 27, 61, 81; politics of, 8, 88, 158, 161
Reynolds, Richard, 56, 195, 207
Richmond, Charles, 3rd duke of, 12, 22, 113, 129, 220, 227; and militia, 141n, 171, 172; and Pitt, 33, 81, 131, 133
Rivers, George, Lord, 153, 163n, 224, 230
Robinson, John, 23, 29-30, 181n
Rockingham, Charles, 2nd marquis of, 195, 199, 227
Rolle, John, Lord, 21
Romney, Robert, 2nd Lord, 54, 196n
Romilly, Samuel, 210
Rose, George, 178, 180n
Rous, John, Lord, 160n, 172
Roxburghe, John, 3rd duke of, 151, 154, 223, 224
Rutland, Charles, 4th duke of, 183, 219, 221, 227, 230

Sackville, George, Viscount, 79n, 80, 88n, 125n, 228
St Albans, 91-2, 192, 202, 228
St Albans, Aubrey, 5th duke of, 19
St Helens, Alleyn, Lord, 151, 153n, 224
Salisbury, James, 7th earl and 1st marquis of, 30, 149, 223
Sandwich, John, 4th earl of, 13, 18n, 124, 184, 185n, 187, 228, 230
Sandys, Edwin, 2nd Lord, 31n, 95n, 160n
Say and Sele, Thomas, 7th Lord, 29n, 80n
Scarsdale, Nathaniel, Lord, 94, 197n
Scott, John, *see* Eldon, Lord
Select committees, 67-8, 70
Selsey, James, Lord, 160-1, 224
Sheffield, 194, 196
Sheffield, John, earl of, 21, 69, 86, 119-20, 141n, 172, 196n, 197n
Shelburne, 2nd earl of, *see* Lansdowne, marquis of
Sheridan, Richard Brinsley, 23
Shrewsbury, George, 14th earl of, 197n, 199
Slave trade abolition, 51-2, 57-60, 120, 137, 210
Smallwell, Edward, bishop of Oxford, 162n
Smith, Adam, 136